Rebel Yell

Michael Buffalo Smith begins *Rebel Yell* aptly with an insight of Charlie Daniels', that the brotherhood between Southern musicians is the unifying force behind the genre "Southern Rock" more than any single musical style shared by bands from the South. Smith then invites us to sit at the table with the heroes and legends of the diverse genre: the players, technicians, crewmembers and friends. I know and love many of them, and they are captured faithfully. Listening to the rambling tale of the extended family my father Duane and his Allman Brothers gave birth to in 1969, the power of the brotherhood is palpable. It is fitting that this history is expressed in the vivid voices of the people who lived it, many who we have since lost. There is no prouder southern tradition than the love of storytelling, except maybe the love of playing music together. There are many twists and turns in this tale, some funny, some tragic, all fascinating and in the end, inspiring. *Rebel Yell* is a gift Smith has given back to the musicians he has always loved, and we all benefit from receiving it.

—GALADRIELLE ALLMAN, AUTHOR OF *PLEASE BE WITH ME: A SONG FOR MY FATHER*

Today there are lots of writers interested in what happened during the seventies—and also the sixties—and Buffalo has remained steady on top of getting the job done, before the others have even started. *Rebel Yell* is an outstanding example of his hard work and dedication.

—ALAN WALDEN, FORMER MANAGER OF LYNYRD SKYNYRD & THE OUTLAWS

A true and fair, tell it like it was, "Keeper of the Flame!" That's our Michael all right. Sho nuff! Oh! He is also a very good listener. Hence the great storyteller.

—BONNIE BRAMLETT, SINGER AND ACTRESS

It's really hard to argue with anything in Michael's book. Every word's a quote! He did an amazing job of compiling these mini-stories that are not drawn out or boring. Recommended!

—ED KING, FORMER MEMBER OF LYNYRD SKYNYRD

Nobody lives, breathes, and bleeds Southern Rock like Michael Buffalo Smith. *Rebel Yell* is as real as rain.

—HARVEY DALTON ARNOLD, FORMER MEMBER OF THE OUTLAWS

Michael Buffalo Smith is the true voice of Southern rock, and *Rebel Yell* clearly echoes that.

—JOHN LYNSKEY, EDITOR *HITTIN' THE NOTE* MAGAZINE

Michael Buffalo Smith has a unique passion for the preservation of the history of Southern rock. *Rebel Yell* is the result of years of loving dedication to the genre, giving him a special ability to present the oral history of this important American musical revolution.

—SCOTT B. BOMAR, AUTHOR OF *SOUTHBOUND:*
AN ILLUSTRATED HISTORY OF SOUTHERN ROCK

Michael is the Flannery O'Connor of Southern music, integrity of music and literature. These [the artists in this book] are only a few of the great people and things Buffalo has written about over the last thousand years.

—COL BRUCE HAMPTON

Buffalo knows the tale of Southern Rock inside out and tells it with flair.

—ALAN PAUL, AUTHOR OF *ONE WAY OUT:*
THE INSIDE HISTORY OF THE ALLMAN BROTHERS BAND

Few people have been in the trenches and know and truly understand the 'nuts & bolts' of the music called Southern Rock. As an author, composer, recording artist, magazine editor and radio personality, Michael is a living encyclopedia who knows and tells the true and real story.

—GREG T. WALKER, *BLACKFOOT*

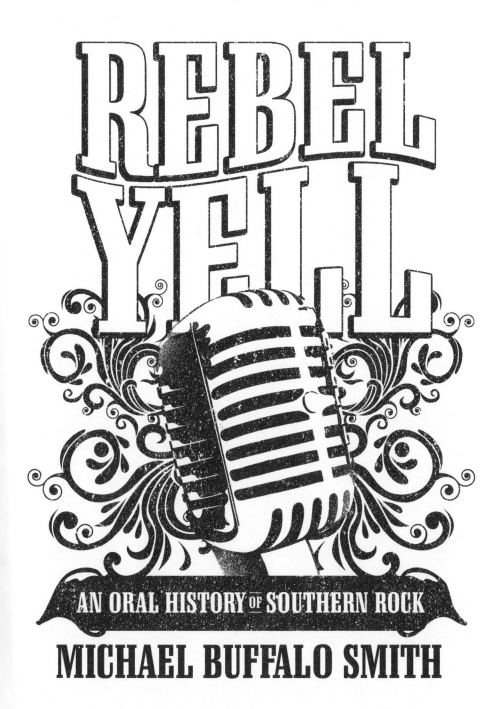

REBEL YELL

AN ORAL HISTORY OF SOUTHERN ROCK

MICHAEL BUFFALO SMITH

MERCER UNIVERSITY PRESS | MACON, GEORGIA

35 YEARS OF PUBLISHING EXCELLENCE

MUP/ P490

© 2014 by Mercer University Press
Published by Mercer University Press, Macon, Georgia 31207
All rights reserved

9 8 7 6 5 4 3 2 1

Books published by Mercer University Press are printed on acid-free
paper that meets the requirements of the American National Standard
for Information Sciences—Permanence of Paper for Printed Library
Materials.

Smith, Michael Buffalo.
  Rebel yell : an oral history of southern rock / Michael Buffalo Smith.
    pages cm
  Includes index.
  ISBN 978-0-88146-495-5 (pbk. : alk. paper) –
  ISBN 0-88146-495-3 (pbk. : alk. paper)
1. Rock music--Southern States--History and criticism. 2. Rock
musicians--Southern States. I. Title.
  ML3534.3.S575 2014
  781.660975--dc23
                                          2014034864

Contents

Dedicated to Scott Greene, my brother of the road.

Also by Michael Buffalo Smith

Prisoner of Southern Rock: A Memoir

First KISS: My Forty-year Obsession with the Hottest Band in the World

Outlaws, Rebels and Renegades II

The Brown Box: Remembering Greenville Memorial Auditorium

Outlaws, Rebels and Renegades

Carolina Dreams: The Musical Legacy of Upstate South Carolina

"We are brothers of the southland
Singers in the same band
Spirits on the wind.
Standing on this stage together
Our song goes on forever
It's part of heaven's plan..."
—Henry Paul/James Peterik/Charles Robbins,
"Brothers of the Southland"

"Travel out across the burnin' sand
Cross the ocean to some distant land
We'll reach the end we'll all be singin'
And we'll all be friends
Back where it all begins."
—Dickey Betts, "Back Where It All Begins"

Foreword

In my forty-five years of working the music business, first in soul music and then in Southern rock & roll, I have met a lot of talented writers who wanted to do interviews, write books, or even make movies. Most of them were cocky people who could never quote me properly, maybe because they could not understand my Southern drawl or wanted to make the story more "Hollywood" style.

One of the nicest, most honest writers I ever met is my good friend, Michael Buffalo Smith, a great guy who has a *true love* for Southern rock & roll—almost as much as me. Buffalo lets you tell the story as it is or was without making changes or misquoting you. He also does not try to write "Southern style," which a lot of other writers try to do when they don't really understand the South, let alone this thing we call Southern music. Maybe it is because he is Southern and understands it better than most. Buffalo also just happens to be a Southern musician, and I am sure that helps him write the *truth* about our profession, which is sometimes hard to find. He writes with sincerity and a love for what he is doing rather than decorating the stories with his own opinions.

Michael Buffalo is no newcomer to the music scene. He has done interviews, reviews, and stories on everyone from Billy Bob Thornton to Chris Hicks, Gary Rossington, Henry Paul, Hughie Thomasson, and Phil Walden and me, always giving each of us the same status and star treatment. Today many writers are interested in what happened during the '60s and '70s, and Buffalo has remained on top of getting the job done before the others have even started. Always far ahead in the game, he stays on top of the new artists as well as the headliners.

Now Buffalo has brought you this new book, which covers a great deal of territory in Southern rock history—more territory than most. I hope you will enjoy his hard work and creative writing of this "song of the South," *Rebel Yell*. Can I get a "Hell, yeah!" on that?

Rock on 2014, Michael Buffalo Smith!

Sincerely & Soulfully,
Alan Walden
2003 Inductee, Georgia Music Hall Of Fame

Introduction

Southern rock. If you asked ten people to define the term, you'd most likely get ten different answers. After all, the classification has always been vague. There are so many schools of thought surrounding this sub-genre of rock 'n' roll that a clear definition proves to be quite elusive.

There is no doubt that Southern rock began around 1969, with the opening of Capricorn records in Macon, Georgia, and the humble beginnings of the band that would become Lynyrd Skynyrd in Jacksonville, Florida.

There's also no doubt that Southern rock is simply a melting pot for all different types of music. The only real common factor is that all of the musicians hailed from the Southern United States.

In reality, the Allman Brothers Band was a blues band with underlying elements of jazz; Lynyrd Skynyrd was a rock 'n' roll band steeped in the tradition of great British invasion groups of the 1960s; the Marshall Tucker Band was a country music band with elements of jazz and blues (and an R&B-style lead singer); the Charlie Daniels Band was pure country rock, and Wet Willie was a straight ahead rhythm and blues and funk outfit.

Then comes the controversy surrounding which bands are indeed *Southern* rock bands, and which ones aren't. Some folks consider ZZ Top a Southern rock band; some don't. Other folks consider Black Oak Arkansas a Southern rock band; others don't. Still others consider Tom Petty and the Heartbreakers a Southern rock band because they hailed from Gainesville, Florida, and their roots were in a Southern rock band called Mudcrunch.

There are many who don't like the term "Southern rock" at all. One of the most outspoken has been Gregg Allman, who says that the term "Southern rock" is redundant—after all, according to Gregg, most all music came out of the South: "Saying Southern rock is like saying rock-rock," Allman has said in numerous interviews.

As for me, I simply use the term "Southern rock" to describe all the wonderful music that I grew up loving. Like Charlie Daniels has said publicly, it's less about what style of *music* these bands play and more about the like-minded *people*. I agree with that. It's the people, the brotherhood. Brothers and sisters on the same musical journey.

The following oral history is assembled from hundreds of interviews that I've had the privilege of conducting over the past twenty-five years. Most of the interviews represented herein have previously appeared in various publications and books, but some of the quotes are being used for the very first time. All of the interviews prior to 2011 I recorded on Maxell cassette tape and transcribed mostly by myself. (I never learned to type, but I can get after it pretty fast sometimes with the two fingers!) The quotes have been minimally edited in order to preserve the conversational style.

In putting this book together, I came to the somewhat startling realization that we have lost a whole lot of the characters herein within a relatively short period of time. Thank God we have their music to remember them, as well as these archived interviews.

I truly hope that you enjoy this walk down the Southern rock highway. This is by no means a definitive history of Southern rock, but I still hope to write that some day. In the meantime, this is a large chunk of history, as told by the people who lived it, and it don't get much better than that.

—Michael Buffalo Smith
Spartanburg, South Carolina

Cast of Characters

Matt Abts—Drummer for Gov't Mule and former member of the Dickey Betts Band

Devon Allman—Singer/guitarist, solo artist, and leader of Honeytribe; son of Gregg Allman

Gregg Allman—Founding member, lead vocalist, keyboard player, and guitarist for the Allman Brothers Band

Don Barnes—Founding member, lead vocalist, and guitarist for 38 Special

Joe Bennett—Rockabilly guitarist of the popular 1950s band the Sparkletones; a guitar teacher in Spartanburg, South Carolina, who taught many of the Marshall Tucker Band guys how to play

Dickey Betts—Founding member, guitarist, and singer of the Allman Brothers Band; also of Dickey Betts & Great Southern, the Dickey Betts Band, and BHLT

Jo Jo Billingsley—One of the three "Honkettes," the backup singers for Ronnie Van Zant and Lynyrd Skynyrd (d. June 24, 2010)

Elvin Bishop—Guitarist of the Paul Butterfield Blues Band who signed with Capricorn Records and ended up recording and playing with many of the artists, including the Allmans

Scott Boyer—Founding member, singer, and songwriter of Cowboy

Randall Bramblett—Multi-instrumentalist, singer, songwriter; a solo artist and former member of Sea Level and Cowboy

Bonnie Bramlett—Soul/blues/rock singer, songwriter; one half of Delaney & Bonnie; the first "Allman Sister"; the first white "Ikette" in the Ike & Tina Turner Review; Capricorn recording artist and actress (*Roseanne, The Doors, The Guardian*)

Delaney Bramlett—One half of Delaney & Bonnie; singer, songwriter, guitarist, producer, conduit for bringing musicians together (d. December 27, 2008)

Bruce Brookshire—Founding member, vocalist, and guitarist of Doc Holliday

Danny Joe Brown—The original voice of Molly Hatchet (d. March 10, 2005)

Mark Burrell—Drummer for the Toy Caldwell Band

Toy Caldwell, Sr.—Father of Toy, Tommy, and Tim Caldwell; husband of Virginia Caldwell (d. January 9, 2006)

Red Dog Campbell—Original roadie, long time road crew chief for the Allman Brothers Band (d. February 21, 2011)

David Cantonwine—Founding member and bass guitarist of Eric Quincy Tate

Pete Carr—Member of Hour Glass with Gregg and Duane Allman; Muscle Shoals and Capricorn session guitarist

Tommy Crain—Longtime lead guitarist for the Charlie Daniels Band (d. January 13, 2011)

Peter Cross—A British lad; a longtime follower of Southern roots music; holds a degree in geography and once traveled the world for five years, hitchhiking more than 25,000 miles

Charlie Daniels—Singer, songwriter, fiddle player, guitarist, author, founder, and leader of the Charlie Daniels Band; known to many as "the Godfather of Southern rock"

Taz DiGregorio—Piano/B-3 organ player, singer, songwriter, founding member of the Charlie Daniels Band (d. October 12, 2011)

Tom Dowd—Legendary record producer and engineer of such classics as Allman Brothers' *At Fillmore East*; Derek & the Dominos' *Layla & Other Love Songs*; and Lynyrd Skynyrd's *One More from the Road* (d. October 27, 2002)

Les Dudek—Guitarist; worked with the Allman Brothers Band during the early to mid-seventies; recorded a series of solo albums

Fred Edwards—A long time drummer for the Charlie Daniels Band

Mike Estes—Guitarist, singer, songwriter; former member of Lynyrd Skynyrd, Blackfoot, Southern Rock Allstars, Artimus Pyle Band

Jerry Eubanks—Plays flute, saxophone, keyboards; founding member of the Marshall Tucker Band

John Galvin—Original (and present) keyboard player for Molly Hatchet

Doug Gray—Founding member, lead vocalist of the Marshall Tucker Band

Steve Grisham—Former and present member of the Outlaws; guitarist, singer, songwriter; also leader of the band Ghost Riders.

Jimmy Hall—Founding member, lead vocalist, sax, and harmonica player for Wet Willie

Randall Hall—Guitarist; former member of Lynyrd Skynyrd

John Hammond—Guitarist, singer, recording artist

Charlie Hargrett—Guitarist and founding member of Blackfoot

Barry Lee Harwood—Guitarist, singer, songwriter in the Rossington Collins Band; also worked with Lynyrd Skynyrd

Warren Haynes—Guitarist, singer, songwriter; former and present member of the Allman Brothers Band; founding and present member of Gov't Mule; former member of the Dead and Phil & Friends

Charlie Hayward—Bass guitarist for the Charlie Daniels Band; worked with Gregg Allman, Dr. John, Alex Taylor

Tony Heatherly—Bass guitarist, singer for the Toy Caldwell Band and later the Marshall Tucker Band (d. May 15, 2013)

Jimmy Herring—Guitarist; formerly with the Allman Brothers Band and Aquarium Rescue Unit; presently with Widespread Panic.

Derek Hess—Drummer for the Rossington Collins Band

Chris Hicks—Guitarist, singer, songwriter; former and present member of the Marshall Tucker Band; former member of the Outlaws

Dave Hlubek—Guitarist, songwriter; founder and present member of Molly Hatchet

Paul Hornsby—Keyboard player, songwriter, producer, engineer for Capricorn Records; was also in Hour Glass with Duane and Gregg Allman

Larry Howard—Guitarist, songwriter; founding member of Grinderswitch

Bobby Ingram—Guitarist, songwriter for Molly Hatchet

Jay Johnson—Guitarist, singer, songwriter; former member of the Rossington Band, Blackfoot, Southern Rock Allstars, and Radio Tokyo; son of Muscle Shoals legend Jimmy Johnson

Ed King—Guitarist, songwriter; founding member of Lynyrd
Skynyrd; formerly with Strawberry Alarm Clock

Al Kooper—Keyboard player, songwriter, producer, engineer;
worked with the original Lynyrd Skynyrd along with a who's
who of classic rock

Pete Kowalke—Guitarist, songwriter, singer with Cowboy

Johnny Lawson—Truck driver for the original Marshall Tucker Band

Tim Lawter—Bass guitarist, singer, songwriter, producer, engineer;
longtime member of the Marshall Tucker Band; presently in
Watson's Riddle, a jazz band, with Paul Riddle

Chuck Leavell—Keyboards, singer, songwriter; former member of
the Allman Brothers Band and Sea Level; studio and touring
musician; present and longtime touring member of the Rolling
Stones

Brad Lesley—Former Cincinnati Reds pitcher; singer, friend, and
ultimate fan of the Marshall Tucker Band (d. April 27, 2013)

Dru Lombar—Guitarist, singer, songwriter; founding member of
Grinderswitch (d. September 2, 2005)

George McCorkle—Guitarist, singer, songwriter; founding member
of the Marshall Tucker Band (d. June 29, 2007)

Justin McCorkle—Guitarist; son of George McCorkle

Rickey Medlocke—Guitarist, singer, songwriter for Lynyrd Skynyrd;
founding member of Blackfoot

Rusty Milner—Guitarist, singer, songwriter, producer, engineer;
longtime member of the Marshall Tucker Band

Moon Mullins—Roadie, crew chief for the original Marshall Tucker
Band

Jimmy Nalls—Guitarist, singer, songwriter; founding member of Sea
Level

Johnny Neel—Keyboard player, singer, songwriter, producer; former
member of the Allman Brothers Band

Henry Paul—Singer, songwriter, guitarist; founding and present
member of the Outlaws; also founding member of Blackhawk

Artimus Pyle—Former longtime drummer for Lynyrd Skynyrd

Paul Riddle—Founding member of the Marshall Tucker Band

Duane Roland—Former guitarist with Molly Hatchet (d. June 19,
2006)

Gary Rossington—Guitarist, songwriter; founding and present member of Lynyrd Skynyrd

Dale Krantz-Rossington—Singer; former lead vocalist for the Rossington Collins Band and the Rossington Band; present backup singer for Lynyrd Skynyrd

Johnny Sandlin—Drummer, bassist; producer and engineer at Capricorn Records; member of the Capricorn Rhythm Section; former member of Hour Glass with Duane and Gregg Allman

Leonard Skinner—Former teacher and gym coach at Robert E. Lee High School in Jacksonville (d. September 20, 2010)

Jakson Spires—Drummer, singer, songwriter; founding member of Blackfoot; longtime drummer for the Southern Rock Allstars (d. March 16, 2005)

Eddie Stone—Keyboardist, guitarist, singer, songwriter; founding member of Doc Holliday; also performed with Grinderswitch and Wet Willie, and in duet with Rob Walker from Stillwater

Stuart Swanlund—Guitarist, vocalist, songwriter; slide guitarist in the Marshall Tucker Band from 1985 until his death on August 4, 2012

Tommy Talton—Guitarist, singer, songwriter; founding member of Cowboy

Hughie Thomasson—Guitarist, singer, songwriter; founding member of the Outlaws; former member of Lynyrd Skynyrd (d. September 9, 2007)

Billy Bob Thornton—Oscar-winning actor (*Sling Blade*); drummer and singer in the Boxmasters

Dan Toler (also known as "Dangerous Dan")—Guitarist, songwriter; formerly of the Allman Brothers Band, Dickey Betts & Great Southern, the Gregg Allman Band, the Toler Brothers Band, and the Toler Townsend Band

John Townsend—Singer; formerly of the Sanford-Townsend Band ("Smoke from a Distant Fire") and the Toler Townsend Band

Butch Trucks—Drummer; founding and present member of the Allman Brothers Band

Donnie Van Zant—Vocalist, guitarist, songwriter; founding member of 38 Special; also records with his brother Johnny as Van Zant

Johnny Van Zant—Vocalist, songwriter of Lynyrd Skynyrd; also
with Van Zant

Alan Walden—Macon, Georgia, producer, manager, songwriter,
promoter; former manager for Lynyrd Skynyrd, the Outlaws, and
Otis Redding

Greg T. Walker—Bass guitarist; founding member of Blackfoot

Riff West—Bass guitarist; former member of Molly Hatchet and
Foghat

Franklin Wilkie—Bass Guitarist; former member of the Marshall
Tucker Band and Garfeel Ruff

Dennis Winters—Guitarist, vocalist, songwriter; founding member
of the Winters Brothers Band

Allen Woody—Bass guitarist, former member of the Allman Brothers
Band; founding member of Gov't Mule (d. August 25, 2000)

Rudy "Blue Shoes" Wyatt—Pianist, guitarist, singer from Greenville,
South Carolina

John D. Wyker—Guitarist, bass player, singer, songwriter; founding
member of Sailcat ("Motorcycle Mama") (d. December 8, 2013)

Tom Wynn—Drummer; founding member of Cowboy

Monte Yoho—Drummer, the Outlaws

Part 1

The Allman Brothers Band

Beginnings

The roots of Southern rock can be traced back to Jacksonville, Florida, in the 1960s. The same city that gave us Lynyrd Skynyrd was also the early developmental site of what would eventually become the Allman Brothers Band.

After several bands did the member shuffle, great bands like the Five Men-Its, the Allman Joys, and Hour Glass morphed into the band that would be signed by Phil Walden to a new label called Capricorn, leading them to relocate to Macon, Georgia.

Pete Carr

I was about fifteen, and I went to see the Allman Joys play at the Club Martinique in Daytona Beach. I had my guitar case with me and introduced myself when the band took a break and asked Gregg Allman to show me some guitar lines. Gregg replied, "That's my brother, Duane's, department." At that point I introduced myself to Duane Allman. That meeting began a friendship, which lasted until Duane's death in a motorcycle crash on October 29, 1971.

Johnny Sandlin

Well, I was in a band called the Five Men-its with Eddie Hinton, Paul Hornsby, and I think at the time Fred Styles was playing bass. Anyway, we were playing and we had heard of them (Gregg and Duane)—I guess at the time everyone in Florida had heard of them through the grapevine. We were doing a gig at this little place kind of out of the way and right off the beach. It was a little Spanish village with a patio outside and a club inside. They had booked the Allman Joys for the patio, which usually attracted more kids. We were playing mainly for the sailors because Pensacola is mainly a navy town. That was the first place that I met them. We kind of kept in touch with them after that because they were the best guitar player and singer that I had ever heard. I had met Bob Keller who was the bass player. But anyway, we all stayed in touch. Eddie Hinton decided to leave the band and go to Muscle Shoals and do session work and that left us without a guitar player and singer. Eddie was both in our band. We called Gregg and them to see if they would help us find some people. In the interim they sent Pete Carr up here and we were going to start a band with him but we never found a singer that worked out for us. We later got a call from them saying that their band had broken up and let's get together and jam and see what we could come up with. So they came up here to Decatur. We got together and rehearsed in our garage. So that's how the Hourglass got together.

Pete Carr

Duane and Gregg told me about a band in Alabama that they knew who needed a guitar player. So I moved to Decatur, Alabama, in 1966 to play guitar for a band called the Five Men-its. Their guitar player, Eddie Hinton, was leaving the band to pursue studio work, and I was called in to be his replacement. Irony and fate have shown their faces to me many times in my life. I would later become the replacement for Eddie Hinton again when he left the Muscle Shoals Sound Rhythm Section in a twist of fate. Johnny Sandlin, Mabron McKinney, and Paul Hornsby were the other members of the band. I remember Sandlin playing me songs such as "It's All Over Now" by Bobby Womack and the Valentinos. I already knew the Rolling Stones version of that song, which I loved, but I also liked Womack's version. Sandlin had heard Womack's version first and did not like the Stones version. They were both great recordings in different ways. Sandlin also got me to sit down with the classic B. B. King album *Live at the Regal*. I credit Johnny Sandlin and Paul Hornsby as both being big-brother influences and teachers that helped me in my music career.

John D. Wyker

I remember the first time I ever saw Pete [Carr]. Duane Allman brought him to Decatur in about 1965 when Pete was about 15 or 16, but not much older than that and he was so thin that you could barely see anything except long wild hair and big Beatle boots with stacked Cuban heels. He talked like the great baseball player Pete Rose, attitude and lightning fast. He was playing guitar like a cocky little mad genius and smokin' Duane Allman. Gregg loved his playing. I mean Pete was a kid, but even back then you just knew that Pete's brain was wired to be lightning fast. Computers were invented years later and Pete was one of the first ones to learn to play hot licks on them too. A few years later, as I watched in the recording studio, Pete and whoever would go back to the studio and take their places. Pete would pick up his guitar and instantly start playing exactly what the song needed, intro, feel, everything and that's the way it went session after session, over and over and time and again.

Paul Hornsby

Eddie Hinton left the "Men-ites" to be a session player. One bleak day in the middle of starvation, Duane Allman called me up and asked "Paul how would you like to have me and Gregg in your band?" Well, it really wasn't "my" band, but I thought it over 30 or 40 seconds and said, "Why, hell yes!" So, it seems we immediately started wood shedding in the Sandlin's garage in Decatur, Alabama.

Within two weeks we had our first booking at Pepe's-a-GoGo in St. Louis. That had been a big town for the Allman Joys. We played there for a month. I don't remember if we used the name Allman Joys or not. We had kicked a few names around. We all figured that a new name was in order by now, but hadn't really settled into one as yet.

During that month, Mabron McKinney, our bass player, was at the St. Louis airport when he ran into the Nitty Gritty Dirt Band. In those days (1967) you noticed a fellow "long hair" and felt a natural kinship. He had never heard of them, as it was before their first hits. They were on a promotion tour for their first LP. In the conversation, he invited them to come by Pepe's to hear us play while they were in town. This they did, accompanied by their manager Bill McEuen. After the first set, McEuen ran to a phone and called someone at Liberty Records in Los Angeles. He told them that he had just discovered the next Rolling Stones. Come to think of it, I guess we were pretty good, at that.

He convinced us to come out to California and promised to get us a record deal. This we did, he did, and the rest is history. We cut one LP for Liberty. Then, Mabron McKinney left the group. He was finally replaced by Pete Carr. Pete was a guitar player friend who just happened to be visiting us when the position came available. He had never played bass before. However, after a little bit of arm-twisting, he jumped right in and continued on bass till the end of the group in 1968. We cut one more LP for Liberty in 1968.

At this time "Beach Music" was the thing on the west coast. Here we were—a band of Southern cats with a Blues-oriented sound, like you might expect the predecessor to the Allman Brothers Band to be. You might say we were the first "Southern rock" band in the classic sense of the word. The producer and record company didn't have a clue as to what to do with us. Our producer had just come from a few hits with Jan and Dean, Bobby Vee, etc. As we had a "black" or "blues" sound he kept referring to us as a "Motown" band—wrong side of the country. Our first record was filled up with horns and black chick singers, etc. We were just eager to please. Anything they suggested, we went along with. We were just a bunch of country boys, what did we know? We did know how to make music! Most of the stuff they had us play on those records, we never played live. We had a set of mostly blues and R&B, sounding stuff that we had put together during the past year together and inherited from past bands we had all been a part of.

We played all up and down the California coast—the Fillmore, the Avalon Ballroom—as an opening act at stadium concerts, etc. The Fillmore was beginning to be noticed in all the rock magazines as the headquarters for the 'Frisco bands like Jefferson Airplane, Big Brother, etc. Bill Graham was the owner of the club and also managed the "Airplane" and several other bands who played there. Bill had not as yet received the "legendary" status that he later acquired after his death. He was just a guy who gave the bands a place to play, and the people what they wanted to hear. He seemed to know what those fans wanted though.

At the time, I never gave much thought to Bill, no more than any other club owner. I do know that he was a personal fan of the Hour Glass. He kept having us back time after time, even though we didn't have a charted record. One thing in particular I remember about Bill was—one night after a weekend at the Fillmore, we were struggling with my Hammond, carrying it down those steep steps out in front of the club. A bunch of stragglers were hanging around after closing time. He yelled out "Give them cowboys some room. They just played their asses off and now they're trying to get their own gear out." I don't know why, but he seemed impressed by that. I've toted it many times since.

We were practically the house band at the Whiskey-a-Go-Go. That was a prestigious place to play back then. We sort of started a custom of jam sessions when we worked there. The biggest acts in the country, when in town, would come out to hear us play and sit in. One such unforgettable night, Janis Joplin, Eric Burdon, Steve Stills, Neil Young, Buddy Miles, and Paul Butterfield, joined us on stage there. The club had to pull the power plug to stop us that night, as there was a 2:00 closing curfew. Most of these acts we had opened up for, and so we had developed a reputation of sorts. This was all without the benefit of a hit record to help us break out of California.

By the middle of the summer in 1968, we had become disillusioned with the whole L.A. thing. Duane wanted to come back east. We did try it back in the old haunts again for a month or two, but it just didn't work out. The band disbanded in August of 1968.

Pete Carr

The Five Men-its band couldn't find a lead singer and we were about to disband. At the same time Duane and Gregg Allman needed new band members and called upon Sandlin, Hornsby, and McKinney to join their band. I was just a kid and they really had no need for three guitar players in the band so I left and traveled around Alabama meeting some great musicians. I would also go back to Daytona Beach and play at the Pier over the ocean. This new Allman Joys band would later be seen in St. Louis by the Nitty Gritty Dirt Bands' manager who persuaded them to move to California and changed their name to Hour Glass. I lived just across the river from Gregg and Duane, about a ten-minute drive, and they had just flown back home from California with a recording of the first Hour Glass album.

They seemed very excited with the new album and it sounded good to me. Gregg was really singing! Gregg was also home for a draft notification, which would have ruined everything for the whole band if he, the lead singer, left for the army. I mean a lot of peoples' careers were on the line. He had to do something, so he drank a few belts of whiskey, went into the front yard, and shot himself in the foot. The next day he got on the bus for Jacksonville. The army people turned him down and the band was saved. Gregg and Duane asked if I would like to fly back to California with them and I accepted the offer. In a twist of fate I again joined forces with the Allmans, Sandlin, and Hornsby when Bob Keller, who was playing bass for them at the time, just got up and left one day before a show at the Whiskey-A-Go-Go on Sunset Blvd. They asked if I would play bass for them and I accepted. I figured if Paul McCartney played guitar first and picked up the bass out of necessity, I would give it a try also. It all worked out fine at the show that night and I became a permanent part of the band.

Duane and I shared an apartment and we would play guitars together a lot. I remember Gregg, Duane and I playing and singing "Long Black Veil" a few times, which is a country standard. It started *Ten years ago, on a cold dark night, there was someone killed, in the town that night.*

I remember us harmonizing on it and it really was a moment separated from everything else we were doing. It was like a close family thing. I remember my mother talking about that song and how my Aunt Gertie would play and sing songs like that. She also sang a lot of country blues because my mother said she used to use a kitchen butter knife to play slide guitar. I wish I could have played music with her, but she died before I was old enough to really remember her. She had epilepsy and I think I recall Mom saying that had something to do with her death. I don't really know. It seems like a dream since I don't remember her except vaguely. I seem to remember her falling from the doorway into the yard one time and people gathering around. Maybe she was having an epileptic seizure. It is like a dream to me now, very vague and shadowy images. I was probably two or three years old.

In 1967 Gregg, Duane, Paul Hornsby, Johnny Sandlin and I, as Hour Glass, played together on the *Power Of Love* album. The Hour Glass had recorded songs in Muscle Shoals, Alabama, at Rick Hall's Fame Studios, which was known for innovative productions and great sound. One song recorded at Fame, "Sweet Little Angel," was later released in a *Duane Allman Anthology* set. This recording is now considered a classic piece of raw electric Southern rock blues. When we got back to California we played the tape we made in Muscle Shoals for our producer, and he didn't like it. He was looking for a hit single, and the Muscle Shoals cuts had no radio top-ten type of hit singles. We went ahead and finished the *Power of Love* album and it turned out fairly well for the time but we never got that radio hit record. We finally disbanded and everybody went their separate ways.

Johnny Sandlin

Oh, yeah, we opened for Buffalo Springfield, and actually played on a show with the Doors and at the Whiskey, Janis sat in with us. Eric Burdon and Paul Butterfield too. Anyone that heard the band fell in love with Duane and Gregg both and they thought that they were great. Which they certainly should have.

John Townsend

I get this phone call one day in 1967 from an old friend and musician Paul Hornsby who was playing with a band called the Hour Glass. Paul had just come back from Los Angeles where his band had just landed a recording contract with a big label. The Hour Glass was made up of a couple of guys I had met during our beach club days, Gregg and Duane Allman, along with Johnny Sandlin, Paul [Hornsby], and a bass player named Bob Keller. Sandlin and Hornsby became music producers later on and produced a lot of the successful Southern rock acts. Gregg and Duane...well you know the story. I declined the offer to go to L. A. with Paul but decided to put a band of my own together and hit the road west some months later.

The Rise of the Brotherhood

Duane Allman went looking for session work, and the story of his first meeting with Rick Hall at Fame Studios in Muscle Shoals, Alabama, has been told many times before. (One Way Out by Alan Paul; Skydog by Randy Poe) The essence of the story is that Duane went to see Rick Hall and asked if he had any session work for a guitar player. Hall told him that he didn't have anything at the time. Duane told him to please come outside and tell him when some work came available, he would be pitching a tent in the parking lot and waiting.

Butch Trucks

Duane, Gregg, and I had played in a band together in '67–68. When that band fell apart Duane went to Muscle Shoals and did the session work that included Wilson Pickett's "Hey Jude," Aretha Franklin's stuff, and most of the other sessions he became known for. After about six months of the studio he got really bored. About that time Phil Walden signed him to management and recording contracts and sent Jaimoe to Muscle Shoals where they hit it off, and Duane and Jaimoe eventually headed to Jacksonville to find more players for the new band that Duane was going to form.

At first he thought it might just be a trio so he took Jaimoe and Berry Oakley back to Muscle Shoals and recorded a few songs. After hearing himself singing on those recordings they all headed back to Jacksonville to grab some more players. We spent about a month or so getting together as often as possible and jamming. Finally after going through many combinations, we were at the Second Coming's—Dickey and Berry's band—house and six of us got into a jam that lasted about two to three hours. It was incredible. When we finished Duane walked to the door and said, "Anyone in here not gonna play in my band is gonna hafta fight his way outa here."

The group was Duane, Dickey, Berry, Jaimoe, me, and Reese Wynans—he went on to play with Double Trouble. Duane knew that we had to have a singer and he knew who that needed to be so he called his brother, Gregg, who was struggling in L. A., and told him to get his butt to Jacksonville. Two days later we had our first rehearsal and learned "Trouble No More," "Don't Want You Know More," and "Dreams." The rest, as they say is history.

Dickey Betts

Berry Oakley and I were both young adults when we met, and we were both still searching for our style of playing. He had so much insight and vision. I was playing nightclubs, and I was making what would be the equivalent now of about $3000 a week. Back then it was about $600 a week, which was real good money in the sixties. Oakley would come around and he'd say "You gotta get out of these clubs, and do your original stuff!" I'd say, "But Oakley, we'll starve to death. I'm married, and I've got to pay rent." But he kept telling me we had to break out of it and kind of starve for a couple of years. I used to kid him, I'd say, "You're like my big brother, but you're younger than I am." [Laughs] He was the real visionary in the band. He and I got together, and we started doing about half cover stuff and half original stuff. The band was called the Blues Messengers. A guy from Jacksonville came down to this club we were playing at called Dino's in Tampa. It was a real big blues club. The guy had a club in Jacksonville that had all this plexiglas that lights came through, psychedelic lighting, an electric dance floor. Jacksonville didn't have anybody in that town that wasn't playing soul music. They were kind of behind the times. He came down and saw our band and said, "Man, I want to bring you guys to Jacksonville. But I've got to change the name of the band to the Second Coming." He thought Berry looked just like Jesus Christ. Oakley hated that! [Laughs] So we went to that club, and we were the only people in that great big city that had long hair and were playing that kind of music. So Oakley said, "We've got to get out and get our people together." I said, "Oakley, we don't have any people." He said, "Yeah we do, they just don't have anywhere to go." So we got out, and some of our hippie friends built us a stage on this lot that some people let us use. They had electricity on it. They had about twenty acres there, and they told us we could play there on Sunday afternoons. So we got one guy to build the stage and another guy to get the electric lines run, and we set up our stuff and just did free shows. And in about two months we had like 3,000 people coming there, and everybody's hair kept getting longer and longer. But Oakley was the visionary. Kind of the guy who could see how to get people together and make things work. And that's kind of what he brought to the Allman Brothers Band.

When the Allmans started out, it was supposed to be Jaimoe and Duane and Berry. They were going to be a power trio like a Hendrix or a Cream. But the more Duane played with our band to get used to playing with Berry, the more we realized that Duane and I played great together. So then it was two guitar players, and Butch started coming around, and we saw it sounded great with two drummers. So we rehearsed that way for about two months. Duane and Gregg were in a big fight at this time. They weren't speaking. We kept telling Duane, "You've got to call your brother, man, because nobody in this band can sing good enough for the kind of band we've got." So we finally got Duane to call, and Gregg showed up and that was the Allman Brothers. But when it started out, it was supposed to be a trio. And of course Phil Walden was going nuts. He was ready for a trio, and all of the sudden he had a six-piece band, and we had to have all this new equipment and stuff. He said, "I've got all kinds of bands, and they have their own stuff." He had been dealing with Percy Sledge and Otis Redding. But a rhythm and blues band didn't have to have all that stuff like a modern band needed.

At Fillmore East

At Fillmore East has become perhaps the most influential and loved live record of the rock era. Released in July 1971, the album went on to earn platinum status, selling in excess of a million units.

As an interesting aside, the iconic Jim Marshall album cover, showing the band and all of their road cases, was not, in fact, shot outside the Fillmore. It was shot in a lot in Macon, Georgia, near the band's office.

Butch Trucks

Those Fillmore concerts were the high points of that part of the band's history. We were really gelling as a group, and Tom Dowd was able to catch it all. After every show we would head to the studio and listen to what we did and say, "We got that one; we'd better do that one again." We knew we were onto something very special.

Elvin Bishop

[On the *Fillmore East* recording] I usually tell people if you remember a particular night from the seventies then you must not have had much fun. [Laughs] But I do remember that one. We used to get together and jam all the time. It was kind of a jamming time, you know. It was the Fillmore East in New York City, and I remember that I went over there after my gig, which was somewhere, and then they had a bomb scare, and they made the people go outside and stand on the street for an hour and a half or two hours. And the thing was, that thing was going so strong, nobody left. Then at 2 a.m. they let them all back in, and we ended up jamming until five or six o'clock in the morning.

From those days until just a couple of years ago, I never saw the Allman Brothers. Our paths just never crossed. Then a couple of years ago I got invited to jam with them during their Beacon run. I went over there, and they were just real nice. We actually opened up one of their shows, just me and Derek Trucks and Warren Haynes. That was so much fun, and I loved playing with them so much. Warren told me that when he was sixteen he played "Struttin' My Stuff" in a bar band.

Red Dog Campbell

The Fillmore East was unreal, man. Bill Graham had that thing, man—it was the place to play. You'd go in there and set your stuff up on dollies. Nowadays we leave a lot of things in the case trays and all like that. But at the Fillmore they had these dollies. And after you played there one time, they knew what your gear looked like. When you'd come back, them dollies were even better, to go with your gear. They put everything on them four-wheeled dollies, and rather than having to carry everything out onstage, they just rolled it out there. So when it came time to change the stage it was bang-bang-bang and out of there. Next band. The Fillmore just sounded good too. Look at that *Fillmore East* album. That's one of the best live ones ever laid down.

Tom Dowd

Oh, yeah, the *Fillmore* album. I had been in Africa for a month doing a show called *Soul to Soul*, doing a film and a recording. I got home on the weekend, and I did not expect to be home by the time I got home because I ran into inclement weather coming out of Africa. I came all the way back to New York. I called in and said I was back in New York and that I was going to take a day and then go home. Jerry Wexler said, "I sure am glad you are here because the Allman Brothers are recording on Monday down at the Fillmore." I thought, that's interesting, and he set up an exquisite recording space. I went down because I had experience with the two drums and the bass and the two guitars and this and that and more or less told them how to lay out the tracks, and they put up the microphones.

It was good crew. I was just being a catalyst about things. As things were going I was sitting in the truck and the Brothers didn't even know I was there. I was sitting in there and I was saying,

"Alright, there is going to be a guitar solo, we are going onto multi-track, and I am just alerting the engineer as to what to look for. About four or five numbers into the show, the second [the assistant to the producer] comes up and taps me on the shoulder and says, "You didn't tell me where to put the horns." I said, "What horns?" I'm thinking that he is being a smart-ass and being funny or something. But no, there are two horns and a harp coming onto the stage. I am thinking, where am I going to put them? Stick them on one of the vocal tracks—I really don't give a damn! Then when I heard what the horns were playing, I beelined it out of the truck and went backstage and as Duane came off the stage, I said, "You son of a bitch—if you ever do that to me again, you're gone and if those horns walk onstage one more time I am pulling the recording." He just looked at me, because I had never spoken to Duane like that. Duane and I were hand-holders. I had never accosted him like that.

They did another show that night and I said, "Now, I want you guys to come up to the studio and I am taking the tapes with me and I am going to play you tonight's show." We argued in between shows and I told them they could put the harp player back in, but don't ever let those horns onstage again or I am pulling the pin. So that night we went back to the Atlantic Studio and I played them the entire show and I let them hear what the horns were doing, and Duane said, "Okay, the horns are fired, they are gone." So then we made it a practice, after every show, 2:00 a.m. we were in a taxi cab and going back up to Atlantic, grabbing hamburgers, hot dogs, Chinese, whatever the hell, and we would sit down and listen to the entire show, both sets. By so doing after the second night, four shows, we would say well we don't have to do "Elizabeth Reed" again, or this song again, and so let's put this song in and this song in and change the next days shows, saying we don't have to do this song, we have it already.

So after four nights the album was together and we knew what was going to be the top priority or pick of songs that were going onto the album. Everybody in the band had come up to the studio every night after the show and listened to every song, and we had all agreed on what we wanted to do, with who and so forth. In listening to the various takes, Dickey Betts wanted to use a solo from one version of "Elizabeth Reed" and the band said, "Whatever he wants, we love this take," so I wired Dickey's solo from one take into another take. They were that close in tempo, you never knew. I used "Hot 'lanta," but I could not use the best version because I could not get rid of the damn horns! Remember we were going onto twelve-inch discs so that we only had seventeen to nineteen minutes on each side, so we were limited as to what we could employ. In going through the "Whipping Posts," because that song closed every show, there was one show where some guy in the audience yelled out and the band cracked up when they heard this.

When it came time to mix the album down, the band was back on the road. I had already decided what seven or eight cuts we were going to use, and I had come up with the correct "Whipping Post," but as tongue-in-cheek so that when they heard it they would crack up, I threw in an overdub of this guy in the back of the audience yelling onto the tape we were using. [Laughs] So when I am asked twenty-five years later to remix the damn thing for CD, we transferred everything that was ever recorded, and it took three or four days. I sat there and listened attentively to everything. I had the band's blessings, and I put "Elizabeth Reed" back together the way it was, and Dickey did not object. I used my favorite version of "Hot 'lanta" because going to digital I could find ways to hide the horns that I could not find in the old analog days. So I switched the take on "Hot 'lanta," and I used the echo version of "Whipping Post," but I did not add in the idiot that screams "Play 'Whipping Post'!" You know, I am still getting mail that I used the wrong tape, can you believe it?! That's how much people know, you gotta crack up laughing. [Laughs]

4

Friends, Family, and Other Love Songs

The band really took off at this point, gaining respect and admiration from not only fans, but their contemporaries as well. That admiration even crossed the pond to England, where Eric Clapton would eventually ask Duane to play on his new album Layla and Other Assorted Love Songs.

Pete Kowalke
The Allman Brothers were just full tilt awesome. The band flat out cooked. I really didn't know what to think. Just powerfully great music. And there was a damn wildly interesting hotel and after hours scene in Macon. Duane was a gentleman, always. He was a really nice guy. Got right down to business too, no fooling around. He really helped push me along and gave me a few Duane stories to tell in the coming years. I am totally blessed for the time and interactions I had with him.

On the whole, the Brothers were extremely kind to us, (Cowboy) kind of like we were their little brothers. But they also respected the music we made and the vibe and wisdom we had within us. Of course we completely loved and respected them and their music.

I remember Berry, and probably some of the others, coming up to me backstage and saying, "Pete, get into black music." They made that point very strongly. And of course, they were right. I was already into it to a point, but their urging took me in a new direction. I probably had a black life or two in the past. [Laughs]

Gregg was more cool and reserved, but also still so good to us. Of course, Butchie was already our friend from way back. Dickey was always really cool and nice to us too. I didn't have too many interactions with Berry, he was like Duane, really cool, down to business, call it like it is, live fast, full and hard, and play your ass off.

One more Duane story. When we were in Muscle Shoals Studios ready to do "Please Be With Me," Duane was going to play the Dobro slide. Well, the Dobro has those little metal baffles, resonating things, whatever they are called. Duane was getting ready to play and one of the baffles is rattling as he plays. So I look at him and pick up this thin little magazine, a real estate mag, you know, shiny paper, a little stronger. I roll it into a tight roll and shove it down one of the f-holes until it comes up against the rattling baffle. The rattling stopped, and Duane took off. That first take was so damned awesome! I really don't know if he knew how good it was. He just played it and then shot out the door and onto his bike and the next place. We all loved Duane. Still do, wherever he is. Feels like he is still around. I will let y'all figure that one out. Yep.

Dru Lombar

[Touring with the Allmans] was only the best, you know? On the road there are some bands that feel like "you can't use this monitor" or "you can't use these lights," you can't do this, you can't do that. But the Brothers said go out there and use whatever you want. And if we got an encore, they'd say, "Go out there and take your encore." They were real supportive guys, man.

Dickey Betts

The thing is, nowadays people are thinking that it never was that way, but it always was a family. And when we say family, we aren't trying to just make up some kind of imagery or something. When someone was down, the rest of us would pull him up, maybe even be mad about it, but we'd stick together and pull him up. That's what we meant by family. That's what the band was for thirty years, and that's what seems to have gotten lost along the wayside here.

Paul Riddle

When I saw the Allman Brothers the first time, Toy Factory opened. At the time, it was Toy and Tommy and Jerry and Ross Hanna—a four-piece band. I sat up chairs in the front row. Watching those two drummers with the Allmans changed my life forever. The first thing that really got me was the drums. And I'm looking at Butch

Trucks's kit—a 22" bass drum, one tom, one floor, three cymbals, no head on the bass drum and packed with a pillow. And then I'm looking at an 18" bass drum, with a 12"and a 14" floor-tom, three cymbals, and they're tuned like Elvin Jones drums. Jaimoe tunes his drums real tight, and they sing beautifully. If people would understand, you can tune a drum up like that and the frequencies cut through everything. Case in point is Johnny Sandlin, who mixed the *Brothers and Sisters* record. If you listen to that album, Jaimoe's bass drum is in your face, it's all over it. I've talked to him about this before. I wish they'd turn his bass drum up live. Sound men have this thing about drums ringing. They are *supposed to ring*. A drum is supposed to ring. It resonates like everything else. So here's this big guy playing all these double strokes on the drums, and you don't do that in rock and roll. And then there's Butch over here just kicking the crap out of the bass drum with his foot. All I could think was, this is amazing stuff. I had never ever heard a better band.

Tom Wynn

I liked them all. They were good guys—focused—massive nads—and they seemed to goad each other pretty aggressively, but it always seemed good-natured and positive at its heart. They had much more of a warrior feel among themselves than Cowboy ever dreamed of. One listen to each band's records pretty well reveals that. Duane was definitely the spark plug, and there were zero questions in anyone's mind about that. He was massive raw energy. I liked him a lot.

It was interesting, and not my imagination—and I don't think Duane would mind me saying—but I saw Dickey blow him away on more than one occasion. As a matter of fact, I'm sure that's why Duane wanted him in the band. Duane really did care about the music first and his ego second. Sure, probably a pretty close second, but the music was first for him. He was a big-hearted guy with a big spirit. So, Dickey was not a threat to Duane. Dickey helped make the songs better.

It was always mighty impressive to watch the same skinny guys you'd just been backstage with, especially Berry Oakley and Duane, and watch them totally dominate an audience of 10,000 people. They made a point of getting up on the tightrope every night, and people had no choice but to watch—and try to keep breathing. It was powerful. And Duane always led the charge.

I have to say Jaimoe was the Allman Brother that I remember most fondly. He was one of the big guys to me much more than the rest of the guys. They were just guys. But Jaimoe, he had been on the road with Otis Redding before the Allman Brothers. He had already been doing it for a number of years when the Allman Brothers were not even a thought. Jaimoe was one of the big guys.

Jaimoe was cool and he loved his job. Once, when both of our bands [Allman Brothers Band and Cowboy] were in New York at the same time, we were all staying at the Chelsea Hotel. Somehow I ran into Jaimoe as he was getting ready to go across town to his favorite drum shop. He invited me to go with him. He was looking at some new drums, and the guys at that shop would customize them in ways I had never heard of. He was excited about it and wanted to share. He's a big-hearted guy and a mighty fine drummer—very delicate touch and the fire seems to come out of nowhere. But, come, it does.

Tommy Crain

I was playing guitar and my brother Billy was interested, but I didn't know he did anything. I came into my bedroom one day and my guitar was sitting up against the wall with a broken string. I went to find Billy and couldn't find him anywhere and then found him hiding up under my bed. He had taken my guitar out and played it and broke the string and was scared that I would kill him. I said, no, let's just play together. Then he got his own guitar and we started sitting together and playing without amps and learning stuff. Then we both got busted in 1970, in Nashville for marijuana. I got out of it by going to this group therapy session thing, but Billy was under house arrest and could only go to school and come home. So every day I would come home and play with him for two or three hours after school. Then the Allman Brothers came out and it just all opened up. We wanted to be like them.

Dickey Betts

[On "Blue Sky"] I was married to an Ojibwa Indian at the time. Let's see, Ojibwa in Canadian is what we call Chippewa. It's a different pronunciation, but it's the same thing. Her name was Sandy Blue Sky, and I started out writing the song "Blue Sky" for her, but then I realized it was a nicer song if I wrote it for the audience, so I decided to keep the "he" and "she" out of it. So now it's almost gospel in a spiritual sort of way. It's ambiguous, sort of like nature and the sky, and it kind of gave it a nice innocent character about it. I wrote that in the Big House there in Macon, in the living room one night at about four o'clock.

Tom Dowd

Now, as for *Layla*—after I did the three albums with Cream which were *Disraeli Gears*, *Wheels of Fire*, and the studio portion of *Farewell*, I did not hear from Eric [Clapton] for about two years. I could not reach him. He was having a love affair going on and was completely out of it. Then out of the clear blue sky I was working on *Idlewild South*, or *Eat A Peach*, I guess it had to be *Idlewild South*, but in the middle of it I got a phone call. Now, the only phone calls that I would take during a session were from my wife, my kids, or Ahmet Ertegun or Jerry Wexler, because it would be something urgent. This was Robert Stigwood, and I thought, " Oh, boy, what does he want?" I figured I had better accept the call.

So while I am taking his call, the Brothers are recording, and they finish recording and they walk into the control room and here I am with the monitors turned off. I had no idea what the hell they had played, and I am talking to England and when the call was done I said, "You guys will have to excuse me, that was Eric Clapton's manager and he is talking to me." Then Duane says, "Eric Clapton," and he starts playing me Cream licks, and says, "That guy?" And I say, "Yeah." He asks me if I am going to record him, and I explained that they were coming here in a couple of weeks and wanted to find out what my schedule is like. He says that he wants to be there when Clapton comes and I have to tell him when. "Fine," I say, "so in the meantime, let's get back to what we were doing."

Sure enough, in about three weeks to one month later, Clapton, and Raddle, Gordon, and Whitlock show up. I know Bobby Whitlock from Memphis, the other two I had never met before, and Eric I know from the Cream days. I said, "What are we going to do?" and they say, oh, this and that. I had warned the studio that the last time I had recorded this guitar player he had double stacks of Marshalls and was going at 120 db and this and that. Well, when we walk into the studio here he is and he has a little Champ and Princeton with him. Literally, he has a Champ and a Princeton. I am thinking to myself, "What the hell is this about?" They start running songs and I am saying, "What's the name of this?" They tell me that they don't have any names of anything yet that they are still just working on songs.

So I get my engineer, I have two or three of them, and I say just keep the two track rolling on whatever the hell they are doing, and we will index it and be able to play it back to them so that I can say, okay, this series of chords should be the bridge for this song, or if you are going to do this song, you need to start on this section. So we are talking this way and they are running endless jams by me and during one of these jams who calls but Duane. He says that he will be playing there tomorrow night with the band and he wants to come by the studio. While I am talking to him, I shut everything down and Eric walks in and he looks at me and I told him that it was Duane Allman on the phone. Then Eric looks up at me and gives me the Duane Allman solo on the back of Wilson Pickett's "Hey Jude." He plays it note for note. I told him that Duane wanted to meet him, and that his band was playing in an open air concert at Miami Beach tomorrow at 7:00 p.m. and he says, "We'll be there!"

So I got a limousine and threw the band in and I take them down and the Allman Brothers are already on stage. I sneak them in from backstage and we are sitting in the barrier that protects the band from the audience. Nobody knows that we are there because we are behind the security line and have crawled in on all fours. Duane is doing a solo and he opens his eyes and here is Eric staring at him and he just stops dead in his tracks. Then, Dickey is like, looking sideways at Duane, and he figures that either his amp is broken or his string is broken off and Dickey starts soloing. You know what I'm saying [Laughs].

Then when that show is over we all go backstage and everyone is hugging and talking and playing licks and then by about 11:00 p.m. we all go back to the studio. I had all the engineers and told them whatever the hell, roll 16 tracks, don't let anything go unrecorded. We recorded everything that was going on. We had Gregg Allman playing organ, Whitlock on piano, Jaimoe on drums for his song, and Jim Gordon was playing percussion, and here Eric and Duane were playing licks to each other and all of a sudden Duane would say, "Oh, no, that's not how I do it, I do it this way," because he would recognize what Eric copied. Then Eric would recognize something that Duane copied and correct him, and here they are switching guitars, switching fingerings, it was like a marriage made in heaven. None of this "I can play better than you" crap. It was a marriage made in heaven. They proceeded to jam until 3:00 or 4:00 in the afternoon. Everyone was exhausted. They talked about when could we get back together to record. They had formulas for two or three different songs. In a couple of days Duane came back, and we did the whole album in ten days. If you look at the sheets of the reissued version we did it in ten days.

Jimmy Hall

The first time I saw the Allman Brothers it was way back. They were playing the Warehouse in New Orleans, opening for Albert King. I was knocked out by their songs, I mean, I had bought the first album. It was their first album that caused Wet Willie to start setting our sites for Macon and Capricorn. One thing I remember about that night was Berry Oakley. Some good-looking girls were standing at the front of the stage, and he made an off-the-wall comment that would be considered sexist today. He looked at them and said, "Forget about hamburger, we're having steak tonight!" [Laughs] Also when I think about them playing there, that's where we recorded *Drippin' Wet Live*. That was New Year's Eve, 1973.

5

Skydog

Duane Allman was killed on October 21, 1971, just months after the release and early success of At Fillmore East. *He was riding his motorcycle through Macon when he collided with a flatbed truck carrying a lumber crane.* Eat a Peach, *the album they were working on when he died, was released a few months later.*

Tom Dowd
The Allman Brothers Band was Duane's baby, no two ways about it.

Dickey Betts
Duane and I were just musical brothers. We would sit up late at night and get us a bottle of ripple you know, and talk about how the thing that breaks up every band is jealousy, and fighting over women. So we had the women thing figured out. Nobody messes with anybody else's girl. But we talked all the time about how easy it was for he and I to get jealous of each other. It was just a human nature thing. It was just something we dealt with straight ahead and talked about it in private. I'd say "Sometimes when you play, I either get jealous or it makes me want to play harder." But Duane was just so assured and straight ahead. When he wanted to get something done, he would just go straight ahead, and nothing would stop him. And that's what he offered to the band. That confidence and the "We can do it!" Not a cheerleader, but keeping everyone's morale up. And of course his playing was incredible. [Laughs] We know about his playing! But when Duane got his mind set, he was straight ahead. And he would inspire people around him. So it was kind of an interesting mix. Berry was kind of the guru of the band, and Duane

was the real fire-breathing, straight ahead, nothing can stop me guy. It was really a good mix.

Red Dog Campbell

Without a doubt he was the leader. What he said went. Everybody respected Duane. If Duane said, "We're leavin' here right now," we were leavin.' That's what made the band so good was that everybody respected his opinion. But Oak was the underlying force. Berry Oakley. Oak did most of the talking. At meetings and stuff Oak did the rapping. When we'd go into a meeting, Berry would bring up the questions. Like I said in the book, one time Phil said to Duane, "Do I have to meet with the roadies?" Duane told him, "This is the band." And in my book I was talking about the gold record deal, where Dixie said she wanted it, and Duane told her "You didn't earn it." A guys tells you something like that right in front of his old lady, that's something. These days that doesn't happen anymore. Sometimes you wonder if people appreciate what you do. It's all business now. You can be replaced tomorrow. The road crew changes constantly. I'm the only original crew man left.

Delaney Bramlett

I met Duane through Jerry Wexler. I had met him before, but we didn't get to know each other or anything like that. I'd seen him doing sessions with Aretha and stuff. But Jerry told me, "You need to get together with Duane Allman. You two would make some classic records, the way you play guitar and the way he plays." I said, "Yeah, but he's got a band." Jerry said, "It's worth a try." So I called him up and asked him what he was doing and he said, "Nothing." I asked him if he'd play some shows with me, and he said, "Yeah! Delaney I've always wanted to play with you." I said, "Well I've always loved your playing." Before I knew it he was at my house. From then on, the Allman Brothers would be on tour and they'd be looking for Duane and he'd be out here on tour with me. [Laughs] He'd call me from the airport and say hey bro, can you come pick me up? I'm here.

Phil Walden, who owned their record company, sued me about seven or eight times for soliciting [pulling Duane away to play without management's permission]. Duane would always say, "Nope, you can't sue him. I'm the one who solicited *him*." So nothing ever came of it. But we got to be best friends, and if you saw one of us you saw the other. And King Curtis rounded out the trio. I mean, me and Duane and Curtis, we hung together and we made some real good music. You know Duane got a little strung out on drugs, and I talked to him and asked him before he got any worse if he'd go to the hospital. He said, "Do you think it would work?" He got to the hospital, and it would have been easy because he wasn't that bad off, but he was like me and had a bad temper. He told the nurse, "I need a little something to calm me down. I'm kind of hurting." And the nurse yelled at him, "Oh all you druggie hippie musicians come here for help and just go back out and do it all again!" It made him mad, so he just got up, put his clothes on and got on his motorcycle and took off. And that's when he hit that peach truck (*sic*) and died.

He was supposed to play with me the next night. We had two shows scheduled. I did the first show, looking for Duane. Then I asked my brother, who was my manager at the time, if he'd heard from Duane and he said no. Well just as I was getting ready to do my second show, my brother Johnny ran out onstage and told me Duane had been killed. I was stunned. I had to do the second show with that on my mind. It liked to have killed me.

Jerry [Wexler] called me and said everybody wanted me to sing at the funeral. I said, "My God Jerry, do you know how hard that's gonna be?" He said, "Yeah, but he's your best friend." Sure enough it was hard just like I said it was gonna be. And see, just five weeks before that me and Duane had gone to Curtis's funeral, because he was murdered, you know. Some Puerto Ricans were fighting outside his motel door and he asked them to quiet down because someone was going to call the cops, and he didn't want to see the cops out there. Well, he turned around and got stabbed in the back. When he said, "You hurt me real bad," the guy stabbed him in the heart. He died on the way to the hospital. Duane and I went to his funeral, and five weeks later I went to Duane's. The trio was busted up.

Tom Dowd

Duane was a pussycat, an absolute humble, soft-spoken, brilliant leader. He never provoked anyone in the band. He was never demonstrative but he was in charge and he got everyone to go the right way whether he did it by playing them something or saying something to them.

Butch Trucks

Duane is the most powerful human I have ever known. If not for him I would be a math teacher at some high school. He was the kind of person that, when he entered a room every one would stop and look—he had that kind of presence. He was a self-taught intellectual. Few people know this but his line about "Every time I go south I eat a peach for peace" was taken from T. S. Eliot's "Love Song of J. Alfred Prufrock." The metaphor has to do with when you eat a peach you make a mess just like when you live a life full of experience.

He reminded me of Goethe, Faust, he wanted to experience everything life had to offer, good and bad. The great thing about him was when the bad experiences began to adversely affect his life, he would stop them. Duane experimented with just about any drug there was. As soon as he realized that they were affecting his music he would stop and never use that drug again.

As for me, I was riddled with self-doubt about my playing. Although I was very good drummer I lacked that confidence. Jaimoe had been telling Duane that I was the second drummer for the band. I think Duane knew on one level that was true, but there was no way that he could have me in the band with my lack of confidence. I think he reached a point where he decided that I was his man but not with the lack of confidence I had. One day we were jamming and things weren't really going anywhere. I did my usual "Oh shit, everybody's looking at me" thing and Duane whipped around, locked eyes with me, and played a screaming riff with a "Come on you s.o.b.!" look. My first reaction was to back off even more. After about the third time he did this I got pissed and started hitting my drums like they were Duane's head. Needless to say the jam just took off with all of the energy I was pouring into it and Duane backed off, looked at me and smiled, and said, "There ya' go." I swear it was like he reached inside of me and flicked a switch. It was an epiphany. I have played from that moment to this with all off the power at my disposal. No more nervousness.

Red Dog Campbell

He was my hero. I mean, I would have followed Duane to the end of the earth. I was older than him, but I respected him enough and loved him enough to do it. Duane had a sixth sense—or a seventh sense, man. He just knew what to do at the right time. There's a fork in the road, right? If you go to the left, there's a pot of gold. If you go to the right, you're in a pile of crap. Duane could walk right up to the fork without thinking and say "Let's go to the left." And he'd come out smelling like a rose. But he was fair. He was honest. He was up front and didn't beat around the bush. You didn't have to hear [drags voice] "Well, you know…I was thinkin'…. It ain't really nice for me to say it, but…." You didn't have to hear it. He'd just say, "Red Dog, you messed up bad man. We're gonna have to let you go." There wouldn't be no beatin' around the bush. I try to live like that myself. I just don't have the tactfulness or the position in life to deal the other way. So I just hit it, bam-bam-bam. [Laughs] I don't really think you can put it into words, on Duane. He used to say, "You guys do all the work. We just come over and have fun." That's really what it's all about. If these musicians say "I'm out here working my butt off, something's wrong." I mean, if he ain't out there playing and having fun, something's wrong. It's at the stage of the game now where it's not work. It's "Hey, let's enjoy ourselves and play." The roadie's the guy who's doing the work to get the thing going.

Charlie Daniels

Duane was a favorite and an influence. I don't believe there has been a musician come along from our part of the country since that early Allman Brothers Band that hasn't been influenced by Duane in one way or another, at least by the caliber and intensity of Duane's playing. I know I have.

Johnny Sandlin

He was one of the most interesting, exciting, and alive people that I ever knew. He was one of the most intelligent as well. Most of the time he was great to be around. He was so dedicated to music, and it was a central thing in our lives. It was that way with Berry too.

Whenever anyone played with Duane he would bring out the best in them. Not that it was a competition, but he was an inspiration. He was one of the best that there ever was.

Charlie Hayward

[With Alex Taylor] We got to do quite a few shows with Duane and the Allmans and we opened lots of shows for them. Then, the next year after Duane died when Dickey kind of took over—that was before Chuck came in—doing some of those big festivals that we played with them were just great.

Bonnie Bramlett

Duane is probably the bonding agent between all of us. And Joe Dan and Twigs and all the guys we lost, and it is a strong bonding agent to go to all these wakes, and the older we get the more we will lose each other. When we go to these wakes I can see all the older guys looking at each other wondering who will be next. The great thing about this time is that people are not taking drugs and drinking, everybody is healthy.

Pete Kowalke

At one point was in Daytona Beach and we—Scott, David Brown, and me—were at the Allman Brothers' house, and they wanted to start a group and invited me also to join. Silly me, my response was "You got Duane, what do you need another guitar player for?" [Laughs] Oh well, live and learn. [Laughs] Later on at another time I was playing the Daytona Beach Pier and Duane came by and gave me his Fuzz Face—you know, the round effects pedal—Jimi Hendrix used one sometimes. I tried it a few times and determined that I didn't like the sound of it and proceeded to go to Duane's house and give it back to him. Can you believe it? He looked at me kind of funny like "Why would you give it back?" [Laughs] I hear that Fuzz Face is in Duane's biography book...but no one got this part of its history in there.

Devon Allman

Man, you know, I think if you ever read his journal entry about love, "I'm happy to be alive and I will give love wherever I can and take it when it is given," something like that, that sums it up—he hit a point where his soul was so pure they had to take him. He had a much bigger job somewhere else. That's the only way I can justify taking someone so young.

Obviously he will live forever in the body of work he left, which was huge for someone of twenty-four. I think the fact that *Rolling Stone* ranked him number two after all these years is an amazing testament to what he did for music as a whole.

You know, I've only been playing lead guitar for five years. I never sat down and learned his licks. I never picked up a slide because of him. I thought it would be a little too much. Not to say I never will, but I wanted to be respectful, you know? I went to his grave once and I just sat there and lost it. There's some kind of ribbon of connectivity. Not so much about music but about family. And I think there were multifaceted reasons behind those tears. For him not being on the planet anymore. For my dad not having him anymore. For my grandmother not having him anymore. For music as a whole not having him anymore. But he will live forever through his great music.

6

Brothers & Sisters

After a period of mourning, the remaining five band members picked them-
selves up, dusted themselves off, resumed touring with Dickey Betts as solo
guitarist. Rather than hire a second guitarist, they would soon add a young
keyboard wizard named Chuck Leavell, and proceed to record yet another
landmark album, and their first to spawn a certified Top 40 hit ("Ramblin'
Man") — Brothers and Sisters.

Red Dog Campbell
As a roadie in the early days you did it all. Matter of fact, when I
started, nobody actually took care of drums. In those days they didn't
really have a drum roadie—or technician—whatever they want to call
'em these days. Everybody has got to have a title. That's why in my
book [*The Legendary Red Dog: A Book of Tails*] it says "roadie" by my
name. I was a roadie thirty years ago, and I'm a roadie today. It hasn't
changed none. In the old days, we used to have to do it all, drive and
everything. I'd set up the drums, and if Kim still needed some help
with the amp line, I'd just jump over and start setting up the amp line
with him. Or I'd help Callahan with the P. A., you know. And vice-
versa. If one of them finished before I did, they'd jump right in and
help me. In those days, you didn't have to say "Hey, can you help
me?" There was somebody right there.

Right after Duane died, we already had to count on one another.
The first tour without him was very emotional. We truly did become
brothers and sisters more than ever before.

Taz DiGregorio
The whole Southern rock thing was a brotherhood, a family, and
we were at that time when we started out. We [the Charlie Daniels

Band] toured with the Allman Brothers Band, the Marshall Tucker Band, Wet Willie, Lynyrd Skynyrd, Black Oak Arkansas, and these people were gracious and loving people who allowed us to open shows and play in front of a lot of people. They allowed us and taught us. For instance, the Allman Brothers Band's Red Dog taught us about road cases. He asked where our road cases were, and we did not know what he meant. It was an education.

Dickey Betts

I wrote "Ramblin' Man" in the kitchen at the Big House. I got a bunch of good songs out of that house.

Chuck Leavell

Well, thanks to Dickey Betts for writing that piece ("Jessica"). It's been berry, berry good to me! As I recall, Dickey first played it to us on acoustic guitar. We sort of toyed with it at first, just getting comfortable with the changes and getting the harmony parts between the guitar, piano and organ. Then we ran through it like, once a night for a few nights in a row until we felt confident about all the twists and turns, and slowly developing some of the transitions that occurred. I don't know how many takes it was, but not many after we really learned the song. I'd guess three or four. There may be an edit in there between takes, I can't really remember, but Johnny Sandlin could probably answer that. As far as the piano part, it just came.... I tried not to think about it, not to "organize" a part, other than to learn the harmony and the other necessary parts. I was just trying to keep up with those guys, and the notes I played on the solo just fell off my fingers. The solo just sort of played itself. It felt very natural, and I was just thrilled to have a song like that with a strong role for my instrument.

Dickey Betts

[On "Jessica"] Well, that wasn't necessarily *how* I wrote it; it was more of an anecdote about what was going on at the time I wrote it. There was a lot of inspiration from Django Rhinehart. If you'll notice, on the melody, you can play that thing with two fingers. And I was trying to get that Django Rhinehart kind of bounce. So that was the imagery I had in my mind, and when [my daughter] Jessica came into the room, I tried to capture that feeling, and it gave it that happy feeling, you know. And the thing with "Elizabeth Reed," I was writing it for this beautiful Spanish Italian girl named Carmella. I didn't want to call it Carmella because—she wasn't married, but she was going with a guy. It was a cloak and dagger love triangle. [Laughs] So I called it "In Memory of Elizabeth Reed" because of that tombstone [at Rose Hill Cemetary in Macon, Georgia].

Les Dudek

I had a band in Florida called Power at the time, and we were doing a lot of shows trying to get a deal in those days. The keyboard player knew Dickey Betts real well because he had grown up in Venice, Florida, and Dickey was from Sarasota. When Duane died we heard that Dickey was going to start a band separate from the Allman Brothers. He was auditioning players, and Peter found out about it and said why don't we go up there and see what's going on. So, we went up and hung out with Dickey for a weekend, jammed with him on the back porch there in Macon. We said our goodbyes and went on home, and then I got the call back. So, I went back to Macon and was working out with Dickey and then Gregg caught wind of the fact that Dickey was doing his own band and kind of threw a hissy on that, so Dickey kind of backed out of it. That band with Dickey did some demos for Phil Walden and we were supposed to be getting something happening but it never came about.

So, they started on the *Brothers and Sisters* album, and I was down there one night when they were cutting "Ramblin' Man" and Dickey would come over and say "What do you think about this?" I'd throw a couple of ideas at him. Then he'd go back out and do it and come back and say, "What about this?" [Laughs] He was talking about the guitar parts. Finally, he said to hell with it, "why don't you just come out here and play with me?" That's how we ended up doing "Ramblin' Man."

I co-wrote "Jessica." I never got any credit for it. Dickey says he still feels bad about that. Maybe one of these days he'll write me a check [Laughs] and put my name alongside his. He was really stumped on that one. We were at his house there in Macon. At the time, I was rooming with Joe Dan Petty, who just died recently. He had wanted me to be in Grinderswitch with him. He was starting a band and that's when I turned him on to Larry Howard and Rick Burnette, cats that were playing with me down in Florida at the time. One night, I was over at Dickey's when they were still doing the *Brothers and Sisters* album. Dickey had the one part of "Jessica" written, the melody on the verse section. He said, "Play this, man. Let's see if we can do something with it." We kicked it around for 45 minutes or so and my girlfriend and his wife were in there cooking us steaks, so he got frustrated with it and put his guitar down. I kept messing with it and I came up with the bridge. I said, "Dickey, come here a minute, man." [Laughs] I said, "Play this after you play that." He said, "What do we do next?" I said, "Walk it all the way up to the top and stop." He said, "Well, what do you do after that?" I said, "Start over!" [Laughs] He was just ecstatic. We ended up not even eating our steaks. We threw the guitars in the back of the pickup; he wanted to go and play it for everybody. Right when we did it, it started snowing in Macon. It was kind of a spiritual moment, how it all came to be. He marched me into Walden's office and he promised me some points on it and this and that. It took us six nights to cut the thing in the studio. At that time, Phil Walden was trying to get me into the Allman Brothers. He said, "Stick with me. I'm going to make you a star. I'm going to put you in the Allman Brothers." I had already had talks with Dickey, and he kind of felt that he pretty much wanted to take over with the guitar slot. I think for a number of years he was kind of the second guitar player under Duane. Not taking anything away from Dickey—he was kind of shafted because, if you look back on the early stuff, Dickey wrote it, like "Elizabeth Reed" and a lot of the good tunes and he played it, too. It's like the quarterback who always gets the limelight, but Dickey was always a real contributor to that band, I thought.

Right after *Brothers and Sisters* came out, Bobby Womack was trying to get me to go on the road with him when Boz Scaggs came into town. Boz had a guitar player that kind of wigged out on him on the road, so he called up David Brown and Phil Walden down in Macon and they told him about me. It was kind of funny because the drummer that was gonna be in the band with Dickey, and I was going to go with Womack, also. We had a cab waiting downstairs and we were gonna fly to L. A. to play with Womack when I got a call from Phil who said I should call Boz. He was in Akron, Ohio. It just sounded better to go with Boz. I went downstairs and pulled my bags out of the cab and said, "I gotta get another cab. I'm going to Akron, Ohio. [Laughs]

Chuck Leavell

To give you a feel for where I was coming from, I had just turned twenty years old. I had what I think was pretty good experience and maturity for that age, and really wanted to be in a good band. I mean a really good band. I wanted a gig with a band like that sooo bad, guys that could really play, and that had something different and special. But it came totally out of left field to be asked to come into the Allmans. As you know, they had gone out as a five-piece band for a while after Duane's tragic accident. I was with Alex Taylor, and shortly after that, Dr. John at the time, and both bands opened up for them quite a bit. We were all so impressed that they went out as a five-piece. That took a lot of guts. Well, they had finished *Eat a Peach*, and had done some dates, and I think they were trying to sort out their future. Gregg was going to do a solo album, and Johnny Sandlin called me in to play on it. As it turned out, the rest of the Allmans came down to the studio, hanging out, and we just started jamming. We had lots of these fun jams between Gregg's solo sessions, and things just felt really good. After a couple of weeks of this, sometimes doing Gregg's music, and sometimes jamming with the Allmans, I got a call to have a meeting with the band and Phil Walden at his office. I didn't know what was up, but when they asked me to join the band I nearly fell over! I was trying so hard to be cool about it, but I'm sure it was obvious that I was surprised. I couldn't believe my good fortune, doing the new ABB record and Gregg's first solo record at the same time! It was a huge boost for me, and I was over the moon to be alive and playing with these great musicians! There's not enough space to tell you about the years that were to come, but I can just say that during my whole tenure with the band I was proud to be there. There were tough times, as we all know...and I wish so much that things had not come in the way of the music, but eventually they did. So I was heartbroken when the band broke up. But Jaimoe, Lamar, and I decided to carry on and formed Sea Level, and that led to a whole other story.

Dickey Betts

[On his solo album *Highway Call*] That album was done strictly for fun. We were making a lot of money with the Allman Brothers Band, and we had some time off, and I think Gregg was working on one of his records, and I just wanted to do a fun record. Get a bunch of guys I know and have some fun. The original idea for that was, I was going to do more of a country jazz kind of thing with Stephane Grappelli. But he will not fly. He would only go by steam ship, and hell, he wasn't going to be over here for six months. I was going to have to go to Paris if I wanted to record with him. During that same period of time I ran into Vassar Clements at a bluegrass festival. I just got a bunch of unusual people that you wouldn't expect, like the Rambos, to play on it. And Conway Twitty's steel player. The thing on there, "Let Nature Sing," that was from my old Navajo friend, he's passed away now about six months ago, but he was a Navajo priest out in Arizona. And one of his things was "let nature sing." When your mind is troubled and everything, just sit and let nature sing. The guys that played on that had never been in a recording studio before. They owned a feed store down here in Manatee. They had big shows they would do on Saturday; they were professionals. They would charge people to come in and everything. They were real good players, but they had never been in a recording studio or anything. So next time you spin that you might kind of get a kick out of it. They were like a bunch of guys who had just been to the city for the first time. [*Laughs. Does backwoods accent*] Hey man! This mike here is real sensitive, ain't it?!

Johnny Sandlin

I loved working on that album [*Highway Call*] because it was slightly offbeat from what we were doing up until then. Dickey had written all these great songs for it, and I got to know him well over this album because we would sit around in my office after recording sessions and play stuff. I had just gotten turned on to Billy Joe Shaver.

He had the *Honky Tonk Heroes* album and we would listen to it almost every night. When we finished sessions at two or three in the morning, we would go listen to music and strum guitars all the rest of the night until daylight. I loved doing it and having the band with Vassar, John Hughey, and Dickey, and of course Chuck Leavell. There was a lot of soul in that band.

Tommy Talton

[Gregg's albums *Laid Back* and *Gregg Allman on Tour '74*] all came about for the same reason we were speaking of earlier, the camaraderie, brotherhood, and the house. You can just call Capricorn the living room. Gregg and Scott [Boyer] knew each other forever. I didn't know Gregg as early on as Scott because they were both in Jacksonville, and they knew each other a little bit better. Gregg loved Cowboy and loved our stuff. Gregg and I actually became really close during that time when we were on tour and recording. He recorded "All My Friends." Don't know if you ever listened to the *Boyer & Talton* album? Essentially, if you look at that album, everyone from the *Laid Back* album was all the same. Except Gregg sang instead of me and Scott. It wasn't some outside idea that happened. It was all the same people. Cowboy started the show, and Randall Bramblett was in Cowboy then and David Brown was on bass, he also played with Boz Scaggs and Commander Cody later.

Gregg Allman

Yeah. A couple of 'em [gigs] stand out. Certainly the closing of the Fillmore stands out. I once took out a 28-piece orchestra and cut what became my second solo record. It was called *Gregg Allman Tour '74*. It was recorded at Carnegie Hall. And you put a Fender bass in Carnegie Hall—the place is built for the spoken word. You put an electric bass in there, you've got a problem, man. We used one 12" speaker cabinet for the bass. It was like a Vibrasonic. And one 8" speaker for the lead guitar. We had six horns, six violas, seven violins, and seven cellos. We had the orchestra leader and everything. I want to do that again, now that I'm old enough to do it. I'd like to do it right. [Laughs] It didn't make any money, but it was ballsy. [Laughs]

They said, what's Gregg doin', is he out of his mind? But we had a helluva lot of fun doing that record. It did pretty good.

Johnny Sandlin

I love Gregg very much. I enjoyed working with him at times and then there were times that I would have never put myself through if I had known what it was gonna be like. I hear that he is doing well now, and I sure am glad. I do love him to death, and I have known him since we were seventeen or eighteen years old. He sings as well as anyone when he is on and he has a huge voice. He always did. When we were rehearsing with the Hourglass we did a bunch of blues-based stuff and his voice was as good as it ever got. It was strong, convincing, and real. He is not a prolific writer, but when he writes he is talented. One classic song is better than fifty that don't get out there. [Laughs]

The Allman Brothers Band called it quits, for the first time, in 1976. In 1978, original members Gregg Allman, Dickey Betts, and Butch Trucks returned with Dan Toler on guitar, his brother David "Frankie" Toler on drums, "Rook" Goldflies on bass, and Bonnie Bramlett on backing vocals. That lineup performed from 1978 until 1982 when they disbanded once again.

Dan Toler

Oh, man. I remember when we used to ride the bus from one town to the next—see, we were side members. Dickey, Butch, Gregg and Jaimoe were the corporate members. Sometimes they would just fly to the next gig, and we would take the bus. It was great! I'd take an acoustic guitar and we'd sit either in the front lounge, it didn't matter. Whatever anybody was into. And I'd just start playing like a 9th chord, a funky thing, you know, like one of those James Brown chords, and Bonnie would start making up words, and Rook [Goldflies], the bass player would be beatin' on the table. Man we'd have so much fun! I remember a couple of times we did that and when we'd pull into the hotel and it was time to get off the bus, we all about cried because we had to quit.

Bonnie Bramlett

I was in the band during the early 1980s, when Danny Toler was playing. The first "Allman Sister." That is probably the biggest feather in my cap. Some people get Grammy awards and all of those awards but to me, to get on the Allman Brothers' stage, or the Charlie Daniels Band, or Toy and the Tucker boys, those are like real men, and they are really not interested in boobs and butt, well they are, but not when they are working. I would say that I was the first with the Allmans, I know I was the first with them. Then Grinderswitch, Ronnie Van Zant, and Charlie [Daniels]. You know there's a certain acceptance by these men in the Southern rock business that I wear like a badge of merit. I said this at Joe Dan Petty's wake. They always treated me like a lady, whether I acted like one or not. They put me way up on a pedestal and make me feel more than an equal. I am not saying that they never made any mistakes because some other women may have had other experiences with these men than I have.

Dickey Betts

[On his favorite ABB album] I can tell you the one that none of us in the band liked at all was *Brothers of the Road*, because Clive Davis kind of ran a producer in on us. And they mixed out all of the guitar harmonies, and tried to really disco-pop it up, and we really were trying to do some kind of hit single jingle kind of stuff on there. [sings] "Straight from the heart, baby my love." You know, some of that shit. So even when we tried to make the best out of having to do some of those tunes, the guy mixed out some of the hardest work we did on it, and even simplified it from that. So none of us really liked that record. That's when we said hey, we're just going to split the Allman Brothers up until the disco period gets behind us. We went to playing clubs, you know, Gregg took his band one way and I went the other. But I love the *Brothers and Sisters* album of course, and I like *At Fillmore East* a lot. You know, *Shades of Two Worlds* is a good record, and so is *Seven Turns*. It's just different periods of time. I can't really say that I like the music we were playing back in the seventies any more than I like the *Seven Turns* record. In fact, the stuff I'm writing right now will probably be one of my favorites when we get it done, you know?

John Townsend

One autumn evening in 1991, I picked up a local paper and noticed that the Gregg Allman Band was playing just a few miles from where I was living at the time. So I got dressed and drove over to the Country Club in Reseda and arrived just in time to see the band getting out of a limo going into the club.

It was great seeing Gregg and hearing all that incredible music after being held captive by alien jingle-writer bondage for so long. After the show, Gregg invited me up to his home above San Francisco to do some writing. I only realized when I arrived at his house that the whole band was staying there and rehearsing for a tour. We got in a little writing, I got to know the guys in the band better. After a couple of days Gregg came to me and said, "Oh by the way, you're in the band." It was the greatest shot in the arm I'd had in a long time. So I stayed up one night and learned a lot of great Allman Brothers songs and for the next year and a half, got to play them with the real guys. What a total blast that was. I owe Gregg a lot for lighting a fire under me and for making me get off my butt and get back in it all the way. And after another nice run, the Allman Brothers got back together and we went home.

Gregg Allman

Well, when you do the same songs night after night, you try to do them different each night. You couldn't do them verbatim night after night, you'd go crazy. You'd probably run off howling into the night. [Laughs] With the band, it's just a natural thing. It's not like we're trying any great experiments onstage. But there's definitely some of that. When one guy starts going off in a certain direction, the rest of us will follow. As for my favorite song, I just finished a solo album, well, it's been out for about a year now. It's called *Searching for Simplicity*. I did a song on there for my brother. We cut "Dark End of the Street." Duane had recorded it with Clarence Carter when he was working on the staff down there in Muscle Shoals. He was always on me to do that song, and my voice just wasn't that thick. I mean, James Carr first did it—it takes a big, fat "Moon River" type voice. [Laughs] I didn't have the voice for it at the time he wanted me to cut it.

Red Dog Campbell

There's a whole bunch of gigs that were just great. Of course, the Fillmore gigs were unreal. Watkins Glenn was unreal. But the gigs in Piedmont Park that were free—*any* free gigs—were just a ball. I mean, anytime you set up in the park and play for nothing, that's a gas, man. Now you have to buy $200 million worth of insurance to do that, so you're not playing a free gig anymore. We had some good gigs with Charlie Daniels too. I could probably write another book just on gigs alone.

Dan Toler

Dickey had done his *Highway Call* album, and the bass player and drummer were in a band called Melting Pot that I had been in back in 1969. They had signed with Capricorn Records, and we ended up opening for the Allman Brothers. I used to stand behind Duane's amp and watch and listen. Great days. But that band broke up and I moved back to Indiana, and I was playing in a jazz band with a trumpet player named Jerry Van Blair, who was one of the trumpeters in the Chase Band. They did that song, "Got to Get It On." So I was playing with those guys and Kenny and Jerry called me and said, "Come on down to Florida, we've got this band happening." Well, while my wife and I were en route to Florida, that group broke up. Dickey was putting another band together, and they left to go and join him. So I said, give me an audition, I'll come up. And so they did. It was on a Friday the 13th, in August of '75 I believe. I missed my first flight. So I made the next one, and we are there driving, and a guy named Larry Brantley, who did all of the Marshall repair work for the band, picked me up in Atlanta. We drove about 110 miles to Macon—about 110 mph! We get there and we're on the Allman Brothers' property, and just about ran over Butch Trucks coming around the curve on this gravel road. Butchie's standing out there about half crocked. That's when I first met him. But I could hear Dickey's guitar about five miles away, and it sounded good. We finally get to the house, and I unpack my old Flying-V and walk into the house. I walked up to where the band was out on the porch. I met Dickey, and we started jamming a little bit. He asked me if I knew any of the tunes, and of course I said *no*. We did "Southbound," and at the end I twinned the lead with him. He looked at the other guys and looked back at me and said, "Well, I guess I don't have to look any further. You got the job." I said, "Great! Great, man! Am I on the payroll? Can I get my first advance?" [Laughs]

The next night we go to Atlanta to play a gig. I had no idea what the tunes were. I'd never played 'em. We did "Elizabeth Reed," "Ramblin' Man," and "Jessica"—I was really lost in the sauce there. It didn't take too long and I picked the songs up.

We did a gig in New York in Central Park, and it was a free gig, a free concert. There was a rumor of Butch and Jaimoe showing up. Gregg showed up too, we didn't know he was coming. But I guess they had been talking a little bit prior to that. Of course none of us knew what was going on. But when Gregg walked out, you could hear that crowd just going berserk! Man, I mean, it was wild. We played a few tunes, and at the end walked back stage and met John Belushi and Dan Aykroyd. We went to a bar and hung out together. Then came time for the Capricorn picnic, and Jimmy Carter was there. I auditioned for the Allman reunion. That was a long, long day. Great Southern was such a cool band. A great band. Dickey and I did some really cool things live at times.

Playing with the Brothers, those were great shows, great venues. An upgrade on everything, of course. We stayed at nice places, we flew first class, except for when we went overseas, we didn't fly first class. The main four guys did, but the rest of us didn't. It was still fantastic. We did JFK Stadium in front of 140,000 people. Talk about a powerful feeling. You could see the relay speakers, three back, just so they could hear it back there. And we were very, very loud. The P. A. was just kicking. But when you get a 100,000 people screaming, you can't hear that anymore. The sound goes down into this faint little thing down in the corner. It's pretty awesome. I mean, we did a couple of shows like that with Great Southern too—we weren't the headliners, but we were on the bill. That was awesome. I think all in all, as far as musicianship and creativity, I think Great Southern was a better band, to be honest with you. Live especially. I think energy wise, Great Southern was just a little bit better.

The day that Gregg, my brother, and I got fired from the Allman Brothers Band we started the Gregg Allman Band. Rook Goldflies was the bass player at first. Johnny Neel came in and played keys with us there at the end, right before the Allman Brothers got together. And that whole thing was just a political change. What it did was it ruined two separate entities—the Dickey Betts Band and the Gregg Allman Band.

7

Reunion: 1989

Spurred by the success of Gregg Allman's and Dickey Betts's solo works, and an outstanding boxed set retrospective of the Allman Brothers Band, the Brothers reunited, combining elements of the Dickey Betts Band, Gregg, and Jaimoe with Warren Haynes, Allen Woody, and Johnny Neel. Following the release of Seven Turns, *Johnny Neel left the band, and they soon added percussionist Marc Quinones.*

Warren Haynes

I met Dickey and Gregg on the same night. It was late '80 or '81. I was always a big Allman Brothers fan, so it was a big thrill for me to meet those guys, and hang out with them, and jam and stuff. Then a few years later, when I joined Dickey's band, I had just signed a deal to do my first solo record. In the same time I got a call from Dickey, and he said he was going to do his first solo record in nine years, and wanted me to sing and play guitar and write some songs. It was two really great opportunities hitting at one time, and I was going, "Man, when it rains it pours." I had gone from having nothing to having both of these things. So I had to choose between them. I made a decision at that point to join Dickey's band (which released an excellent album featuring Warren, *Pattern Disruptive*). I did that for about two and a half years. Again, that was stepping up to a nicer situation, and also, because of the musicians in the band—Dickey and myself, and Johnny Neel was playing keyboards and Marty Prevat was playing bass, and Matt Abts, who is now in Gov't Mule, was playing drums. We had a really excellent band, and toured for about two and a half years. Then that thing was kind of coming to a halt, and I decided I was going to take that opportunity to do my solo record. That's when I got a call from the Allman Brothers saying,

"We'd like you to join." It was really strange timing. Here I was preparing to do my own record again, and I got a call from the Allman Brothers. Once again, it was an opportunity that I couldn't turn down. I mean, getting a chance to work with an institution like the Allman Brothers, that's a once-in-a-lifetime situation. I never really knew that they were thinking about getting back together. And they never kept it a secret; they didn't want to get back together. They just said, "We're never going to play together again." But somewhere along the line, with Stevie Ray achieving success, and being so good at bringing blues back to the people, and Robert Cray coming into the picture, and the Grateful Dead was doing great, they started seeing opportunities for the Allman Brothers to be a valid entity again. Knowing that if the right combination of players could be brought in, it could be a great thing. So they had a little meeting, and they brought me and Johnny Neel into the band. Then they auditioned bass players, and they auditioned Woody, and he got the gig. It was just a great feeling, that first year, knowing that the Allman Brothers Band was coming back full force. I had always been a big fan. I'd grown up listening to that music, and it was just a great opportunity for somebody like me to come in, and be allowed to interject my personality into it. That's about all you can ask for, as far as being in a band that's been around that many years. I can't imagine another band from my past like that who would give me that much musical freedom, and be so enjoyable to play with.

We tried to bring that spirit back. I think Woody deserves a lot more credit than he got, because the bass player's role is more understated in most bands. But Berry Oakley was such an aggressive bass player, so unique, that when they lost Oakley, having just gotten over the loss of Duane, that was such a huge loss for those guys that a lot of people thought they'd never get it back. But they were gaining momentum from a fan base standpoint, and they had some great bass players through the years. I mean, Lamar Williams, who passed away as well, was a really great bass player, too, but he didn't play in that style that Oakley did. Until they hired Woody, nobody ever did. He brought a lot of that fire back in and deserves a lot of the credit.

Allen Woody

Artimus Pyle introduced me to Butch Trucks. Talk about it being a small world. I've been to Jerusalem with Artimus, we have been down some highways together. We were working on an APB [Artimus Pyle Band] record down at Butch's studio that never got released. Warren, Matt, Johnny Neel, and Marty Prevatt had just finished recording the Dickey Betts Band album there, and then we came in. We were working there when Butch heard me playing and said that they were re-forming the Allman Brothers, and he thought I'd be the one for the bass position. Artimus had told him, "Man, he was born to do this gig." So I went down and auditioned and got the gig the same day.

Warren and I were casual friends. We had met just prior to that. And you know who introduced me to Warren? Artimus Pyle, once again. But we were in the Brothers, and one night on the bus, we were listening to Cream, and I turned to Warren and said, "You know man, with the right drummer, we could have a power trio like there hasn't been in thirty years." And he said, "Yeah, with me and you and Matt Abts." So we went out, we were playing the Greek Theatre, and we went out to the Captain's Cabin to hear Matt play. We did a little jam, and it got reviewed in the paper. Like we were a regular band. They raved about the interplay between people, and everything. With that in mind, we formed, if you will, Gov't Mule, and it turned out so cool, and was so rocking, we started going out on the road in between Allman Brothers gigs. It was like, wow, this is our band. And you know, you don't want to work for somebody else your whole life, you want your own thing. The Brothers had reached a point where the creativity had died way down, and we were feeling like we had a lot of creativity we needed to get out. So we were on the road with the Black Crowes. We were backstage with Chris Robinson and some of the others, and Chris said, "I hope you guys know that you're poised to happen and you really need to get out and do your own thing." So we had pretty much already decided, and gave our notice after the Beacon run in 1997. So we've been together, a little family in a tube, going down the highway for five years now. We just finished our fifth year. But I couldn't ask for two more creative and special musicians to play with.

Red Dog Campbell

I liked it. [The Warren, Woody, Dickey lineup] I mean, the difference between Allen and Oteil, is Allen would stay in the pocket more, and his flair outs had a little more drive to 'em. Allen was more of a driving bass player. Oteil is more of a finesse bass player, and when he comes out of the pocket sometimes he loses the feel. The tune is pumping—book, boom, *book*—like a train coming at you. And Oteil will come out of the pocket and play these jazz licks. You lose the pop of the thing. It changes. But he comes right back and it goes again.

Johnny Neel

I had been playing at the Bluebird Café. It is now pretty prominent, but before it was a little joint, you know, I did a benefit for him (Dickey Betts) with an organization that he was involved with at the time but then he heard me play a slide synthesizer. I was playing through a Marshall with a wheel on the slide lick. That is how I got involved with him. I worked with him for about two years, and then I quit, and then he called me to write the album with him. Then I hooked up with Gregg Allman and wrote a song called "Island" with Gregg on *Before the Bullets Fly*, and then I got involved in the Allman Brothers reunion tour. Then I did *Seven Turns* and then we separated and I went to work for Huey Lewis's people. I enjoyed working with the Allmans.

Billy Bob Thornton

Warren works harder than anybody I know. I was in New York last year making a movie called *School for Scoundrels*, and Warren and his wife invited me and my assistant, and we went over to their apartment there in New York. He took us to his favorite local Italian restaurant. That's the last time I saw Warren. But I talked to him on the phone a couple of months ago.

Butch Trucks

Warren is one of the greatest guitar players alive today. He is also a great singer and songwriter. He brings all of these elements to the band and a solid presence that gives us a real focal point when we play. He does take charge of the music when we play, and I doubt if we could play the way we do if he didn't. He does it in such a way that he pulls everyone together without stepping on anyone's toes. It is a very tough thing to do and he does it very well.

Devon Allman

Man, Warren Haynes made a really large impression on me during that first tour I was on with the Allmans. We were in Philadelphia on the bus, and we were ready for some munchies. So me and Warren and Allen Woody got off the bus and walked to a 7-11 about a block away. Along the way there were about five homeless people, a real bummer scene. So we went into the store and everybody got a little somethin' somethin.' And this guy in there took this huge tray of donuts, bagels and pastries, and was just about to tilt it into a huge garbage tub. Warren says "Stop, stop! What are you doin'?" The guys says, "These are old, we're throwing them out." So Warren asked him to put them in a bag. The guy made three or four big bags.

Warren handed one to Allen and one to me, and he took a couple and he says, "Come on guys." We were walking back to the bus and he stopped and gave every homeless person five or six of these pastries. And it hit me like a freight train. This guy is a rock star, and most people would not even think to do it. But Warren did. And that stuck with me forever. You're never too cool or too important to just be a human being.

Warren Haynes

[Talking about his first big break] I would say being hired by David Allan Coe as guitarist. I never thought about playing a country gig before, but they called and offered me this gig, and it was my first chance to record on a major label and to tour on a national level and stuff. I talked to Coe on the phone, and I told him I wasn't a country guitar player, and I might not be right for this job. He was like, "Well, I'm looking for a blues-rock guitar player to add a nice edge to my sound." I thought if I can play like me then I'll be into it. It was really through playing with him that I met Gregg Allman and Dickey Betts and all those guys. That was my first opportunity on a national level, plus I met a lot of the people I'd become involved with later.

Chuck Leavell

Warren has been a friend for a long time. You probably know that I produced his first solo CD, *Tales Of Ordinary Madness*. That was a wonderful experience, and I'm very proud of the outcome. Too bad that it sort of got lost in the shuffle…maybe one day it will get the attention it deserves. Matt Abts is a helluva drummer. I worked with him on a Betts tour ages ago. He's one of those guys that had to be born with a pair of sticks in his hand. I was very glad that Woody and Warren got him for that spot. It's been a groove to see them mature. Their new CD [*Life before Insanity*] is the shit—it's Mule to the next level. There is no doubt in my mind that if they keep at it, they will be huge. Maybe even on this one. As for the New Year's Eve gig. What fun! Warren was a champ to ask all those players to come…Randall Bramblett, Bernie Worrell, Derek, everybody. He's like that, though, always finding a situation to invite interesting musicians to play together. I love that tune on the new CD, "Bad Little Doggie." Just great! Mule Rules!

Johnny Neel

I remember that Woody could make me laugh to the point of tears. He talked about seeing someone walking down the street and make me cry laughing. He was very sensitive and spiritually aware. He was confused about parts of his life as we all are, but overall he was a good-hearted soul. He and Warren and Matt were such a thing, in Gov't Mule, I just loved it. That is the kind of magic he was about, and it [Allen's passing] kind of messed me up. We all kind of sat back on that one.

Warren Haynes

Well, it wasn't nearly as complex as some would have you believe. When I joined the Allman Brothers, Woody and I joined in '89, it was just going to be a reunion tour. But it went so well, we decided to do it the next year. Well, that went even better, so we decided to do it another year. But they had this past history of never

staying together over three years at a time. I don't think it was ever
my intention to be in the Allman Brothers for eight and a half years.
But it was a great experience and a great opportunity, and I wouldn't
trade it for anything. I write a lot of songs that don't necessarily fit
into the Allman Brothers bag, and I always wanted to first and
foremost do my own music, and I was able to in the Allman Brothers.
I was able to write songs in the band, and I was able to be one of the
singers in the band, and given a lot of musical freedom, as we had
talked about earlier. But I still wanted an opportunity to record and
perform a lot of the songs that I was writing that didn't fit into that
genre, so to speak. For three years, Woody and I juggled the two
bands. We'd get off the Allman Brothers bus and get on the Gov't
Mule bus, and we'd get off the Gov't Mule bus and get on the Allman
Brothers bus. We went from one tour to another and another, which
proved to be a very hectic schedule. It was rewarding, but it was
tough, you know? Eventually we just figured out that Gov't Mule
was really starting to gain some momentum, and that's where our
heads were as far as a musical future. That's what we wanted to do,
and we didn't want to pass up the opportunity to do it the right way.
So we thought about it, and the only way we could convince the
world that we were serious about it—and that it wasn't just
something we did when we weren't playing with the Allman
Brothers—was to do it full time and allow it to gain the steam that it
needs. Last year we left the band, and this was the first year that
we've had the entire year to do what was best for Gov't Mule, and it's
been a great year. We're really excited about it. It was great to make
decisions based on what was good for the band, as opposed to
saying, "Well, the Allman Brothers are working here, here, here and
here, and what's left we can figure out, if and when we want to
work." See, to leave an institution like that is never going to be an
easy decision. We had to do it to kind of show ourselves and the rest
of the world that we were very serious about this. A lot of people
read more into it than there really was, you know.

Gregg Allman

When Warren and Allen left the band, I don't think there was any doubt that we wanted to keep going. I knew replacing Warren wouldn't be easy. There's only one Warren Haynes. There's also only one Derek Trucks/

8

Brother Dickey

In 2000, the band forced Dickey Betts out of the band citing "personal and professional differences." Dickey immediately formed the Dickey Betts Band before reuniting with Danny Toler to resurrect Great Southern.

Red Dog Campbell

Well, I'll put it this way, in a nutshell. It's just thirty-three years of being together, right? And things going down. And finally it all just comes to the surface. You couldn't say this happened or that happened. You know what I mean? It's thirty-three years. And like back in the early seventies, Gregg's thing with Scooter wasn't the most popular thing in the world either. It's just a marriage, man, and somebody's just pissed off: "Go live with your mama for a while, *bitch*! I ain't even talkin' to you!" In a nutshell, that's it. I mean, a bad marriage doesn't happen overnight. You started gettin' up wrong six months ago.

Dickey Betts

I can tell you pretty much what is happening, and it's becoming more obvious if you've read any of Butch's quotes on the Internet. Butch [Trucks] has kind of taken over the band, in my opinion. The way I see it, and I was there when all this shit went down, and I really didn't realize how much pent-up resentment, and damn near hatred, I guess, Butch has for me. And a lot of it has to do with the fact that he kind of blames me for the Allman Brothers not getting involved in his business things. To put it simply, Butch has finally taken over the band. And the first thing he does is get rid of me because he feels I was keeping the other guys from going along with his business ideas. I'm not sure Gregg was going along with them either. We had meetings and voted on it and all, and Gregg and I and Jaimoe would all vote against these things because we felt like it was a conflict to mix Allman Brothers business with Butch Trucks's business. But I just saw on the Internet that the Allman Brothers had gotten out of the deal with Sony and were signing with what they call the ABB Record Company. Which, I have an idea, will be the Flying Frog Records. So really I think that's what is the problem in the band. But if that's what they want to do it's fine with me. I certainly don't want to be involved with it if that's what they are going to do anyway.

It surely saddened me. It broke my heart as a matter of fact. And to think that Butch Trucks would get in there and mess things up the way it seems he has done. That's kind of pitiful. I was kind of hoping that the Allman Brothers Band would all say "Let's do a farewell tour," and everybody go do your own thing. And leave the thing in a more graceful or dignified way. But it turns out we end like all of the other bands end, with differences that just can't be dealt with.

The thing is, they kind of trumped up these things on me, when that's not the problem at all. It wasn't my playing, or any kind of substance abuse.

About the playing, there was one absolute train wreck on those tapes, and Derek and I laughed about it when it was over. Derek started the wrong song. We started "Black Hearted Woman." And he was so positive he had the right song that he came in playing real loud, and it threw the whole band off. We almost had to stop playing before we could figure out what the hell was going on. Because "Black Hearted Woman" starts in a 7/8 time, and Derek came in with a 4/4 time thing, and everybody was second guessing what song we were playing. That was the only thing I heard on the tapes that was outstandingly out of whack.

Butch Trucks

When he [Dickey] would start drinking it got very difficult. All I'll say is that we reached a point to where we couldn't do it anymore. He was beginning another slide into drinking, and I decided that this time I would not go with him, so I called Gregg and Jaimoe and told them "No more." They agreed, and we decided to do the summer tour without him and give him time to get himself back together.

That famous "fired by fax" said in essence that he had some serious problems that he needed to get help with. We were going to do the summer tour with another guitar player, and in the fall we would get back with him and discuss continuing the journey that we had been on for all of these years. Rather than getting medical help, Dickey hired a lawyer and sued us. As Jaimoe said, "Dickey quit" that day.

Jimmy Herring

The way it came about, I had known Derek since he was eleven years old. His manager, Bunky Odom, was a friend of Bruce's and he kept coming around to our shows and saying "Wait 'til you hear this kid. You'll think you're listening to Duane Allman." We're kind of like, "Yeah, right." But then he came and played a show with us in Chapel Hill, and he put all of us on the floor. His essence was right up front. All the things we had been struggling to find, he already had it! We were just knocked out by him, and our relationship just grew and grew, and we're the best of friends—all of us are. I was on tour with him about two or three years ago when the ARU [Aquarium Rescue Unit] wasn't playing as much. Butch came to the show one night, and he liked the chemistry that Derek and I had, and he wanted to form a band. He asked if I knew a bass player. I told him I knew the Michael Jordon of bass players, and that was Oteil. So Butch said let's all get together at this time down in Florida. We'll rent a bed and breakfast and we'll rehearse. And that was Frogwings. That's how I met Butch. Actually, I had played with him once in 1993 when Dickey missed a show and I sat in with them. Not long after Frogwings formed, Warren Haynes and Allen Woody left the Allmans, and they wanted to get me and Oteil to come in. But Dickey was still there, and I knew they needed a slide player. I said, "I'd love to be in the Allman Brothers, don't get me wrong, but I'm not a slide player." I said, "You should get the best slide player in the world, your nephew." At that time, Derek was only seventeen. They felt like he was too young, or maybe Butch was a little bit concerned about bringing in a family member who was only seventeen years old. So they ended up getting Jack Pearson, who is just an extremely good musician. I love Jack Pearson.

So with Oteil in the Allmans, one of my best friends was in the Allmans. Then when they got Derek, two of my best friends were in the Allmans. Plus I had played gigs with Butch and Marc, and I'd played with Jaimoe when the Allman Brothers were broken up back in the mid-eighties. So I knew everybody in the Allman Brothers except Gregg and Dickey. So when Dickey didn't play the summer tour, they asked me, I guess because I knew everyone. I felt very lucky to get the call, but I was also very skeptical about doing it. I mean, Dickey is one of the reasons I started playing guitar. It was great, but during the summer, I started talking to Phil Lesh about the band he wanted to start putting together for the next year. I said, "Phil, I don't know what to do. I'm in the Allman Brothers Band." He goes, "I know. That's unbelievable!" He was real happy for me, but he still wanted me to be in his band. Having to choose, I was in a tough spot. My decision was based on many angles. Number one, I played with Phil before I played with the Allman Brothers, and he had mentioned he may want to put together a full time band some day, and I had told him that I would be interested.

Then the Allmans called me. By the end of the summer, I was real comfortable with the gig. The gig was the easy part. The hoopla surrounding it was tough. I mean, *Dickey didn't retire*. He didn't leave on his own. He wasn't happy about it. And the guy can still play. He's awesome. It made me feel like I was standing between him and his rightful place, regardless of what their problems together were. That's none of my business. I never asked them about it. Whenever they would start to tell me, I would say, "Please don't tell me about it. I don't want to know." So I went ahead and took the job with Phil. One reason is, this is Dickey's road that he paved here. All I can do is basically drive up and down the road he paved. With Phil, I could pave my own road, even though we are playing Grateful Dead's music, and even though there are the inevitable comparisons. But both of those gigs were great, for different reasons.

With the Brothers, you get to stand there and swing the bat hard. You get to play loud, and you're playing huge venues. With Phil, it's more about open-ended experimentation and you're not playing that loud. And you're not swinging the bat that hard, because you aren't trying to hit a home run with Phil. You are playing totally team sport.

You know what I mean. With Phil, it's like Dixieland music, three or four guys are playing at the same time. Phil doesn't want you to fall into the thing of you play rhythm for him while he solos, he plays rhythm while you solo—he's not into that scene. He's looking for everybody to open it up, you know. Whereas with the Brothers, it's more like "you swing the bat."

Tom Dowd

Dickey and I get along famously, and I have to look at him sometimes, and only because of that common 1940s background do I realize where Dickey is coming from sometimes. Now, Dickey is the first to say that we used to sit on the back porch with my grandpa and that's how we learned and so forth. Dickey was extremely sensitive to Django Reinhardt and Stephane Grappelli, and he did not know who they were. He was sensitive to Grappelli particularly; if you listen on *Beginnings* and *Idlewild South* some of his solos start like the Grappelli violin solos, and they start on row strings and go up, now all of a sudden he is a blues, jazz, rock guitar player. He never just jumped on it like that. He set a foundation and then slid into it. I recognized that right away from my jazz sensitivity days, and I could not say that to him for fear that I would upset him, so I choose to leave him alone, because what he is doing is beautiful. I would admire him and tell him that the way he started that solo is magnificent, and that what you are doing is great don't change it, try and start every one like that. I would tell him to try and do every lick with that touch you have right now, because I never wanted to criticize him because I would send him off on a tangent that would take him a week to recover. But on the other hand, if you just stroked him, oh, he would come up with some exquisite playing.

Bonnie Bramlett

That is not fair to ask [about Dickey Betts] because he is like Michael Jordan to me. When he is an Indian, he is so spiritual, a great leader, he does not force opinions but he shares information. When he is a cowboy, he's not—let's just say that he is not anything like the Indian when he is a cowboy. I love him either way. I always have and I always will, and his wife doesn't mind. It is okay for me to love him.

Matt Abts

I first met Dickey in the early eighties. During that time, I had moved down to Florida and I was playing with a friend from the Virginia area. My dad was in the Army and we moved around a lot, so I ended up in Virginia. I worked the East Coast right after high school for six or seven years, and we all gravitated toward Florida, where the weather was nicer. [Laughs] So I was playing in Florida with a friend of mine in a Top 40 cover band, and that's where I met Dickey, down in Sarasota area. Gregg was living down there at the time too. Dickey used to come into clubs we played in, and we had some sort of jam relationship going. After I moved out of the area, Dickey had a band called BHLT, which was Dickey, Jimmy Hall, Chuck Leavell, and Butch Trucks, during one of the times when the Allman Brothers were broken up. At one point, Butch couldn't make the gig, and Dickey had my phone number, so he called me. I was in Virginia. I ended up touring with them that summer, and working with Dickey from 1984 until '89. We had a number of guitar players, and then Warren was brought in around 1986, and we went on to do some playing. In the meantime, Warren had brought Johnny Neel in. I played with Dickey for about five years through a bunch of different configurations until it ended up with me, Marty Privette on bass, Warren Haynes, Johnny Neel, and Dickey Betts. We did the record [*Pattern Disruptive*]. That was the best band, but it only lasted about a year before the Allman Brothers were reunited, and Warren was invited to join them. It was a great learning experience, and I met a lot of people from the whole Allman Brothers family. I had a great time and I enjoyed it very much.

Dickey Betts

[On the Great Southern Reunion, 2002] Well, we are doing an acoustic project right now. Danny and I have been doing a little playing, about once a week for the last month or so. Last night, we had Dave Stoltz, the bass player, down. So we had him and Danny and myself. So we are getting a good idea of how it is going to sound. We had a helluva night last night. We played and played and played and played. Dave brought his stand up bass, which really sounds cool. All it is, is the neck of a bass on a tripod with a pickup in it. It really has a great sound because of the technique he uses. And playing with Danny—his playing has just gotten better and better. And Frankie Toler was here. Frankie was down. His name is actually David Toler, but we all call him Frankie. It's a little private joke. You know Frankie played with Gregg Allman, he played with my band, and with the Allman Brothers. He is great. Like I say, it's great playing with Danny. He's really developed a unique style over the years. That's not to take anything away from Mark May. He was great, but he had things he had to do. His record company was on his tail and his band was all splitting up, so he kind of bowed out.

So we are doing this acoustic album. Yeah, well, I didn't really plan it, but it's turning out to be all the influences who have influenced my playing over the years. We're doing a tune that was written back in the 1940s by a guy named Horace Silver. He was a jazz piano player. He wrote a song called "The Preacher," and he featured trombones on it. He did it to a stripper beat. [Hums the melody] And the western swing guys back in the fifties picked it up and put a swing beat to it. So we're doing that, and it's got a real nice chord change and a lot of room for melody, so you really have to stay on your toes. And I'm doing "High Falls," which is nominated for a Grammy tonight from the *Peakin' at the Beacon* album. We are also doing "One Stop Be-Bop," which was on the last record, but this will be acoustic. That's my Charlie Parker influence. I'm playing about ninety percent gut string on this album. Just because it makes me work harder. You can't bend any strings on a gut string. You can bend maybe a half tone—maybe one fret. You really have to play the lines straighter, which makes me play a whole different way. So that's going to be interesting to hear. We're doing a [Bob] Dylan tune, "Tangled up in Blue," and a Billy Joe Shaver tune, "Georgia on a Fast Train," which I do in a kind of Django Rhinehart-type beat. Then I've written a thing. It's pre-bluegrass. Like the old European, kind of Ireland sound. Gaelic. Almost like a battle song. I call it "Beyond the Pale." It really sounds nice. It has kind of a pipes sound in it in places. I'm going to do "Change My Way of Livin'" and get Matt Zeiner to sing that one. It's a tune I wrote a few years ago, but I'm going to do it as a slow blues. And then I've got a few acoustic slide things I am going to do, so it's really a lot of the influences that have incorporated into my music. Like I say, I wasn't really planning it that way, but as I started looking down the list I saw that I had just about covered everything that I had studied.

Billy Bob Thornton

I was real close with Cash and Willie. We open for Willie a lot. And I loved him and Waylon and Kristofferson. All those guys. I'm real close with all of them. Yeah, when Cash died, it was a real bad week. We were playing on tour with Willie, and the last date of our tour was Farm Aid in Columbus, Ohio. Just before that we played Cleveland. And I got a call from Dickey Betts, and he was playing Columbus right before we played down there. And he wanted to know if I wanted to come and jam with them. I was like, shit. Of course I wanted to. [Laughs] At the same time it scared the hell out of you. This was right after Dickey got out of the band, and he was out with his own band. He had Danny Toler on guitar. So me and the guys in my band went down and got on the bus with Dickey and hung out for a while, and he said, "You gotta come up and play with us. What do you want to play on?" I said, "Gosh, what are y'all playing from the Allman Brothers? I can probably play one of those. I know 'em pretty well. He started naming off a few and he named off "Southbound." I said, "I know "Southbound." So I played drums on "Southbound." That was one of the biggest thrills of my life. I was nervous as hell. Dickey said, "Yeah, we got you a Marshall setup and a gold top up there ready for you." I said, "Dickey, [laughing] I'm not really a guitar player, man." He said, "What do you play?" I said, "I play drums, really." He said, "Get back there."

Phil Walden said something to me one time that was a pretty good quote about Dickey. He said, "Ronnie Van Zant wasn't afraid of anybody in the world except for Dickey Betts." And he said, "Nobody made Dickey nervous except Toy Caldwell." [Laughs] But I know Gregg and I know Dickey, but I never really knew Butch or the other guys.

9

The "New" Guys

Oteil Burbridge and Derek Trucks joined the band in 1997 following the departure of Allen Woody and Warren Haynes, who were devoting their energy to Gov't Mule full time.

John Hammond

In many ways Derek Trucks has gone beyond what Duane was doing—and you have to remember that Duane passed right at the time he was getting started. They have the same enigmatic source—wherever it comes from—they have got it. It is hard to compare.

Warren Haynes

Derek is amazing. I've known him since he was eleven years old, and he was amazing even then. He's got the depth and maturity of someone three times his age. It's really a special gift he has, and to deal with it the way he's dealt with it, he's such a great person. He's so down to earth and genuine. I could tell in all the times we've been around each other and played together, he's going to always remain a student of music. That's what it's all about, learning. You're always going to be learning. When you're eighty years old, you're still going to be learning. He has such a great attitude about it, and he'll get up and play with anybody, anywhere, anytime, which is really what it's all about as well. I have a deep respect for Derek as a musician and as a person.

Allen Woody

Oteil and Derek are dear friends of ours, always have been. We really love Derek, and are proud of what he's doing, too. Jaimoe and Gregg Allman are very dear friends of mine and will remain so until one of us drops and is planted in the ground. Jaimoe is a wonderful drummer, a wonderful musician that taught me about playing music, a lot about listening to music. It's the same with Gregg. Thank God he's straightened up. The real Gregg Allman, when he's not screwed up, which these days he is straight all the time, he's a wonderful guy, man. He's a singer's singer. He's best blues singer that's ever been poured into a white body. He's extremely knowledgeable about people like Little Milton. I knew who Little Milton was, but I'd never been into him. Gregg got me into him, and now we are on his new record [*Welcome to Little Milton*]. It was a joy. Once again, I learned tons about music from Gregg and Jaimoe. I learned about writing music with Gregg. And Warren too. Warren is a great writer.

John Hammond

Well, Warren is just one of those dyed-in-the-wool great players, a very steady even keel, great chops. Then, Derek is phenomenal and he's just a kid. I had stayed in touch with Butch [Trucks], and he would tell me about his nephew and how good he is, and like Duane Allman reincarnated—yep, *sure*. Then I heard him play and he was right! Unbelievable. Those guys have still got it. I don't care what they have been through and all their changes going down, because I knew them all. I toured with them when they first started, and I was hanging down in Macon. I knew Dickey really well and all those guys. What a scene that was. I mean, you know, years go by and stuff, but when you got it you got it. Gregg can sing his ass off and that's the real deal.

Red Dog Campbell

It's changed [the music business]. It's a business thing now. Like the new bands coming out today. Everything is so business-oriented. In the seventies you had free style music. You had great music. The visual thing was not the important thing. The important thing was the music. The hippies just stood up there and played. Nowadays everything is just so business-oriented. You audition for the gig, and Disney puts out a band like 'N Sync or Backstreet Boys, one of them groups. You don't have that camaraderie. Everybody is expendable these days. Let's say the bond is there, it's still business. In my case, with Gregg, Butch, Dickey, and Jaimoe, right? There's a bond there that has been established over thirty-three years. So you can't just push that aside. But yet, it's still business oriented. You can't just forget it and say, "Let's get rid of him." Like the thing with Dickey.

10

Birth of the Mule

The three-piece power trio formed by Haynes, Woody, and Matt Abts began to catch fire, and the band became a cult hit, shaking up concert stages across the land with powerful originals and eclectic covers. You never knew what cover song the guys might toss into the mix, from Cream to Alice Cooper, Prince to Black Sabbath.

Matt Abts

They [Warren and Woody] were just more stressed out at the time because they were doing double duty. At this point it's all Gov't Mule, so there's no dividing it. At that time, we were just getting started, and it was fine then. Everything turns into what it is supposed to turn into over time, you know? That was a good time, and this is a good time now.

Allen Woody

One thing I feel about the Mule is that we are there for each other. I'd do the same for them anytime. Sometimes you have to thank your Maker that you're in this position, playing great music with good friends. You don't want to ever take for granted that God Almighty has put you in the same plane with guys who are dedicated to making good music. I read one time that John McLaughlin said this, about that really fancy double-neck guitar with the design with all of those vines on it. He said the reason he had those was because he felt a musician should be like a vine growing up a tree, where you are constantly evolving upward as a musician, and as a human being too. I mean, it kind of goes hand in hand.

You can't be a great musician and be a miserable schmuck. I guess you can for a season, but trust me, it'll wear off. You're on this path, and hopefully it's always a path of increased enlightenment and God-consciousness, and you get closer and closer, then one day you leave this tent they we call a body and hopefully go to a better place. You have to, hopefully, become more decent, instead of less so, and become a better player instead of less so, and become more creative, instead of less so.

Matt Abts

When Johnny Neel and Warren were invited to join the Allman Brothers Band, it was the end of the Dickey Betts Band. I would see them almost every year when they would play the Greek Theatre. We all remained friends, and I was happy for Warren. It was a great break for him, and it brought him a lot of well-deserved notoriety. I would get up and jam with them, and there was this whole brotherhood thing going on. Talk kept coming back to Allen, who I didn't know at the time, and we talked about doing the trio thing. Warren had this solo project he had been working on since before he was in the Dickey Betts Band, and I knew he had to finish that up. He had a lot of New York players on it, and Chuck Leavell produced it. We all had stuff we needed to get out of our system. So in early 1994, Warren gave me a call and said that he and Woody had been seriously talking about the trio thing. So he called me up and formally asked me what I thought about it. Of course I thought it was a great idea. So we started scheming at that point. So the next time the Allmans were in town, I took them to a club I had a gig at called the Captain's Cabin in North Hollywood. Just a little rock club where we did a blues jam every Sunday. So that's how the band actually started. We initially went in and said, this is cool, let's record it ourselves. So we went to Telstar Studios in Sarasota where we had all done a bunch of work. It was owned by Bud Snyder, who is the sound man with the Allman Brothers. We recorded on our own with no record company, and then by the end of 1994, we got signed with Sony/Relativity, and that's when we went in to do that first record.

In August 2000, Allen Woody was found dead in his New York City hotel room. The Mule was limping. But rather than shoot it, Warren and Matt rallied, performing a series of acoustic duets, and recording The Deep

End, a tribute to Woody that featured some of the greatest bass players in rock history. They would later tour with Dave Schools (Widespread Panic) on bass and Chuck Leavell on keys, before settling into a permanent four-piece lineup.

Warren Haynes

I talked a lot with other bands who had lost band members, you know, talking to the guys in the Allman Brothers and Phil Lesh and Blues Traveler and with the guys in Metallica and people who have been through these things and have managed to keep moving forward. They were all saying the same kind of thing, "I know you don't feel like you can do it now, but you can." And of course people are encouraging us to keep the music alive, and the music was Woody's legacy and it is very important.

Artimus Pyle

Allen touched many people and this has never been more evident than it was Thursday night, September 21, 2000, in New York City at Roseland Ballroom at the "One For Woody" benefit for the Savannah Woody Educational Fund in memory of Allen Woody. I had a horrendous flying experience (and I hate to fly) that included an emergency landing in Greensboro, North Carolina, but was able to share the experience with fans of Allen's who were en route from Louisiana to New York just for the show. They recognized me and knew just where I was headed! The concert was like the old days. Allen would have loved it. Everyone wearing tie-dye, incense burning, a true feeling of camaraderie with the players who were all there for Allen. The whole night was like a flashback to the sixties with peace and love as the purpose of the party.

Warren Haynes

There is always speculation as to how he [Woody] would feel about it [the benefit concert]. I think the bottom line there was keeping the music alive. After so many years of hard work we had finally reached a point where we were spreading the word really good, and right before he died it was on the horizon, things were getting better for us, ticket sales were up, and the record sales were up. There were more people coming to the shows who had never seen us and more and more kids that were coming to the shows. And they were telling us it was their first Mule show, and all my friends are just digging it. You could just feel it growing and something big happening. It was something that we acknowledged, you know, all of us talked about it before Woody died, and he never really got to see it come to fruition to the extent that Matt and I are seeing it now. But you start thinking about the music being the most important thing. That the music should not die along with Woody. So many bands could have given up but didn't, and Allman Brothers are a classic example. If it was not for the fact that the Allman Brothers moved on past Duane's death and past Berry's death and eventually many others, then Woody and I would have never gotten that opportunity to be in the Allman Brothers in the first place.

Part 2

Lynryd Skynryd

11

Jacksonville

In summer 1964, teenage friends Ronnie Van Zant, Allen Collins, and Gary Rossington formed the band the Noble Five in Jacksonville, Florida. The name was changed to My Backyard in 1965 when Larry Junstrom and Bob Burns joined the group. A couple of years later, the name changed yet again to the One Percent.

In 1970, Van Zant decided he wanted a new name—something memorable and different. They decided on Leonard Skinner, a play on the name of a physical education teacher at Robert E. Lee High School, Leonard Skinner, who was always giving them a hard time about having long hair.

In 1970, Phil Walden's younger brother, Alan Walden, became the band's manager. Over the next couple of years, the band experienced some lineup changes for the first time. Junstrom left and was briefly replaced by Greg T. Walker on bass. At the same time, Rickey Medlocke joined as a second drummer and vocalist. Medlocke grew up with the founding members of Lynyrd Skynyrd. In 1972, Medlocke and Walker left the band to play with Blackfoot. When the band made their second round of Muscle Shoals recordings in 1972, Burns was featured on drums, and Leon Wilkeson was Larry Junstrom's replacement on bass. Also in 1972, roadie Billy Powell became the keyboardist for the band. Lynyrd Skynyrd had their band together. They would soon record their debut album, Pronounced.

Leonard Skinner

I was a gym coach in high school for Ronnie Van Zant and the others. We had a dress code at the school that said sideburns could not come below the ears; hair could not touch the back of the collar; belts had to be worn; shirt tails had to be in; and socks had to be worn at all times. It was among the duties of the coach to help enforce these rules, which I did. They got sent to the principal's office, and I became the most hated man at school. [Laughs]

Rickey Medlocke

Well, Blackfoot had relocated up into New Jersey, and what happened was some of those stupid little tiffs that bands get into and we were not really going anywhere. For me, I was just frustrated not going anywhere or doing anything and everything just going awry. I actually called Ronnie up after I had gotten hold of Allen Collins first and told him that I needed a gig. I told him that I would be able to drive a truck, load equipment or whatever y'all need done. Then, Ronnie asked me if I still played drums and I told him, sure I could do that, but in reality I had not sat on drums in a long time. We had a great drummer, Jakson Spires, at the time. So, I opted to go because Bob Burns was leaving, and he says that you can come in and do the bill. So, I took off for Jacksonville and got with Lynyrd Skynryd right there in 1971. You know, from 1971 until 1973 I opted to leave [Blackfoot] and do that. I sold my gear and kept my guitars and a few things and hung around this band house we had in Princeton, New Jersey. I kind of brushed up on playing and all that kind of stuff, and they sent me a plane ticket down and flew down to rehearse. In Jacksonville that night, I was sitting in rehearsal and working up the material that would later come out not only on the *Pronounced* album, but on *Lynyrd Skynyrd's First and...Last*. That's what started it.

Ed King

I played on the first three albums along with the *First and...Last* album...which was actually the first album [that had been rejected by various record companies]. I was recruited to play bass on the first album, *Pronounced,* but, during rehearsals Leon came out to the rehearsal cabin. While there, the band played "Simple Man" with Leon on bass. I had never heard the song before. After hearing Leon play bass, I decided he should be the bass player. He's the best I've ever heard. To this day, I never write a bass part without asking myself "What would Leon play?"

As a matter of fact, the last two songs we recorded, "Free Bird" and "Simple Man" contain my bass parts that are very far removed from all of the other bass parts on that album. Mainly because I had caught the vision from Leon of how the bass should be played for this band.

One night, after the first album was done but not released, Ronnie came to me. I was sitting on my bed playing my Stratocaster. He put his arm around me and said, "Ed...you're really the worst bass player I've ever played with." So the next day Ronnie and Gary went out to this ice cream factory where Leon was working. They asked him to return to the band. Two days later, with Leon on bass, we wrote our first two songs with the new lineup. "Sweet Home Alabama" and "I Need You." Not bad for the first day.

Derek Hess

I believe if my memory serves me well, just before Leon [Wilkeson] joined Lynyrd Skynyrd, there were some players hangin' around at the old Comic Book Club downtown, and that place was rough. Myself and probably Barry [Lee Harwood], Leon and some others were jammin' around one late Sunday afternoon just having some fun, I seem to remember that Ronnie [Van Zant] walked in and sat around and listened. The jukebox had one of their very early recordings on a 45 on the box. I remember it kept getting played a lot. The song was "Need All My Friends," and I liked it and was surprised it didn't end up on their first album. I thought it was as strong or even better than the other tracks.

Randall Hall

I was in a band called Running Easy, and we were doing all instrumentals, and each song was worth about three songs, they had so many changes in 'em. We ended up opening for Skynyrd. That was on the Tribute Tour, which you can see on the [tribute tour] video. That was the first day that I met any of them guys. It was like 1972. Downtown there's a place they call Friendship Fountain on the river, and we opened up for 'em. That's the day I met Allen Collins. He came up to me and said, "Hey you ol' hot dog you, you're damn good!" After that we started getting gigs opening up for Skynyrd before they were even known about. That was when they had two drummers—Rickey Medlocke was drumming and Bob Burns was drumming. And Ronnie helped us get on the "chittlin' circuit" [small clubs throughout the South] with one of the agencies out of Atlanta, Paragon I think. He just believed in us. He introduced me to Allen and Phil Walden there at Pinocchio's in Atlanta. We went up there to audition. We were gonna do our audition after their show. Before we could do it, Ronnie took me upstairs to one of these little balcony booths, and Phil and Allen were sitting there. Ronnie said, "I want y'all to meet Randall Hall. He's seventeen. Mark my words, you're gonna hear from him some day." We had to start doing cover songs. We had been doing original instrumentals, but we said, well, we'd better start singing something. [Laughs]

One time we went over to Ronnie's apartment he had at the time.

He said, "What do you feel like hearing?"

I said, "What about some Allmans, like *At Fillmore East*?"

And he said, "You don't want to listen to them guys. Why don't you listen to Merle Haggard?"

I said, "Merle Haggard??" [Laughs] I wasn't into it then. I was just interested in guitar at the time.

But he said, "You don't know what you're missing."

Rickey Medlocke

When you are young and full of piss and vinegar and trying to do something, to be honest with you, I don't really think that anyone knew at that time what the band was really capable of. It was very raw back then. We had an incredible writer that we were playing with named Ronnie Van Zant. When I first started working with him, he had the most unusual way of writing songs. What we would do is go out to Hell House, and we would play those songs over and over again without him even singing. He would just kind of sit in the corner in a chair and keep thinking about writing the lyrics in his head. He never even wrote anything down on paper; it was all in his head. He would just step up to the microphone and start singing. It was incredible. When I look back on it, because we have some good writers now, but with Ronnie it was like genius; it was like an artist painting a picture. He could see it in his head, and I think it was gift he was blessed with and is genius. Some of my favorite writers have been Bruce Springsteen, Ronnie Van Zant, Bob Seger, Sting, and Don Henley, people of that caliber. These are guys that paint the picture and allow you to see it in your head.

Don Barnes

I used to ride my bike over to Allen's [Collins] house and listen to records. His mom was great and very sweet. I remember walking into his house and he had this Vox amp there and she would just smile and be really proud of him. At the time you are part of the history in the making and we were just kids together. They were one of the first bands from Jacksonville to make it on their own material. There is a lot of musical history in Jacksonville.

Ed King

Hearing "Sweet Home Alabama" on the radio for the first time. That was a great feeling. Ronnie'd say, "That's our 'Ramblin Man.'" There were lots of great times on the road, especially before the band made it. Those times traveling in a beat up car towing a trailer—the reward is the journey.

Doug Gray

We [the Marshall Tucker Band] took Ronnie out on the road for the first time the same way the Allman Brothers had done for us. We played Hickory, North Carolina, and Lynyrd Skynyrd was opening for us. We were traveling all the way to the west coast. When we reached California two months later, we walked into this shop, and all of the sudden, we heard their song on the radio there in Los Angeles. I turned to Ronnie and said, "Guess what buddy, your time has come." He just smiled.

Alan Walden

I opened Hustler's Inc. on April's Fool Day, April 1, 1970. There was no magazine at that time, and we named it for "someone who's a hard worker," hence, let's hustle! I set it up as a publishing company, number one, and as a management company, number two. I went on a talent search for that "special" band and auditioned 187 bands in one year and I only kept one. The thirteenth band I auditioned was

Lynyrd Skynyrd. All it took for me was hearing their song "Free Bird" one time. I changed my lucky number from five to thirteen!

I took them to Muscle Shoals and recorded them with my friends, David Johnson and Quinn Ivy at a studio named Broadway Sound. Then I took them to my other good friend, Jimmy Johnson, at Muscle Shoals Sound. Jimmy really sunk his teeth into the band and literally taught them how to record. He gave them great advice and pushed them hard to get the best sounds. He helped polish their whole concept. While working with them after living there for five months, trying to get something going, I found myself broke again. The Allmans had broken wide open and business was booming at Capricorn.

Nine record companies had turned us down. I don't mean, "We like you but you need better material." I mean, "Not interested! No need to contact us again." Atlantic, Columbia, Warners, A&M, RCA, Epic, Electra, Polydor, and even Capricorn all passed after hearing "Free Bird," "Gimme Three Steps," "Simple Man," "I Ain't the One," and about twelve other originals. Their comments were, "They sound too much like the Allman Brothers." Now I ask you...put them on back to back and tell me they sound alike? We all came from the South, played hard, had long hair, drank, and chased women. But we did not sound alike! The Allman's had their jazz influences and we were a straight ahead juking band. I remember one executive telling me to turn that noise off while I was playing him "Free Bird."

I had one hundred dollars in my pocket when I left Jimmy and Muscle Shoals. I had encountered problems with some of the other partners and was looking at starting all over again. I got about thirty miles out of town when the old Cadillac broke down with a bad fuel pump. The wrecker service left me out there waiting until after 5:00 p.m. so he could charge more. They spent all but ten dollars. Add $90,000 in debt back home, and you might understand how bad it was. I walked out into a cotton patch shaking my fist at the sky, shouting, "I am going to make Lynyrd Skynyrd happen even if it kills me!" It was my solemn oath.

We had to hit the clubs again. We played a hell hole [in Atlanta] called Funocchios, which was a real fruit and nut bar. The booze was good, the women were wild, and we stayed until I thought I would die there. Then we had a run-in with the manager. Ronnie's grandmother died, and he did not want to sing. When Ronnie and I went to see him to tell him the band would still go on but without Ronnie, and Jeff Carlisi was also bringing his band, the manager's reply was "The old bitch is dead and you will go on!" When it was the last song ["Free Bird"] on Saturday, Ronnie started throwing amps onto the dance floor, smashing chairs, and breaking bottles. He totally wrecked the joint. People screaming and running, cops rushing in. I reached him just as the cop was about to bust him with a billy club. I screamed "His grandmother died! Help me, don't hurt him!" We got him outside with the help of the police only to find out I had to go back and collect the money for the week.

Ed King

High intensity discord and bad management (and bad material) caused the breakup of Strawberry Alarm Clock [Ed's pre-Skynyrd band in California]. In 1970 we did a three-month college tour in Florida. That's when I met the guys in Skynyrd. That was a real fun tour, the most fun I'd had in years. We got ripped off by the promoters day after day. Totally screwed over. But we made the best of it. Haven't had that much fun since. When the tour ended, I told Ronnie to call me if he ever needed a guitar player or bass player.

Alan Walden

During these years Lynyrd Skynyrd rehearsed constantly. When they were home they went to rehearsals like most go to straight jobs. Judy Van Zant, Kathy Collins, girlfriends, and families supported them. They had a place in the swamp called "Hidden Hills" and a deal with the local police to turn off by 5:00 p.m. everyday. They may have always been broke, but they still knew how to have fun with each other. We continued to improve our equipment and our shows. We would write, rehearse and then try the new ones out in Atlanta or Jacksonville or Gainesville, Florida. The good songs stayed in the set and the bad ones went to the trash can. I wish I still had copies of the bad ones. They were great too!

We changed members several times but there was always Ronnie, Allen, and Gary. And Ronnie was the undisputed leader. He was a natural poet with the gift to write about what he felt, what he knew, his life, and the things he understood. No fantasies. The *real deal*! We became the Ten Musketeers! All for one and one for all! Wild, crazy, drinking, fighting *rednecks* with a capital "R" and proud of it! I had drank with some of the best, with Johnnie Taylor—the best—but when I met Skynyrd—whew—I went under the table. Those guys could drink. Straight from the bottle—and they were still teens at the time.

We met Al Kooper while still playing the clubs. He was starting his own "Southern" label, Sounds of the South. Even though it was short lived we used it as stepping stone. When we signed the recording contract on the hood of my pickup truck in the Macon Coliseum parking lot, Ronnie asked me in front of the other musicians what I thought of the contract. My reply was it was the worst I had ever seen—worse than most of the old R&B contracts.

His reply was "What else we got? Nothing." I said, "Gimme that damn pen" as he reached for it. We could wait no more. The band could not starve any more. We had already been in the clubs too long. They signed, and he went back to Jacksonville and started writing "Working for MCA!"

Derek Hess

One day around Christmas in the early seventies, and *Pronounced* had been out maybe a year or so, Ronnie [Van Zant] and Gary Rossington walked into a music store I was working at. We were casual friends at the time, and he told me he was looking to buy a starter drum set for his younger brother, Johnny, for Christmas. And all through the conversation and transaction, the both of them would drop these little remarks, maybe hints along the way as to when was I going to start doing what I really loved and was good at. I didn't catch on right away, but as soon as we got outside to load the drums, he just matter-of-fact blurted out, "Would you like to play drums for Skynyrd?" Well of course I was a little stunned to say the least. Then he stated they were thinking about letting Bob Burns go and looking to replace him. What was my reply? There wasn't much of one, I think, because Ronnie could see I was a little perplexed at the ambush, and he knew Barry and I were going at it pretty hard to get where they were. And I will tell you, that band busted their brains out to make it happen. Such a shame to see it go down in such a way and at a time when they were heading for superstardom, America's Rolling Stones, you know?

Soon afterward, I heard "Sweet Home Alabama" and was blown away. I was like, where did that come from? So well put together and well played, and yes, I was listening to Bob Burns. I thought he must still have the gig. Later, it was suggested to me by several friends that maybe my missing that opportunity kept me on this earth for a while longer. It makes me shudder. That had to be fright beyond words.

12

Sounds of the South

With the great buzz circulating about the band, Al Kooper decided to start his own Southern record label, Sounds of the South.

Al Kooper

I was producing this record down in Atlanta. I came through on tour in Atlanta and I had some friends in the Atlanta Rhythm Section. I knew them when they were called the Candy Men, in the late sixties. I met them when I lived in New York. We became friends, so I called them and told them I was coming through for a week in Atlanta. I told him that when we came through we would have a great jam session. So that is what I did. They had a great studio. I came back, and as a matter of fact, I was recording my back-up band and they were making their own album called *Frankie and Johnny*. This was about 1972. So we were there for one month and worked every day from noon until about eight.

Then I met someone that I went to summer camp with. He was a manager of a club, and I thought I could just go to his club and chase some women. Record all day and then chase women at night. That's what it's about. This place is called Funocchio's on Peachtree Street. It was a rough place, and there were lots of fights going on and stuff. We had a private balcony and we would tell the waitress to go tell that girl in the orange sweater that we were inviting her up here. We loved going there. The first week we were there they had a band called Boot playing. I went and sat in with them. In those days you played for a week at a time. It was not a one-night thing like it is now. You would be there for one week. Boot played there for one week and the next week I saw it was Lynyrd Skynryd. I said, "What the hell is this?" Then they played and I thought, boy this is a weird band. They were doing originals. I always liked that.

A couple of them really started getting to me and I thought, this is really good. The singer is barefoot and walking around and throwing the mic stand around. By the third night I had heard some of the tunes, and I was hoping they would play them again. By the end of the week, I was completely sold and felt like they were a great band. So I offered them a deal. We went back and forth on that and I heard lots of great bands in Atlanta. I didn't even want to go home. I had my roadies go back and pack up my stuff and got a place to live in Atlanta and decided to stay there and start a label. That's what I did. Skynyrd was the second album I released on my label, and it just knocked all the other bands into the toilet unfortunately.

Alan Walden

I knew from the beginning we needed MCA on our side. I made sure we gave them a deal that would give them a chance to make millions. We recorded *Pronounced* for $22,500. Can you believe it? We did not try to borrow a lot of money. We did not call everyday. We were a working machine, fully tuned and oiled. Independent! When I met Mike Maitland, he was shocked. I was all business and not into hanging out in the Hollywood scene like most. With him I laid out some of the best marketing and promotion plans ever. I got the Who tour when all others failed. I got the best dates for the band and built a foundation the present band lives on. Take away "Free Bird," "Gimme Three Steps," "Sweet Home Alabama," "Simple Man," "I Ain't the One" and what do you have left? If these songs were dropped from the set, would you pay to see them?

I did very career-minded booking while their manager. I had the long run in mind constantly. I caught a lot of crap from the band sometimes because they wanted to make a certain amount all the time. Once we played a $10,000 date; they thought all the dates should be $10,000. We might play Nashville for $35,000 and the next day be booked for $3,500 in a market undeveloped. Then once they said no more under a certain price, they complained of working the same cities over and over. They should have concentrated on the music and the shows and left the bookings and business to the pro. It amazes me how bands hire a manger and as soon as they get hot want to tell him how to do it. Or fire him because he is too smart for them. They should stick to what they know best. MUSIC.

During this time I also was thinking of their latter days when they would no longer tour. Like now maybe? I had set up profit sharing and pension plans for their older years. I got them life insurance—things they did not want to keep at that time. They wanted it all in *cash*! One visit to the road I discovered $90,000 in a briefcase. Smart. I took it home and straight to the bank. I tried to remind them it wasn't that long before that we all had been broke. The wheel of success had turned. I was the money miser. And they just knew the success would never stop. *Pronounced* was a smash, and *Second Helping* was as well. MCA was thrilled and now had reps meeting us in every city. *Second Helping* came in for under $30,000.00. *Both* smash albums for under $50,000.00. No wonder MCA loved us so much. I was setting them up for the kill. We had not borrowed money and it was a prime time to renegotiate their recording contract. It would have been a multi-million dollar deal—my biggest deal to date.

We were also getting prime concerts now with the Allman Brothers in Atlanta at Braves' Stadium, Clapton in Memphis, ZZ Top in Nashville, and heading to pick off the Eagles at the Orange Bowl in Miami. The band was now the showstoppers. They killed and killed. No one could hold up behind "Free Bird!"

Al Kooper

I was from New York and they were from Jacksonville, so you know, we didn't have too much in common. One thing that we did have in common was we worshiped the band Free. On every album we did at least one track that was a tribute to Free. On the first album it was "Simple Man" and on the second album it was "I Need You," second track. "On the Hunt" was the third one. All three of those songs were where we were going for that Free thing.

Alan Walden

We were at the Orange Bowl with the Eagles, and I was doing an in depth interview with *Creem Magazine*. They had spent two days traveling with me and this was going to be *the big story*. Ronnie told me he needed to talk to me right after the show, and he and I went back to the room together. When we sat down, he informed me the band had voted to replace me as the manager of the band. The wind went out of my sails. I can't tell you how bad and shocked I felt. This had been my whole life for the last four years. No one loved the band anymore than me. Not Ronnie, not Allen, not Gary or any of the rest of the band. Ronnie had been best man at my wedding. The only people I invited were the band. I thought of Ronnie as my closest friend. There was anger, hurt, pain, fear, and numbness. Ronnie said I could beat the hell out of him, that he would just cover up the vitals and let me have a go at him. I couldn't. He asked me if I wanted to know who voted what. I was still wrestling with the verdict. I knew Ed King didn't like me, but the rest of the guys were supposed to be my friends, too. I knew I had done a superb job for this group. But something had gone wrong. Here we were with the whole world at our feet and now BOOM! I must admit that also came a feeling like concrete blocks falling from my shoulders. Now I did not have to worry about their future like I had been doing. The truth of the matter is no one was looking after mine or seemed to care but me.

I went home to Georgia to lick my wounds. I have never been the person to stay with someone if they did not want me, and this was my biggest disappointment in life. Now they wanted that big Hollywood super manager to take them on to superstardom. I waited a couple of days, prayed over it, and then called Ronnie. I offered to meet with them and try to correct any problems, and I did go out to see them. But it was not the same group of guys. They were now "the machine" as Ronnie called it. No more Brotherhood. My control was gone, and I knew it. I could have stroked them all and maybe stayed in the picture a while longer, taken a cut in commission, and become the yes-man. Gary, Dean, and Ronnie came to the Capricorn Picnic that year, and Ronnie and I ended up in a room alone again. I won't go into details, but I lost it with him this time. Here was the guy whose back I had been covering for four years even when we were up against very bad odds. And now he's letting them all stab my ass in the back. I knew Ronnie could kick my ass one-handed, but I was so angry this night that did not even matter. I was furious, and after I had my say, I saw a tear coming down his face. Then I lost it and left with tears flowing as I left the hotel. I knew for sure then it was all over for me with them.

The next day he asked me if I knew I had a bull by the horns the night before. I knew exactly what he meant. Now that it was over I made the suggestion instead of us ending up with a big lawsuit, we should try to find the new manager together and keep the lawyers from getting rich. I had seen these guys rise from poverty and work every inch of the way. I still loved them and tried to understand why they were doing this. I had been around enough acts to know these things happen sometimes and there is not much you can do to stop it once it gets going. No one ever doubted my honesty at least. They did say I was a money miser and I do count money well. Forgive me, but isn't that what a manager's job is? Would you rather have one who could not count?

Al Kooper

Yeah, well they would go out there [to "Hell House," the band's non-air-conditioned rehearsal space in Jacksonville] and just get it all together. They wouldn't even jam, like when you are working with a band and there is a guitar solo on the song, the guy comes in and tries to play a solo. They wrote all the guitar solos out, including "Free Bird." Every bit of that was planned out before I came into the picture. Every guitar solo was played exactly the same. I have never met a band that did that nor have I met a band since, and it was pretty amazing. Ronnie was a great leader, and you know we banged heads many times during the making of the three records I did with them. It was always in an okay way. I would say something, then Allen or Gary would say, "Oh, man I don't want to do that, it sucks. Al, just let us do what we do." Ronnie would say "Gary, I don't like that idea that Al is suggesting either, but I don't want to stop him from speaking his mind. Even if we just use 10 percent of that idea, it's something we wouldn't think of ourselves, so I will always listen to him." And I thought, there was a wise guy. So I did get some things in there. I think that a great way to judge a producer is to listen to the album that they make *after* they split with the producer. You know what I mean? It is understandable. I think that the first album has a certain sound and whether it is good or bad it doesn't matter, it has a certain sound. There were little things that I like to do that were appropriate for them. When we split up I was rooting for them to make a great album. I remember the day when the next record came to my house and I put it on the turntable and looked at the record and said, "Okay, kick my ass"—and I thought it was the worst album they had done.

Ed King

I really enjoyed working with Al Kooper. I believe had it not been for Al, no one would've heard of Skynyrd. He was the visionary behind the band and how it should be presented to the world. We didn't always agree with Al but I certainly enjoyed his presence.

When we drove up to Atlanta to record "Simple Man" we played the song for Al in the studio. He hadn't heard it. He didn't care for it and said, "You're not putting that song on the album." Ronnie asked Al to step outside. He escorted Al to his Bentley and opened the car door. Al stepped in. Ronnie shut the door and stuck his head in thru the open window. "When we're done recording it, we'll call you."

Al came back a few hours later, added the organ part, and it was a keeper. I don't think any band before or since, making its debut album, could get away with doing that to the record producer. There was a healthy respect happening there...and that is a really funny story that reflects that.

13

Street Survivors

With a pair of successful albums under their collective belt, Skynyrd's drummer, Bob Burns, quit the band due to stress. Enter Artimus Pyle, a drummer living in Spartanburg, South Carolina, who was friends with the Marshall Tucker Band.

Fred Edwards (former drummer, Charlie Daniels Band)

What a bunch of good friends. We played with them in a bar in Jacksonville, Florida. We became buddies. Their drummer Bob had just left the band. Then Charlie said to them, "We know this guy that we met at the Warehouse in New Orleans. His name is Artimus Pyle, from Spartanburg, South Carolina. Do you want to give him an audition?" Well, the rest is history. God bless my friend Arti. This guy was the first one to leave the scene of the plane crash to get help. The former Marine ran for four miles to get help for the victims. All this with broken bones. My Pyle. My friend Forrest Gump. [Laughs] This is a drummer who will do anything to serve. Drummers are a different breed of musician.

Artimus Pyle

It was exactly like this. I drove to New Orleans during the early seventies' fuel crunch. I was at Mardi Gras. I went down there to audition for Charlie. He had two drummers at the time, and he was pushing his new album. He had that song out called "Uneasy Rider." So I went to New Orleans with a friend named Sonny Matheny who eventually ended up working for Charlie for years, running sound. Then he went back to Tennessee Tech and got his degree, and now he's the principal of a high school in Roanoke, Virginia. But Charlie loves Sonny. So, Sonny and I were at Mardi Gras. Charlie came up to me and said, "Artimus, the drummer that was going to quit decided not to quit, and if I took two weeks off right now to go back to Nashville and work you in, it would hurt my album sales something awful. And I need to keep these dates." So Paul Riddle from the Marshall Tucker Band, another great person, called Charlie and said, "Boy, do I have a drummer for you." So Paul was pushing me to Charlie. But this drummer Gary Allen that was gonna quit *didn't* and Charlie was just honest with me instead of giving me some big ring-around-the-rosy, some big story; he told me the truth. He told me he knew of a band that needed a drummer, and he was going to hook me up.

So, Charlie played his gig at the Warehouse there in New Orleans, off the beaten track away from the French Quarter. There were thousands of people, and I watched Charlie and his band play. Charlie's bus pulled out of town, and Sonny and I were gonna leave town, too, after Mardi Gras. Sonny got a gig driving a bus and working on the road crew for Charlie. I didn't get a gig, but Charlie had invited me to come to Atlanta to a club called Richard's and jam with him that night. Dickey Betts also jammed with him. There were two sets of drums, and Charlie let me set up a third set of drums. So, when I left out of New Orleans I found this fifty-dollar bill in my pocket. There's no way anybody else could have done it. and I didn't have a dime. Sonny and I probably had just enough money to get us back home to Spartanburg in my Volkswagen bus. It was Charlie. Then he turned me on to Skynyrd. There was this gig in Atlanta at the stadium, and it was Marshall Tucker, the Allman Brothers, Charlie Daniels, Wet Willie, Lynyrd Skynyrd, everybody. Paul Riddle invited me to go to that show after Mardi Gras and I had jammed with Charlie at Richard's and everything was great.

Then I left town and went home to Spartanburg and was working construction. I was working at an airport installing aviation electronics at the Spartanburg Airport. Then Paul called and said, 'We're playing a big gig in Atlanta and do you want to come?' And I said, "Sure." I went, and that's where I met everybody that day. I met Ronnie Van Zant and everybody. Ronnie's face was all beaten up. They had just been in San Francisco and got into a big fight. Ronnie looked like the devil, all black eyes and cut up and everything. He had taken on a whole gang by himself because everybody else hid under the bus, I guess. And between Charlie Daniels and Paul Riddle pushing me and talking me up, saying this is the boy for you, which was unbeknownst to me. I went home and I got this call from Ronnie and he said, "I want you to play drums for my band. I was gonna fly five drummers down to Jacksonville, but what I want to do is have you come down to Atlanta and play with Ed and Leon." So, he hired me over the phone. He said, "I need a fire set under this band, man. Can you do that? We are right on the fence. We're getting there, man."

So, I went to Atlanta where I was supposed to meet up with Leon and Ed King at Alex Cooley's Electric Ballroom. I drove up there in my bus with my drums in it. Well, two or three blocks from the place, my engine overheated and vapor locked. I just pulled up my emergency brake, unloaded my drums, rolled them up the street to the Electric Ballroom, and left my Volkswagen bus sitting on Peachtree Street with the emergency blinkers on. I went in, set up, and played with Ed King and Leon. Ed took me next door and made me a Caesar salad, and I ate. I figured enough time had gone by so I went back to my bus. It had cooled down so I started it up and drove up to the Ballroom and got the gig. So it was Charlie Daniels and Paul Riddle believing in me and being good guys. And Ronnie said after he had met me he realized that he was talking to somebody that talked to him on the same level. I wasn't talking up to him; I wasn't talking down to him. We became friends. I watched Ronnie whip everybody in the band's ass—Leon, Billy, Allen, and Gary. I used to go to their defense all the time because Ronnie couldn't whip my ass. He was tough for a musician, but I had just gotten out of the Marine Corps. I was young and wiry. You'd have to kill me at that point. Ronnie was the same way. He respected me and I respected him. I could have argued with him twenty-four hours a day about some things. About some of the policies—it was his band, but when he would start getting drunk and abusive, I was the only one who could talk to him.

Jo Jo Billingsley

Bob O'Neil was doing their lights, and he was a friend of mine from back in Memphis. He told me that they were going to be hiring some singers, you know. I had just seen them perform with Eric Clapton, and I thought they were really good. At first I thought he was saying they were going to hire the three black chicks that were on the album. Lo and behold they called me! [Laughs] I was just so thrilled to get to go up there and everything. That's how it happened, Bob gave them my name and they called me and I went to Nashville where I met them.

I just walked in and Ronnie saw me and said, "She'll do just fine." [Laughs] Hired me on the spot. And I knew Cassie [Gaines] because we worked at a restaurant called Panchos in Memphis together. I knew she was a singer, and she knew I was a singer, but we never sang together. I thought she was real cool, and I had seen her sing in a play and knew she had done some Broadway stuff. So after they hired me, they asked me if I could help them find another girl singer. I had tried to be friends with those other girl singers in Memphis, but they wouldn't give me the time of day, so the first one I thought of was Cassie. I called her, and she had already moved back to Oklahoma, where she was living in a Victorian house on this farm for $45 a month, and working at a country club. I told her about Skynyrd and everything, and she literally had to go and buy the album because she had never heard of them. She listened to the album and she called me back and said, "Hey, they're pretty good." I said, "Yeah, they are." I asked her to go with us, and she said, "Should I?" and I said, "Yeah, let's go, let's do it!" We both had two weeks to pack and move to Jacksonville. We had a few rehearsals there in their studio in Jacksonville, and then we were in London, England, on tour. We were rehearsing there in the theater owned by Emerson, Lake, and Palmer. It was a big theatre with no seats in it. It had a huge stage, and upstairs was all of Keith Emerson's keyboards and equipment. It was really a cool place.

Gary Rossington

Me and Allen and Ronnie had this dream to make it big, and we were gonna try to make it until we died. That dream came true for us.

I remember us three talking about it on the way back from England the first time. "We did it!" you know? That and playing with the Rolling Stones and meeting Paul McCartney and John Lennon out in L. A. The people you get to meet in this business that you never dreamed you'd meet. I met Jack Nicholson over in England at Knebworth, and we sat there in the dressing room and talked. Met a lot of big movie stars. A lot of people come to rock shows you wouldn't think would. Some of my favorite people are the athletes. Ryan Klesko and John Rocker and Randy Johnson—a lot of football and baseball players—Doug Flutie. They always have free passes because they play at all the big stadiums, and they're big shots in their towns. [Laughs] It's fun to meet them because I'm a big football and baseball fan. I watch every game of football, and I'm a big Braves fan. I like to watch the teams that I know somebody on. Those have been my highlights and also doing some charities where people thanked you, or you knew it really helped some people out. A lot of people come up and say how much a song meant when they played it at their brother's funeral, or some people just got married and they played "Free Bird" or something, and they get excited telling you about what the song means to them. Things like that.

Jo Jo Billingsley

Singing with Skynyrd was fantastic. I thought I had died and gone to heaven. They were really my favorite band anyway. But getting to literally be with them on stage was amazing. They're such awesome musicians and great guys. They treated us so good. Ronnie was such a gentleman, he wouldn't let anybody mess with us. And every show was sold out, and the energy was just awesome. The fans just loved it so much, so the energy was outstanding.

With the release of One More from the Road in 1976, Lynyrd Skynyrd's live version of "Free Bird" was forever stamped into rock history, becoming one of the most loved live cuts of all time.

Tom Dowd

The Allman Brothers *At Fillmore East* album taught me something, and it worked years later with Skynryd when we did the

One More from the Road. The first night I thought the band was going to stay in some community outside of Atlanta in a house, and instead they got into trouble and got into some fights. The next day when we went down to rehearse in the afternoon for that night's show, I told them that they didn't have to do this song or that song again, and they were like what do you mean? I told them they had done it well the night before and that we should insert this song or that song. So I was doing the same thing for the Skynryd band that I had done to the Allman Brothers and not repeating the same show every night. So this made them change their set list, and we would rehearse in the afternoon so that when they did it that evening it would come close to good, if not excellent. After the first night, the second night I had a case of bourbon, a case of champagne, and five cases of beer and all the floozies you could find in a suite in a hotel room. And we sat there and listened to the first night's show, and we listened to the second night's show, and tomorrow night we should do "T for Texas," because we have not done it, and we haven't played this song in three years and we had better rehearse. Well, we go back in at 2:00 in the afternoon and rehearse for three hours, and when they did the show that night, they killed three more songs. And that is the way that album transpired, but I was doing it to keep them out of clubs where they would go get arrested. The last thing I needed was two of them in jail and then I wouldn't have a show, do you know what I'm saying?

Jo Jo Billingsley

There were 250,000 people there [at Knebworth, 1976] who had paid. And there were another 150,000 people around who had not paid, that had just gathered. They had a flea market set up there. People came in on every mode of transportation, from bicycles to Harley's, planes, cars parked all the way back to London on the side of the road. No kidding. And the stage was huge—we were playing with the Stones! They had that stage built all up, and you had to have a special pass to get anywhere near the stage. It was really cool, 'cause me and Cassie were coming up the platform, and who other than Paul McCartney was coming up at the same time. We stuck out our paper for him to give us an autograph, and he snubbed us. I thought—*uh!* We were both heartbroken. I thought, the nerve! I've loved him all my life. We were all backstage—there were so many entertainers there, because it was Hot Tuna, 10cc, Todd Rundgren's Utopia, us, and the Rolling Stones. They had hired entertainers to entertain the entertainers. There were jugglers and clowns.

I bought the dress that I wore at the flea market that morning. I went out there and found that dress and grabbed some scissors and split it down the front, because I had that leotard. Allen and I were close, and I remember him trying to decide what to wear. He didn't even want to take a bath. I said, "Allen, there are 250,000 women out there who paid to see you." So they all got cleaned up, and he had that red shirt and red pants, and I said wear that! It was perfect for the day because they had those big red Stones lips everywhere.

Gary Rossington

Allen [Collins] was crazy. You know how you have certain people in your life that you consider your best friend, well he was one, too. We were like the three musketeers at one time. And then we were the two musketeers. [Laughs] And now, I guess, the one. But he was crazy. I don't mean "crazy" crazy, but crazy for life. He loved life and loved doing anything he wanted to do and would do it in a big flamboyant way. If he wanted to buy a car, he'd get the biggest and best, the most flashy and coolest car. He'd get the best. He was just a flashy kind of guy. When he played the guitar he was exciting and flashy. He just has a lot of rambunction in him. I loved and miss him a lot.

Barry Lee Harwood

In May of 1977, I was in a car crash and almost killed. I suffered broken bones in my leg and left wrist and was pronounced dead. I was so scared to do that session [*Street Survivors*] as I had no lateral movement in my left arm but I could hold a bar and play a Dobro. I will never forget, after that session, Ronnie and I went out to a bar and he was telling me he wanted to do a country music project and he wanted me to be a part of it. Ronnie was a special man, and he always had a song he wanted to sing for ya' and tell him what you thought.

Gary Rossington

I love playing it. ["Free Bird"] It's kind of like an anthem these days. Everybody knows it and wants to hear it, but my feeling is everybody has a certain time in their life when they heard that song a lot. Something was going on that they remember, and they relate to it. People have said, "Man, we used to dance to 'Free Bird' in high school. That's how I met my wife." Everybody's got stories, there's good and bad stories about it. Not just "Free Bird" but certain other songs. And that's a great feeling to know a song touched somebody that way—one that you wrote or helped write. Telling some kid to just be a "simple man," or telling him to just do the right things, and it's a great life, you know?

Jo Jo Billingsley

One time we were doing a show with Peter Frampton and Bill Graham was the promoter. It was when Frampton had the big live album with "Show Me the Way." Bill Graham was the promoter. We were up on this high-rise stage, and we were looking down at about fifty black limousines and one white Rolls Royce. And I asked Mr. Graham, I said, "Mr. Graham, who's so special to get that white Rolls Royce?" And he just kind of smiled at me. When we got done and were ready to leave that white Rolls Royce pulled up to pick me up, alone. And inside he had a bottle of champagne and some roses just for me. That was so special to me. All the promoters just took such good care of me. Alex Cooley, and my friend Bob Kelly from Memphis. Later on they said he committed suicide, but I know he didn't. He would have never done that. He would never harm himself. And there was Tom Dowd, the producer. The first time we recorded, I had never recorded before in my life, never been in a studio. He pulled me aside, and I didn't know who he was. He said, "Jo, you're a natural. Just go with it." He made me relax. Later on when I found out who he was I just said, "Man...." And then later on when we saw him in Atlanta for the world premiere of the movie *Free Bird*, we ran up to each other and got pictures and all, and I said, "What are you doin' here?" And he said, "I produced the movie." And I said, "Okay." [Laughing] I really put my foot in my mouth. He was just so precious.

14

The Plane Crash

October 20, 1977. The band boarded a chartered plane in Greenville, South Carolina, bound for Louisiana State University in Baton Rouge. Near the end of the flight, the plane ran out of fuel and crashed into a swamp. Ronnie Van Zant, Steve and Cassie Gaines, Dean Kilpatrick, and both pilots were killed on impact.

Artimus Pyle

The very last show I did with the band was at the Greenville Memorial Auditorium, as you know. And I had been a Marine, and there were lots of Marines around. They were working the Toys for Tots thing. I remember talking to a couple of Marine Corps guys that were in their dress blues, and I had my children with me. Heidi Diana, she was like a daughter to me, but she was actually my niece. I had my son Chris and I had little baby Marshall with me that night. I even remember what I was wearing. I used to wear a lot of light stuff. I had on white linen, cotton, almost like medical scrubs. I will never forget that night. I felt good, I was in my home town, I had lots of friends there, the Marine Corp was there, I was supporting Toys for Tots, I had my children with me, the band sounded great, I had my brand new monitor system. I could hear every thing perfectly. I had it all tweaked out after working with it for four days. Ronnie was happy because he knew I could hear what he was singing or saying clearly. He was my singer, man; I was his drummer. We had all of this eye contact. I had designed this drum setup so that I could see and hear him better. That was the best the band had ever sounded. Everybody was relaxed; we had a brand new killer album out that we were proud of. We had that little movie thing they were playing in the theaters. We all felt so good. I think that's why they partied so hard there in Greenville, because we'd been home and everybody had been being good boys and girls, so they were back on the road and getting it out of their systems. I'll never forget. Nazareth was the opener. A great band that just recently lost their drummer. We played many, many shows with them. Great guys. So, I have a great, fond memory of Greenville Memorial Auditorium, because it was the place where I played my first and last major shows with Lynyrd Skynyrd.

Greenville was just the fifth date on what was to be a ninety-five-city world tour.

We were going to Australia. We were going back to Japan. We were going back to Europe for the twelfth time. The first show was Statesboro, Georgia. I had just received shipment four days earlier on my new monitor system that I had designed with Bose speakers and a 24-channel board and EQ. I was really proud of that. We went from Statesboro to Miami, Florida. Then we went to St. Petersburg. Then to Lakeland. From Lakeland we came to Greenville. We were headed to Baton Rouge, Louisiana, when we had the plane crash. So we were only five cities into this world tour.

I remember the night before, my wife, Pat, had fixed this big vegetarian spaghetti dinner, and we were gonna have everybody come over after the show. All of the limos were going to bring everybody over to my little place in Campobello for this major dinner. Well, nobody made it because everybody had hangovers. A few guys in the crew came over and made that beautiful drive from Greenville, through the countryside, you know, Michael, how beautiful it is. We ate vegetarian spaghetti and this great salad. I sent the limos back to the plane, and I drove my Jeep over to the airport. I was the last one to get there, and I drove up on the tarmac—because I could—and I drove right up to the plane—because I could. I stepped directly from my Jeep onto the back stairs of our airplane. I kissed Pat goodbye, and she drove off in the Jeep. Two hours later I called her after I had gotten out of the plane crash and found that farmhouse. I called her from Johnny Mote's farmhouse, and I said, "Pat, we had an airplane crash, and there were people killed. I am alive. Tell the kids I love them. I have got to go." And Pat was crying. The whole conversation took less than thirty seconds. And she said, "Okay honey I understand." I walked back out of Johnny's house and there were all sorts of rescue vehicles coming up to the site of the crash. Johnny put me in his truck and we drove through his fence and through his field until we got to where I had come out of the swamp.

Ronnie was asleep behind the bulkhead. They had the cockpit, and then there was a little area where the galley was, which was the kitchen in our airplane. Then began the first quarters. So Ronnie was sleeping behind the bulkhead. You could shut the cockpit door and the door to the lounge and the kitchen was completely dark. And it was daylight when we were flying, so Ronnie went up into that area and was sleeping. Also, when we flew at 10,000 feet, the floor was cool. It was like an icebox in there, it was so cool, that aluminum aircraft metal. And it was October. So Ronnie slept on that because it was like sleeping on a slab of ice, and he was all hung over, so it felt good. Instead of having an ice pack on your head, he just put the plane on his head. I'm sure it felt great.

Derek Hess

Our band Running Easy was playing at a bar, and I got a message to call home, my wife had called. So when I got the news from her, we really didn't have much information, didn't know if it was a commercial flight or whatever, and I felt some worry, but honestly thought that maybe there were no major casualties and certainly not what was to come. So we all went home, not knowing anything else, and on my ride home I tuned in to our local FM rock station, where they were pretty hard on the coverage. By then it was revealed that in fact it was a charter, that the whole band and crew were on board, and there were fatalities. Of course I was sick at my stomach at the sound of that. They had no names as of yet, this was about 2 a.m. So when I got home, I sat up and just listened, and took it all in. As I recall, there was huge anticipation and word they would report the list of fatalities soon, and when the time came, I just shuddered. It was so unbelievable. It was terribly sad to hear the names, but I really couldn't believe Ronnie's was one of them. You just thought he was invincible. We attended the funeral and I remember seeing Billy Powell with the damage to his nose. I was able to approach him and tell him how sorry we all were. Maybe a year or so later, I was in a backstage area at a Blackfoot concert I think, and who would walk up to me, and I really didn't see him until he was right up on me, but Billy [Powell]. He seemed genuinely happy to see me, and equally candid. Just very warm and friendly, just wanted to say hello. I asked him how were things, and he said just doing it day by day, and looking forward to getting back to playing on the big stage. I knew then what a great man he was, and he was so very engaging and wanted you to know you were his friend.

Charlie Daniels

We were playing in St. Louis when we got the word that the plane had gone down. We gathered around and said a prayer before we went to the stage to perform. At first, the rumor had it that the plane had crashed and they were all dead. We were just devastated. It's still one of the saddest nights I can remember. Ronnie was my friend, and I loved him.

Pete Carr

My group, LeBlanc & Carr, had just released an album, and we signed with Peter Rudge, who was Lynyrd Skynyrd's manager. He was also the manager for the Rolling Stones. We started promoting the album and were put on the 1977 *Street Survivors* tour. I don't remember a lot about it. We hadn't done much before the tour came to a tragic end. We all did a show in Miami and afterwards, since Lenny and I grew up in Daytona Beach, we wanted to do a show there for the hometown people. So we went to Daytona and were going to meet back up with Lynyrd Skynyrd at the next show. Well, when we arrived in town to play the next concert we heard on the radio of the plane crash that took the lives of some of the members. We, of course, were shocked. That was the end of the tour. I had known a lot of the band members from when I used to go to Jacksonville, Florida, and play in clubs there. They were from Jacksonville and I had seen them there a few times in the clubs.

Jo Jo Billingsley

They had played those four shows without me. They let all of us girls go in Las Vegas. That was my last time to sing with them. That was August of '77. I had a stomach virus, so I went home to my mom's in Mississippi. I was under a doctor's care, and just wanted to rest because we had 286 days that year that we were booked. We had about fifty-five days off, and about thirty of them were traveling. Leslie [Hawkins] went first and asked for her job back, so Ronnie hired her back. Then Cassie [Gaines] asked for hers back. Then they did those four shows without me, and then Ronnie called me. It was the night before Greenville. My brother and I had made plans to go over and meet them in Little Rock a couple of nights later to party with them. He called and told me he wanted me to join them in Greenville and come back into the band. I thought, well, that's music to my ears. I said, "Yes, of course." While I was talking to him I felt this strange feeling and I heard this word, "Wait." My spirit was talking to me. I said, "Well, we were planning to come to Little Rock anyway. Why don't I just meet you there?" And he said, "Good, bring all your stuff." I went back to sleep there at my mom's, and that night I had the most vivid dream. I saw the plane smack the ground. I saw them screaming and crying, and I saw fire. I woke up screaming, and my mom came running in going "Honey, what is it?" I said, "Mama, I dreamed the plane crashed!" And she said, "No honey, it's just a dream. " And I said, "No mom, it's too real!"

They had already sent me the itinerary, so the next day I called Greenville, South Carolina. I called everybody on the list. Finally, late that afternoon Allen called me back. He said, "Jo, what in the world is it? I've got messages all over Greenville from you." I said, "Allen, it's that airplane," and I told him about my dream. He and I always sat in two seats up front, facing each other. We always sat there. I said, "Allen, please don't get on that plane." He said, "Jo, it's funny you'd mention that, because I was looking out the window yesterday, and I saw fire come out of the wing." I asked him if Les Long had checked it out. Les had flown that plane for years and knew it like the back of his hand. But he had been training these two new pilots. When he told me who the pilots were, I thought, "Oh no," because they had been on tour with us and I thought they were unprofessional. Instead of sleeping while we were getting ready and playing and all, I'd see them down at the bar and such. One of them asked me one night if he could come up to my room with me. I said, "No! Don't talk to me!" But when he told me it was those two guys, it really scared me. I said,

"Please, please don't get on that plane!" Well, when they left Greenville they took a vote that it was going to be their last time to fly on that airplane. They were going to start flying commercial. They were gonna fly from Greenville to Baton Rouge and then to Little Rock. And of course it crashed in Mississippi, my home state. Ronnie always called himself the Mississippi Kid; we never knew why. And then he died in Mississippi. I was completely devastated. I was up celebrating with my band from Memphis because I was going back on the road with Skynyrd. We were all upstairs at my drummer's house, and she came upstairs and said I had a phone call. It was my mother, and she said, "Honey, I don't know how to tell you this." She just started crying, and she put my brother on the phone. He said, "Honey, the plane has crashed and Ronnie is dead." My heart just sank. About that same time a news bulletin flashed across the screen, and I thought—*Oh my God*. I drove home in the rain and nearly had a wreck I was so upset. We made arrangements and flew down to Jackson, and we were some of the first to see Allen and them. The first thing I thought was, *God saved my life.* The Lord gave me that dream to warn me, and I did the only thing I could do and warned them. It was so weird because some of them thought that maybe I had something to do with it, but I had nothing to do with it. At the funeral, Ronnie's daughter Tammy was hanging around me, and I told her she needed to tell her daddy goodbye, so I took a rose off of his casket and gave it to her. I was standing there beside Robert Nix (of Atlanta Rhythm Section), and I'll never forget it, Lacy [Van Zant, Ronnie's father] came up and reached down and scooped up a handful of the dirt and wiped it across my mouth and said, "Kiss this ground you're walking on." And walked off. I thought, *my God*. And Robert is a big guy, I guess 290 pounds and six-foot-five. He just picked me up and put me in the limousine and took me to his and Susie's house in Atlanta, and I stayed there for about two weeks. It really disturbed me that I wasn't on the plane and was saved from it, but somehow got the blame for it, it's just weird. But Robert took me into his studio in Doraville, and played me a new song. He told me if I felt moved to sing along, to go for it. He dimmed the lights and gave me a glass of wine and played "I'm Not Gonna Let It Bother Me Tonight." Pretty soon, I copped the attitude and decided I wasn't gonna let it bother me neither. I started singing, and I looked up and Robert and Rodney were dancing in the control room, and he said, "Baby, it's a smash hit!" We finished it. But he made the mistake of calling someone to tell them, and the next morning when we went in, the musicians had changed everything. They turned me way, way down in the mix. Robert was one of their songwriters and their drummer, and he had played for Roy Orbison. Later he found out a lot of things that had been going on he didn't know about and he quit the group. But they [the Atlanta Rhythm Section] had it out for me after that, they thought I caused that too. One of their roadies tried to kill me backstage in Savannah, Georgia, at a show my band Alias did with them. I was nearly killed, and I quit singing for a long time after that. Seven years. I thought if this is what music is all about, I don't want no part of it.

Ronnie Van Zant, one of the South's true poets, was dead. For many, it was unfathomable. His legacy and legend would only grow over the years, with many left to wonder what other great music he would have produced had he not been taken so young.

Johnny Van Zant

The last day I spent with him, Donnie was there too, just being out there at his house. He really had his stuff together right before he passed away. We'd gone out there to do a *People* magazine interview. That was a special day for me. There were a lot of them to be honest, but that one, maybe because it was the last one, sticks out in my memory.

Donnie Van Zant

He was physically in good shape too. So many years before that, he wasn't. But he had been lifting weights and swimming.

Don Barnes

Lacy [Van Zant] was so supportive when we [38 Special] were just sleeping on a mattress in a van. He would talk about perseverance and keeping your chin up. Lacy is a great guy, and we go back to when we were kids. We all grew up on the same street,

Donnie and Steve Brookins were all friends. Lacy was the patriarch of the whole group. He is a great man, and when the tragedy happened [the plane crash], and I was the one who flew out with Lacy to identify the bodies, the strength that this man displayed was monumental. Lacy was in denial on the plane and hoped that there was a mistake and that his son was not dead. I had to find out who was where, and we had to get to the funeral home to identify the body. After seeing Ronnie at the funeral home and paying last respects with Lacy, I felt changed because this man had helped me at an early age. He had co-signed for me to get an amp when I was young. He felt I wanted it bad enough to make something of myself as a musician. Up until then I was giving about 80 percent of my talent, but after seeing Ronnie dead and remembering his kindness, I try to give 100 percent.

We then went to the hospital and saw all the other people who were hurt. They all looked at Lacy through stitches and swelling and he told me not to say anything about Ronnie. He just stood there and said that Ronnie was fine and you just get better and rest. This man had just been to the funeral home and seen his son dead and decided to keep that to himself for these guys to heal. I told him that it was the strongest thing I had seen a man do. They were ripped from their life and career, and there is justice that they can get back out there. Johnny does a great job and they perform very well. Everything was taken from them so quickly. Ronnie would have wanted them to go on. I have nothing but great respect for him and the Van Zant family.

Jo Jo Billingsley

Ronnie was awesome. He was just such a gentleman. He was brilliant and very quiet, at least to us, the girls. Until he got high, and then he got pretty rowdy. But he was a gentleman. He would never mess with anybody unless they messed with him. And he'd always try to warn them. He'd warn them two times, and the third time he'd just hit 'em. He called it cold-cocking. He was a Golden Gloves champion in Florida. He gave his dad Lacy a black eye when he was like three years old. Lacy would get down on his knees and box with him. Ronnie was in good shape, he really was. He was strong. And he was so creative. He was a great man. I really, truly believe that he was a prophet of God. And early on Satan got his focus off track. He was proud too. I remember one time they told us that we could no longer continue to ride in limousines because it wasn't in the budget. Ronnie said, "We will always ride in limousines. I will ride in limousines 'til I ride in the back of one with flowers on top." It was a very prophetic moment. Everything he ever said came true and that's the sign of a true prophet. I knew then that there was greatness in Ronnie. He was just so charismatic; people were just drawn to him. I was praying one day, and the Lord told me, "Ronnie's with me." That blessed me. I thought, "Thank God."

Henry Paul

I went to Ronnie's funeral, and that was the end of an era. Very emotional. The last time I saw Ronnie Van Zant alive I was playing a show with him in Winston Salem, North Carolina, and he and I were on the bus drinking whiskey together. He was intoxicated and telling me that he was the Prince of Dixie. I was sitting over there drinking and going, "Fuck you. What the fuck is the Prince of Dixie?" He said that Duane Allman was the king, and he was the prince. He had the whole thing figured out. We got back to the hotel and were riding the elevator up, and Ronnie and I were just cranked up. We got to the top floor and the door slid open and we came spilling out and we knocked over one of those ashtrays full of sand. It was a scene. Gene Odom was there and he said, "Is everything okay here—are we cool?" And I said yeah. Ronnie went his way and I went mine and that was the last I saw of him.

Randall Hall

Mine and his [Ronnie's] was always a great relationship. I never saw the bad, because I never worked with him. He treated me like, with a little brother kind of attitude. He took me under his wing, like I said, hooking us [Running Easy] up with agents and trying to get us going. He did anything he could on his end to help us. Sure enough, he got us on some gigs. I remember doing one with Bloodrock up in Atlanta. It was alternating sets all through the night. But as a person, he was always like, "Hey, good to see you again, man." The last time I saw him, I was not working a whole lot playing, so I was working at an apartment complex as the in-house landscaping guy. I was digging a hole out in front of an apartment, and he just wheeled up. It was him and some of the other guys, coming to get one of the roadies that lived there. And I was digging a hole with filth and dirt all over me, you know. And he said, "Randall, what the hell are you doin'?" I said, "I'm digging a hole." [Laughs] I had to knock the dirt off my hand to shake his hand. He said, "Man, you're too good to be doing this shit. Why are you doin' it?" I said, "I got to make a buck right now, you know?" A few months later his plane crashed. On that night, we were gigging out towards the beach, and at the time there were conflicting reports. Nothing was really accurate. They were saying Leon was dead, but he wasn't. We didn't get the full report on what really happened 'til the next day.

Charlie Daniels

When I think about Ronnie I think about shaking of hands. He would do that all the time. He would reach out and shake hands. If I had to name two people that were deeply loved I would say Elvis Presley and Ronnie. These are two people that have been revered so much by people since their deaths in 1977.

Gary Rossington

First of all, he was like my best friend. We went bass fishing all the time together, and camping and doing things outside. We were teenagers doing things like that. I don't remember any of the bad things or any of the bullshit things or the business stuff. And I remember playing live onstage with him. It was always great. He was a great guy and great fun to be with, and I miss him a lot.

Derek Hess

I knew Ronnie just enough to know that he was a man of quiet dignity and honor. Unpretentious and unassuming and just knew his place. A self-confident man, he seemed to walk out of another time almost—a time of chivalry, he was just a plain, old gentleman. I truly liked being around him. Now of course I never had to endure any of his disciplinary actions, as we all knew he was known for. Glad I never had to quit his band. It was usually your ass if you did.

Fortunately, I think he respected me, and the level of playing our band was at. It's hard to believe he's been gone longer than he was alive. A true classic and stylist.

Don Barnes

Basically, you can listen to Ronnie and get a biography of Ronnie through his music. Like I said, he was a true real life poet. The "Ballad of Curtis Loew" song was written about a house that was literally up on concrete blocks, just a wooden shack. It was a little store and there was an old black guy that sat around there and sang.

Ed King

Ronnie was two people. When he was straight, he was one of the finest people I'd ever met—when drunk, he was a madman. Unfortunately, towards the end of my tenure with the band, he was drunk the whole time. That's mainly why I left. Working with him just wasn't fun anymore, and he was the only reason I wanted to join the band anyway.

One of my fondest memories of Ronnie, one that displays his genius, was in January 1975. I had written this entire musical piece in my hotel room. We were working on *Nuthin' Fancy*. He came by the hotel room to hear it and all, I told him was "It sounds to me like the song should be about a train." It took him only fifteen minutes to write "Railroad Song" that night. Ronnie never wrote anything down—ever. But as long as the band could remember the "groove" of the music, the lyrics would always come back to him.

One other thing comes to mind—and this is so cool. Many times in rehearsal while writing the band would be playing—it'd get loud—and Ronnie, after completing a verse or two of lyrics in his head, would walk over to me. He'd cup his mouth to my ear and sing me the song! On at least three occasions I was the first person to hear what he'd come up with. I remember hearing "Saturday Night Special" this way and my jaw dropping. He was an inspiration. I wish we could've parted on easier terms.

Danny Joe Brown

He [Ronnie] was a helluva fighter. Not just a fighter, but a *helluva* fighter. That boy could whip some ass. [Laughs] I drank a couple of tall-boys and got into a fight. My best friend actually fought him. I picked up Gary Rossington and put him up on the stage so he didn't get into it. But Pee Wee, my friend, got into a fight with Ronnie and they duked it out on the dance floor. It was at a church dance, believe it or not. [Laughs] St. Andrew's church dance in Jacksonville.

Tom Dowd

Ronnie was a gem. Ronnie was a brilliant writer. We spent most of our time together traveling on the road for a day or two at a time, or if I had them for a day or two in the rehearsal hall in Jacksonville and in the studio. But we very seldom socialized until the very last album when I was rehearsing them up in Jacksonville, and Ronnie said that I should stay out at his house instead of a motel. I stayed for about four days there and that was about as close as we got. I can say that Ronnie was a true consummate professional.

There are two artists when we were recording that would look at me and say, "I want to sing tomorrow" or "Let's sing a week from Thursday." I would agree and we would set up a schedule for them to come in and sing. There would be songs set up ready for them to sing. Ronnie was one of those, so was Rod Stewart. They would walk into the studio and say, "Play me this song" and I would play the song they were looking for, and then they would sing. Now, we were not in the studio thirty or forty minutes and they would sing, maybe one verse, stop the tape and come into the studio and sit down and listen. Then they would say that they were not ready today; let's do it tomorrow, and just get up and walk out the door. They knew where their instrument was and would not sit there and sing for six or seven hours and not hit the note.

On the other hand, with Ronnie we would be making a track and I would be working on the band, and he would always have a bottle of Jack in his hand, and he would put it down on the end of the console and he would say that at 2:00 p.m. tomorrow he would be ready to record the song. Then he would walk out the door. The fact that he put the Jack down on the console meant that he was going home and have something to eat and have some tea and he would come back in the next day, and if it was one of those days when he said, "No, not today." Then the Jack would stay on the end of the console again. On the other hand, if he heard himself sounding good, then he would go through it in half an hour, and then he would be feeling really good and know that this was the day, and do two or three songs in about two hours. He knew when he was ready to deliver and knew when he was wasting his time and running up the bill. He would just walk out the door. I was talking about how the other musicians were coming in at 2:00 p.m. clear eyed. I never had to say anything to him because if he was going to try to sing tomorrow, whatever the hell he was doing, he would stop when he walked out that door, until the next day or two days later. Just a dead stop, because he knew he was not ready and that was the kind of person he was.

He had been asking me during the year between the live album and *Street Survivors*, if I would help or teach him how to produce because he was working with two groups. One was Molly Hatchet, and the other was 38 Special. He used to say, "Donnie is a better writer than I am, and Johnny is a better singer than I am." Now this is Ronnie talking about his brothers, and that's the way he felt about it. It just killed me when, after his demise, that Donnie is trying to sing and Johnny is trying to write, because if he was alive he would have punched them both out if you know what I mean! [Laughs]. Because he said Donnie is the better writer and Johnny the better singer, but they switched hats and he is ready to kill them. That is not his game at all, or how he saw their careers. Ronnie was an avid fisherman, and he used to love to get with Gary and Allen, and they all had bass boats on the St. John's River. Ronnie had said to me while we were doing the *Survivors* album that his next album was not going to be a Skynryd album. He and Waylon Jennings and Merle Haggard were going to make an album together. He asked me if I was interested and would I help him do it. I told him it would be my pleasure. That was the next endeavor. I could just imagine these three guys with their wry wisdom writing, "Okie from Muskogee," or whatever. I could just imagine the three of them and what it would have been like, and I looked forward to doing that. It never materialized, but I thought, what an album that would be!

In the meantime, he was working with 38 [Special] and [Molly] Hatchet trying to get albums out of them. Ronnie was intelligent. He was belligerent or whatever you want, I don't care, I never had a problem with him. He and I would dispute on something, but we'd discuss it. One night at a band meeting, he said, " There are two people in this world that if I had an argument with, I won't hit!" And I knew who they were, Lacy and me. Other people giving him the same static he would have punched them out on the floor.

Dru Lombar

The bad boys. [Laughs] I grew up with them guys in Jacksonville. They were the bad boys but hard working and committed. Ronnie Van Zant was a great talent. A great writer and singer. That's a sad situation, that whole thing. They lived maybe a little too fast.

Artimus Pyle

Ronnie hired Steve Gaines and brought him into the fold. He loved Steve. He wrote with Steve. He would actually leave the stage in front of 200,000 people and let Steve sing a song by himself. Now, most singers are not that confident. They're afraid to get their little wiggly ass off the stage because somebody might forget them. Ronnie had total confidence in himself, his band, and Steve. It didn't bother him a bit to take a break and walk off stage. I'd sit on the drums and look over and watch Ronnie admiring Steve playing with his band. What kind of self respect and respect for others is that? It was the best!

Al Kooper

Ronnie was an amazing bandleader. I have never seen a better bandleader in my whole life. No one was trying to lead that band if he was the leader. You know how there are fights in bands—well, they didn't have anything like that because he would have whooped 'em. He was a tough little [expletive] and he was a nice guy too. He was not just tough, but he was bright. He knew how to run a band.

He did a great job. I have never seen anyone run a better band in my whole career. The thing he did that was different from other bands was that he wanted that band to sound the same every night. He was not interested in improvisation at all. There was no improvisation in that band at all, except when they were first rehearsing that song. They had a place out near the swamp where they would rehearse and there was no air conditioning or anything.

15

The Rossington Collins Band

The surviving band members—Gary, Allen, Billy, Leon, and Artimus—made their first post-crash appearance at the Charlie Daniels Band Volunteer Jam in 1979. Gary and Allen decided at that time that they wanted to continue on in some form, whether it be with other survivors from Skynyrd or in a new band with new players. One thing was certain, going back on the road would be some time in the future for all of them, as they endured months of grueling rehabilitation while recovering from the tremendous injuries suffered in the plane crash.

Barry Lee Harwood

They healed up and when they figured out that they still had music to share with the world, they called me and offered me the job. I was free at the time, and this time I jumped at the opportunity to play with these guys and help them get back what had been taken from them in the crash. They felt like they had been robbed and were missing out on sharing their music with the world. I guess it's hard to end like that—having the last thing you did as a band was have a plane crash. The mood was upbeat and like we were on a mission to show the world that even though it was not Skynyrd, that this band was just as good and had a lot to say.

I was married at the time so I had to move my whole family back [from Nashville to Jacksonville] with me, but since I had lived there most of my life it was no big deal and kind of like coming home. The band was for the most part together; we just had to find a drummer as Artimus had broken his leg in a bad motorcycle wreck. We all agreed to call Derek and offer him the job, which of course he took, and the band was complete. We locked ourselves in the rehearsal room and started writing and getting ready. Our first warm-up gig was in Gainesville and it went great: the people responded very well to what we were doing.

It was an honor to play with them, but I had played many big shows before, so I was not as nervous as I had been at other gigs. It was a thrill to be part of that music and a band that has such a huge place in history and peoples' lives. Our official coming out party was at the Super Dome, and I have to admit that it was a huge rush to play that show and know that I was part of something that to this day is a huge part of the musical history.   ·

Derek Hess

I had heard of the formation of a new band and knew that Barry Lee was going to be a part of it. Again, I was very envious but also happy for him. I think they had been getting it together up in North Carolina, at a place called Bat Cave, North Carolina, where Arti was recovering from a motorcycle accident. I'm not sure if I knew it was his kick drum leg then or not. It would've been irrelevant to me at the time anyway. I think I knew they were trying a chick singer, the 38 Special backup singer, Dale Krantz. I didn't know anything about her. Seems that Arti wanted the band to listen to and consider a friend of his who was lead singer in his band, Studebaker Hawke. I don't know if that ever transpired, but I believe they were pretty impressed with Dale and her lyric-writing ideas and ability. I think when she opened it up, they were sold. And very intuitive on their part—no one could stand in Ronnie's place. Good move. It's a bit gray here, but from all of the hearsay and opinions flying all about, it was said that Arti wasn't too happy with his bud being out and wasn't sure about the chick singer thing, whoever it was, one could understand that. Nothing personal I'm sure. I don't think there was any question about it as things came along. And the leg was certainly an impairment. Very frustrating for him. Out of the blue, very early in the morning, middle of the week, I was jolted awake by the phone that was ringing. No answering machine or voicemail back then. So I finally answered it, and was floored to hear Billy Powell's voice on the other end. You can't imagine the surprise. I had to stop and reassure myself I wasn't dreaming, really. He proceeded to tell me that it was looking like Arti was not doing it with them this time, or at least not now, and everybody was back in Jacksonville and they would sure like me to come out that next afternoon to Allen's rehearsal studio, bring my drums, and see if things could work. I couldn't believe my ears. I was up the rest of the night. At the time I was working for a ship chandler, which is the business of supplying commercial ocean-going vessels with food supplies and just about everything you or I would need to survive. That job surely sucked. I would do deliveries in the freezing rain and cold in these derelict trucks. It was so depressing. So with an aura of "this can't be happening," I made my way out there.

Dale Krantz-Rossington

Actually, I had sung with 38 Special for a while. I had sung with Leon Russell in the fall and winter of '76, and the 38 boys had heard about that and decided they wanted some background vocalists at the time. We opened for Lynyrd Skynyrd in the spring of '77, which was an eye-opener for me. I had worked with 38 Special for several months before opening for Skynyrd, and I remember standing in the shadows watching Skynyrd and I was just overwhelmed by the sights and sounds—I was blown away. Then several months later after the plane crash, I was still affiliated with the 38 bunch, until they were ready to look for a new singer. And of course that caused some feathers to be ruffled, I must say. When I quit 38 to go and sing with Gary and Allen, I mean. Of course that was just the beginning of a lot of feathers being ruffled.

Derek Hess

I was warmly welcomed into the Rossington Collins Band, and we proceeded to drop the hammer. It was awesome and powerful. Those guys rehearsed at almost stage level. I'm thinking, we plowed through what was later to become "Prime Time," and the fellas were just grinning ear to ear. I was trying to remain conscious don't you know. Allen blurted out, "Now that's what I'm fuckin' talking about." They were signing me up in less than an hour.

Dale Krantz-Rossington

I was totally confident in my belief that Gary and Allen especially, but all of them, deserved their rightful place on the stage. I was only there...I totally understood all the grief they were going through, that they were consumed with over the loss of Ronnie and Steve and the rest of them. I couldn't understand why every one was so tough on Gary and Allen and the survivors. So a little bit of the cheerleader in me came out—and the Baptist preacher. The press had a lot of funny adjectives for the way I came off, but I was not educated enough in the Skynyrd history to know what I was up against. So part of it was ignorance [Laughs]—and part of it was an idealistic, almost worship of Gary and Allen and all they had gone through. I was gonna go out there and kick anybody's ass, if you'll pardon the expression, that didn't feel they deserved to be up there. You can hear that in the lyrics. "They're alive and well and ready— are you ready for the big boys?" That's a pretty simple statement. And "Opportunity"—another of my favorite songs, was for those who doubted the reasons they had for going back to work. Everyone wasn't ready for them to do music again, except of course for them. They needed it. So it was easy to be tough. You had to be tough standing between Gary and Allen, can you imagine? [Laughs] Have mercy.

Derek Hess

I could hear the woman [Dale Krantz] had chops, but I didn't realize how incredible her delivery was until we were cutting the first album. She would sing along for scratch vocals as we laid basic tracks, and when we played it back we were all just juiced to hear how much energy was there. I think she only re-sang parts of two or three tracks. Amazing. Allen always called her, "you wailin' bitch!!" With affection, of course.

Mike Estes

Allen was always fabulous, I thought. I was so intrigued; I had to find out where he lived and everything. I wasn't a stalker, but I guess I was just short of being a stalker. When I was in high school I went to a library and found a Jacksonville phone book and looked in it. The Rossington Collins Band was listed in it. I couldn't believe it. So I called it up, and this guy named Craig Reed answers the phone. I was living in Ohio at the time, and it turned out Craig's from Ohio, so we just got to talking. He was their production manager. I was a junior in high school at the time, so I'm sure I aggravated him to death. I told him I had a band and needed a name for my band. So he got Allen Collins on a conference call, because Allen was coming up with all these cool names, but Craig couldn't remember 'em. Imagine this. My favorite guitar player. I'm a junior in high school, on the phone with Allen Collins. I said about two words. But he says, "You can have that name Helen Highwater, but you gotta swear to God you'll do something with it." So I did. I played under that name, and opened for Allen, and he showed me all kinds of stuff. He'd come and sit in when we were playing clubs down in Jacksonville. This was just at the start of the Allen Collins Band. He showed me everything on the guitar, and moved me up to the next level. I was lucky, I got to learn from him right there at his house. He had so much patience with me. To this day I still don't know why he let me hang around, but he did.

Randall Hall

Allen was a guy that had perfect pitch. He was real hyper as a kid. They used to give him Ritalin to combat the hyperactivity. He had such a tolerance level. He could do more of everything than anybody. I remember having a contest between him and one of the road guys to see who could string a guitar the quickest. He beat the roadie! And he had it in tune without even putting it on a tuner. I was going, "My God."

Derek Hess

[On the breakup of Rossington Collins] That is a rather delicate subject. After an incredible first year, an album that was holding its own in the charts—I believe it got to #9 in some very worthy company—we were having so much fun. It kind of had a euphoric sensation swirling around the whole miraculous happening. After tragedy struck again with the passing of Allen's wife, and just getting caught up in all of the trappings of the big time rock and roll lifestyle, something just went out of the bubble. We were convinced by the record company to get in the studio in a rather hurried fashion. We would pick up a nice bonus if we got our second record out by a certain deadline. So we bit on it but were really unprepared. Allen had a pretty serious car accident a week before we were to go, and he was really struggling with the loss of his wife. He absolutely adored her, and had two young daughters. He just seemed lost. It was very hard to see this happening to him. About this time, it became evident that Gary and Dale were in a pretty serious relationship, and that seemed to drive a wedge between Allen and Gary, and the normally free-flowing productive juices just bogged down. There was a lot of bad behavior to get into out in El Paso, and that just further worsened the entire situation. It was a catastrophic crash and burn outcome, and it just got worse when we got down to Criteria studios in Miami for mixing and mastering. Every imaginable poison that could be thrown our way was, and we barely got the album finished. After lots of anguish and discontentment everywhere, multiple canceled shows, RCB performed a benefit concert here at home. Little did we know, it would be our last. Man that was hard to swallow.

A few weeks passed, and Gary announced that he and Dale needed to get away to clear their heads and think about the future. We got a call from them from somewhere in Wyoming, and they said they were done. I was stunned. Such an awesome new beginning for the survivors, and just a tease for the rest of us. And it was all over. It was very hard to deal with it, I assure you. A few months went by, and I guess Allen, Leon, Billy, myself, and Barry wanted to carry on, so we tracked down my old band mate Randall Hall, and somebody thought about Jimmy Daughtery. We became the Allen Collins Band. Recorded one really good record, and at the time of its release, our record company, MCA, was now in the arms of Motown Records. I think they went, "Allen Collins Band—who?" Very little album support from them, they just cleaned house, so we were pretty much on our own. We toured a little, a couple of eventful shows. It just seemed that Allen wasn't into it. I know he was just beaten down. It was over.

Dale Krantz-Rossington

[On the Rossington Band] Those were sweet times for us. There wasn't so much of the pressure. I mean, Rossington Collins was tough to have to leave. It was a difficult situation at the time. Allen had lost Cathy. We had been mourning her for over a year, and the music was getting further away, and unfortunately, drugs were the predominant factor in that after we lost her. It was tough to leave that band, but once we did that we still missed the music. This was a wonderful way to get our chops up and wail, and God, Jay [Johnson] was a great rhythm guitar player, as well as a lead. He had a solid rhythm that could always take it right on up a few steps. We had a wonderful time back then. We believed in the songs we were writing and we enjoyed working with the younger guys. It's a judgmental business we're in, but some of the old stuff finally got to take a back seat for a little while. We needed that.

Jay Johnson

I was asked to play guitar for some demo sessions on Gary and Dale Rossington. They had been recording demos with the Muscle Shoals Rhythm Section in late '85, but those tracks came out very slick and streamlined, not quite like the raw, powerful "band" feel that Gary and Dale were looking for. So they were back with a hand-picked band trying to find some magic.

Gary had been listening to a lot of Van Halen stuff at the time and wanted to find a young guitarist with that kind of heavy pop/rock sound, one totally against the grain of his own style. That was, of course, right down my alley. I was thrilled to be asked to play. Gary was my favorite guitarist from Skynyrd, and I was more than honored to play with him. The tracks went well, and I went on with my band, figuring that "that was that," so to speak. A week later Gary called me from Wyoming to ask me to finish the album and to join the band officially. I was knocked for a loop. Life was never the same after that.

That band lasted just over three years. Gary, Dale, and my dad, Jimmy, shopped the project constantly to few interested companies. Finally we got a bite and started recording again. We finished the first Rossington Band album, *Returned to the Scene of the Crime* for Atlantic records, who released the LP in late 1986 with little or no fanfare whatsoever. The album fell off the charts as though it had an anchor attached to it. Gary tried in vain to get a tour started right after the release but was thwarted in the process by two band members who bailed out on us at the worst possible moment. I feared that Gary would drop the project altogether, discouraged as he was, but I stepped in and played cheerleader until Gary finally agreed to try another tour using new musicians. We snatched up drummer Mitch Rigel from Radio Tokyo and we brought in Tim Sharpton on keys, who I had written songs with some years before. We did a three-month tour financed totally on Gary's American Express card. It went well and we were added as opening act to Kansas's 1987 summer tour where we made good friends with Steve Morse, one of the finest gentlemen on the planet, who would appear as a guest on the next LP. As we were wrapping up our second LP, *Love Your Man*,—this time for MCA records—Gary had entered negotiations to reunite Lynyrd Skynyrd. Next thing we knew we were on a two-year Tribute Tour with Skynyrd that took us all over the USA. What can you say? It was a young rocker's dream come true.

The Rossington Band was a great—but short-lived—group consisting of some of the best players anywhere. Tim Lindsey is one of the finest bassists ever, and Dale Krantz-Rossington is one of the best singers of all time in my book. What a voice! I'll always be thankful that Gary and Dale gave me the opportunity to work and write with them and I'm proud of the two records we all did together.

Randall Hall

They had the Rossington Collins Band in about 1980. I was a candidate for that too. Gary and Allen used to tell me, "We're putting this thing together, and we're gonna do some of Skynyrd's songs and some of ours." It was between me and Barry Harwood. It was me one week and Barry the next. Finally they just decided on Barry. Then that ran its course. They did a couple of years of that and two albums. Then Gary and Allen parted ways. I guess Gary started hooking up with Dale or something, I don't know. So Allen came out to see me playing locally, him and Barry Lee Harwood. And it happened that Jimmy Doughtry was playing drums with me in this band the Moody

Brothers. An old-time lounge act that had been around for years. I learned so much from those guys. They said, "Man, you gotta come join this band." So that's where that came about. We rehearsed out at Allen's house. His six-car garage, one of them was made into a studio, you know. We did that album, and we were starting to work on a second one, but Allen was just losing it. He had been through so much tragedy in his life. The worst was losing his wife. After that it was just like he didn't care anymore. He began to party to the extreme.

There were many but for me one of first things I recall was when we were nearly finished with cutting tracks on the first album, and some overdubbing had begun, some of the brass from MCA Records came out to hear their new artists, and how the album was coming along. The president of the company along with some of the A&R folks came along. We all gathered in the control room, and Allen says to the engineer, "Don't be shy"—meaning the volume he played it back at. So about thirty seconds into the track, Allen charges up to the console, switches on the big playback speakers, and jacks the throttle up; meanwhile the co-owner is standing there with us, and very much concerned. Then Allen reassures him that MCA will cover the damages, with an intimidating chuckle. Well, we just howled, and those tracks just rocked the house. It was awesome. They all looked at each other when it was over, just flabbergasted. You could tell they were just stunned and blown away at how great it was.

Another memorable highlight would've been some of the large shows we did. The New Years Eve, 1980–1981 transition. All of our families came up to Atlanta at the Omni, which was probably the largest indoor facility of the time. My dad was there with my oldest brother, my family. My two kids were eleven and five at the time. At the stroke of 12 o'clock, the kids all came out on stage with us, my daughter was up on my shoulders, fireworks were going off, the front of the stage had this great firework effect that sizzled like a curtain of sparklers. When the thing heated up, it sort of raised up from the heat, like a curtain would do. Some of us were standing at the very front cheering with our fans, and I almost lost my balance while leaning back to get me and my daughter away from the monster. It was all good though, and we cleared the stage and went into the renowned instrumental "Free Bird." And you know how that goes over. The entire spectacle. Pre-show and everything the simulcast DJ's could think up was broadcast nationwide. It was fabulous. I actually have a board mix from that show. And it is strong. Don't tell anyone though. [Laughs] Three days later, we came home to a front page write up with huge color live photo, and a sold out coliseum. I can't say enough about that feeling. There are many wonderful highlights of our very short existence, but one more I must share is when I received my first gold album. I was thrilled, and almost as thrilled when I gave the adult family members their very own gold records. I think a few of the cried. I had arrived!

Other than the Rossington Band and the Allen Collins Band, former Lynryd Skynyrd members would form two other groups, Alias and the Artimus Pyle Band, who would record two albums for MCA Records during the early 1980s.

16

From Tribute to Legend

Ten years after the plane crash, Skynyrd reunited for a full-scale tour with the surviving band members, Gary Rossington, Leon Wilkeson, Billy Powell, and Artimus Pyle, along with original guitarist Ed King and Randall Hall, who would sub for Allen Collins. Collins had been paralyzed following a 1986 automobile accident.

Randall Hall

My wife and I were at the place where we used to live in Jacksonville. We'd heard some talk about it, the possibilities of something happening. Then out of the clear blue he [Allen Collins] calls me up one day, all hyped up.

He said, "Hey buddy, are you gonna be there for me?"

I said, "Yeah, sure. What is it?"

He said, "You gonna be there for me?"

I said, "Sure, what is it Allen?"

He said, "Oh, it's this Skynyrd tribute thing they're putting together. I just don't feel like going out there in a wheel chair. I don't feel like playing as much. I know you got it. I want to know if you'll be there for me."

I said, "Well, of course."

He said, "I told them guys if they don't use you I'd shut the whole m.f. down. I told 'em I want you and nobody else. I've got people calling me from all over that want to do it. I want you and you only to do it."

I said, "All right man, I'll do it." So that's how that happened.

Derek Hess

Yes, that's true. We, the remnants of the Allen Collins Band thing, were sitting around at the band office listening to Gene Odom talking up this grand idea of putting together a quasi-Skynyrd show, with the ten-year anniversary of the plane crash approaching. After we all thought about it for a bit, and we weren't doing anything at the time, we thought hey yeah, that might appropriate. God knows who else was thinking about it, but the next thing I know I'm on the outside looking in, and the rest is history.

Dale Krantz-Rossington

I have to tell you honestly that in '87 when they started talking about a tribute to Skynyrd, I was very afraid of it, because I didn't want to see Gary going back to so much weight on his shoulders. But, oh well…. Thank God they didn't listen to me, huh? [Laughs] I have learned over the years that Skynyrd is bigger than all of us. It is way bigger than any one of us. It has a life of its own. It started out as six shows. It was going to be one show as a tribute, then it was six. Then everyone was saying, "Hey, there's fans in Texas. There's fans in Nebraska." Then a hundred shows later we decided we couldn't let each other go. It was too good. The rest is new Skynyrd history.

Randall Hall

Well, I can talk about it now. We had a lawsuit that ended a year ago. It took six and a half years to resolve. But it's public knowledge now. At the time I couldn't say nothing. They were contriving other reasons, saying it was something it wasn't, but in essence, the band's management wanted to cut my pay in half. After being with them almost seven years at the time, they just wanted to take half of my percentage of the gross, and I said, "No way." None of them came to see me. They had their manager call my attorney about it. I said, "Call me and talk to me about this!"

My attorney said, "No. I don't see any reason for you guys to do that [fire him]. Randall is there. He does his job. I don't see any legitimate reason for you to do that. And it wasn't everybody in the band's decision either. Months later Johnny called me and said, "I want you to know I fought for you tooth and nail." He said, "If my name wasn't Van Zant, I'd probably be gone too." [Laughs] It was about them making more, and me making less. I was an equal shareholder at the time. They tried to say it was because I was late for rehearsal. Bull. I was the one that had to pick up Billy all the time, because, no driving for Billy. And Billy would want to stop on the way and pick up something. And we'd be late. And they tried to use that as an excuse. It was more than that. I think it was greed, man. It all happened conveniently after Allen was gone. Because if Allen had been around he would have fought that tooth and nail. I think it was more Ed and Gary, I'm not sure.

Allen Collins died on January 23, 1990, from chronic pneumonia, a complication from the paralysis he received following a 1986 auto accident.

Mike Estes

I was at work, and I heard it on the radio [that Allen Collins had died]. I knew he was in bad shape, but I didn't know it was that bad. I had tried getting ahold of him a month earlier but couldn't because he was in the hospital. Nobody would tell me where. So when I found out about it at work, I took the next week off. It about killed me. It was terrible. It wiped me out. I actually had a gig that night that I had to go play. It was very hard. I went and saw his grave after that and had the closure thing. But I had told him while he was alive how much he meant to me. I still miss the crazy guy. He was so much fun to hang out with. Always on fire. I always said when I had that Skynyrd gig I'd give it up in a minute if Allen could come back. And I would have.

I'd been knowing Gary and them for a long time, and Ed King had me come out on the road with them for about a year between '92 and '93. I was writing a lot of songs. Randall Hall was still in the band then. Right after that they fell out with Randall. I don't know what happened. He told me they fired him. They told me he quit. Only they know the truth, I guess. But I was out there, and I got comfortable writing with Johnny and Gary and Ed, mostly Ed. When Randall left, we were down in Florida doing pre-production work on the *Endangered Species* acoustic record. They were gonna just do it with two guitars. I was running their board for 'em as a paid engineer. I'd never engineered in my life. One night Ed had to go out of town for something. I was staying at Ed's house. Gary called me over to see if I wanted to write. We started playing at about eight o'clock that night and didn't finish until five in the morning. I knew all of the Skynyrd songs, and we jammed on some of those and some Free songs, all kinds of different stuff. He had actually asked Greg Martin of the Kentucky Headhunters to take Randall's place, but Greg was undecided or told him he couldn't do it. Well, we'd had a little too much to drink that night, and Gary turned to me and said, "Hey man, you want the job?" So I told him I'd give him until tomorrow and let him ask me again. I didn't want him to make a decision like that drunk. So he called me the next day and said, "Hey, I meant everything I said, and I want you in the band." The next few years were the wildest ones of my life. I went from running their board to playing in the band.

Ed King

I guess I stuck with the reunion band because I was chasing some kind of dream. I was under the impression that just maybe we could write some music that mattered and that maybe Johnny Van Zant would do a good vocal. I was misguided, I guess. I did it to myself.

The '91–'93 version of the band was fun. Custer was a great drummer and we had some great live shows. Artimus left the band because…you'll have to ask him. It's way too complicated, and I'm not sure I understand why. But that version of the band Ronnie would've been proud of. We were tight, energetic, and inspired. Every night was a musical surprise—I had a blast.

In September of '95 I went into congestive heart failure while on the road. I had been diagnosed with an enlarged heart back in late '92. I caught a really bad cold and the infection landed in my heart. The only remedy is a heart transplant. I held my own from '93 thru '95. Though touring did get a bit rough at the end.

I had hoped to get a new heart and re-join the band eventually. But the band kind of deserted me, and maybe it's just as well. The doctors say my health is doing a lot better than they expected, and that I may not need a new heart for five years. By that time, they say new technologies might be available so that I won't need the new heart at all. Who knows. [Author's note: Ed did get a heart, and he's doing great!}

I had thought the guys in the band were closer friends. I was mistaken. Took me a while for that to sink in. I didn't expect them to support me financially, but I didn't expect them to forsake me either. The way they handled my "leave of absence" was a disgrace. I should be grateful to be away from their influence, and I am.

Mike Estes

When Ed got sick with that congestive heart failure, we were finishing a tour up. I had to learn all of his parts in one night. Which, I need a year to learn all of Ed's parts. I got by, but it just wasn't the same without Ed. They hired Hughie Thomasson to come in and play for Ed as a temporary replacement, supposedly. I was a lot happier playing with Ed than with Hughie, and I made it known. Then I was told that Ed wasn't going to be in the band anymore, and I went off the deep end. I didn't quit, they *fired me*. No doubt about it. But it may have been because I was fighting hard to keep Ed in the band. I thought that he was a big part of the sound and the history. Not that Hughie isn't a great guitar player. In his element with the Outlaws, he is wonderful. But it just wasn't the same. It didn't have the same feel. I was just dissatisfied with the whole deal, and maybe the feeling was mutual. But now I have Ed on two songs on my new record. He's great. When I played with him, I just stood beside him, and sometimes it was just unbelievable.

Rickey Medlocke

I will be quite honest with you. When I got back with Skynryd, I was very beat up. I had been slugging it around in a van and riding around with guys in a truck and, at forty-six years old—and that is not an old guy—but the thing about it is when you are sleeping overnights and sleeping in a seat straight up, you wonder what you are doing. When I got the chance to come back with this I took advantage of it. My dad says that you can't drive a car until you learn to ride in the back seat. Those words are constantly repeated in my ear all the time. That is why when I took a break from lead singing it gave me a chance to play guitar. I have great confidence in myself, but I am not going to come from an egotistical place. I play guitar and think I am good but then I listen to Clapton, Hendrix, Eric Johnson, Van Halen, and then I realize I am not as good as some of the other guys. I am not one of those guys that brags about his playing. I learn constantly from other people still today. The greatest compliment that I have had in the last probably twenty-five years of my life came from Billy Gibbons. We did that tour with ZZ Top, and I used to eat dinner at the crew meal every night with Billy Gibbons. He looked straight across the table at me one night and said, "Hey Rickey, I have got to tell you something. I was just listening to you play, man, you have the butter tone." I said, "Yeah, those old Marshalls are really something." He said, "Let me tell you why they are the butter tone. It's because you have the butter spreader in your hand." He said, "Your hand is smooth as buttermilk and don't ever forget it." He looked at me over those dark sunglasses and said that I was a really great guitar player. It blew me away.

On July 21, 2001, bassist Leon Wilkeson passed away. The band continued to forge onward, hiring Ean Evans as bassist.

Gary Rossington

[On Leon Wilkeson] He was just such a nice guy. So down to earth. Leon was just Leon. He did so many funny things. We used to call him "Leon Spillkerson," because he always spilled his coffee or his Coke or drink. He was always doing so many things at one time, it caused him to spill things. And every time he came in or out of a room something would get knocked over. He was so funny. Out on the road, one of us would hear something fall or something and we'd say, "There's Leon!" [Laughs] He used to always press the alarm or bell buttons on the elevator—they're emergency alarms really, you're not supposed to touch them—but every elevator he'd ever get into, he'd push those buttons. So you could always tell Leon was coming by the bells ringing. Now, sometimes elevators would stop when you did that. He'd do that, and we'd get mad at him. But he was just a great guy. He was amazing. I really miss him a lot. His loss is still fresh in our hearts, you know.

Derek Hess

Leon and I, once we were laying the lumber, musically, were like old long lost pals that found each other again. When we played together, it was like a freight train. It was with little effort for our parts to just lock in like a rock. It was like a mental telepathic communication. We rarely discussed or hashed out how to make our parts come together. We could lay down our basic tracks in record time. When we were done, it was depressing. We really rolled. At sound checks most of the time it would be me, Leon, and Barry with Billy some of the time. We would have some very productive moments. A gas.

On a more personal one, on one relationship note, I would have to say that Leon was really my favorite. We hung out a lot. I would drag him out in the boat sometimes, and actually got him to go camping with Billy, Timmy Lindsey, and myself once. He loved it. We rode around in the river most of the night and had a ball. He had quite the moral conviction tucked away in his being, and it would be hard to realize that sometimes. I know a lot of people didn't perhaps see that side of him though there was no doubt with whoever was fortunate enough to spend some time with him. He was all ears and loved to talk at length about just about anything. And he would make you feel very comfortable. We really hit it off great, lots of shenanigans from the two of us. All through the Skynyrd reunion years, he was always very mindful about calling me on my birthday and at Christmas. He would end the call with, "Love your guts." I loved that man. How I do miss him.

On March 13, 2006, the band was inducted into the Rock and Roll Hall of Fame. It was a long time coming for the legions of fans who had petitioned the HOF for years, asking that the band be inducted.

Artimus Pyle

[On being inducted into the Rock and Roll Hall of Fame] My take on that was when Kerri came and told me, the first thing out of my mouth was "Thank you, Ronnie." and I feel like I don't deserve to be in the Hall of Fame because I can think of about 1,000 people off the top of my head that do deserve it. I was Ronnie's drummer, and he was my singer and I will gladly ride in on the coat tails of Ronnie Van Zant.

I was there, I showed up and wore a tuxedo. I played "Free Bird" in a tuxedo, and I went up there and we did a show on the *Intrepid* the day before the Hall of Fame. This was on the *U.S.S. Intrepid*, for first responders families and 9/11 fire police and military families. We just basically wanted to do something that was more accessible. The tickets for the Rock and Roll Hall of Fame were very expensive, and people could not afford to do that. So we did that show the day before on Sunday. I put a band together with some gigantic musicians and it was just for fun and for all the right reasons. I was really proud to be inducted into the Rock and Roll Hall of Fame with Miles Davis, who is one of my heroes. And I got to meet another one of my heroes, Herbie Hancock, and he actually commented on my playing. He said I was a powerful player. It was a dream come true. I had all my family up there. I had a couple of buses and took my youngest son up there, River, and my wife, Kerri. It was all good. We were able to enjoy New York. It was great.

Part 3

The Marshall Tucker Band

17

A Rumbling in Spartanburg: Early Times

Once upon a time, there was a young local band in Spartanburg, South Carolina, called the Rants. The band included Toy Caldwell on guitar, George McCorkle on guitar, Franklin Wilkie on bass, Ross Hanna on drums, and David McCutchen on vocals. The year was 1965.

Franklin Wilkie

My first band with Toy Caldwell was called Magar's Madmen. It was a three-piece with Kenny Magar on drums. We were in the seventh grade, and Kenny was in the ninth. We played all instrumentals, no vocals. Right after Kenny, Toy, and I met a guy named Jimmy Trout. He had a Falcon station wagon and played keyboards, which he was always carrying around in that wagon. He was older, and kind of helped us get organized. The band that came out of that was the Ramblers. We had these red and white shirts with a block "R" on the pocket and black pants. We were doing "Green Onions," early instrumental stuff. When that band broke up, we still had those shirts that had an "R" on the pocket, so we had to come up with another band name that started with "R," and that's how we got the Rants.

Toy Caldwell, Sr.

We were behind them from the very beginning. They would practice a lot in the basement, and it would get so loud, you could watch a coffee cup dance across a table from the vibration. They loved it loud.

Rudy Wyatt
Everybody was fascinated with Frank's bass tone. He was playing with a pick and using an Ampeg with one fifteen [-inch speaker] and a "cow horn" Dan Electro bass with two lipstick pickups. But he got a lot of punch out of that bass. Everybody used to say he had the absolute greatest bass tone they'd ever heard.

That same year, Toy's brother Tommy was performing with Doug Gray, Ross Hanna, and Randy Foster in a band called the New Generation. The boys were heavily into the Motown sound, R&B, and British Invasion rock. They recorded a 45 on the Sonic imprint in 1965, called "Because of Love, It's All Over" written by Tommy and Doug, and recorded in Charlotte at Reflections Sound Studio.

Doug Gray
Tommy and Toy's Aunt Iris made these orange jackets for us with the New Generation for a talent contest one time. We entered this contest where I had to sing "Hold On, I'm Comin'" and "When a Man Loves a Woman." Unfortunately, this R&B group called the Ebonies beat us out that night.

Franklin Wilkie
Their claim to fame was their version of [Percy Sledge's] "When a Man Loves a Woman." That was their showstopper. Doug could really sing that one.

Doug Gray
I had been in a band called the Guildsmen back in 1962. We didn't do much. We played at the Amvets clubs and stuff. Then came Tommy Caldwell, who would ride his bike over to Allen Avenue where I lived at the time, in Cleveland Park. He found out I liked to sing. I remember one time, about 1964, when it was snowing, and he and a couple of his friends came over and said they had a band and wanted to know if I'd like to sing. The first thing we learned was "For Your Love." And see, I'd never learned a structured song before. Everything I had ever sung had been blues, just whatever I felt like singing. I remember Tommy telling the story

several times, because that day they had rode the bikes over in the snow—and that ain't easy. That band, the New Generation, went on for a while, and I got out in 1967 to go to Vietnam and came back. Then Toy had to go and came back. Then we formed the Toy Factory.

Franklin Wilkie

I was in my second year at Spartanburg Junior College—now Spartanburg Methodist College—when we put together a band called the Puzzle, with George McCorkle's brother, Chuck; David McCutcheon from the Rants; Steve "Smitty" Smith (son of Senator Horace Smith); David Ezell, and Wayne Casasanta. Toy had done the early sign-up with the Marines, and every once in a while, he would come up from Paris Island on weekends and jam with the Puzzle at these different fraternity parties.

I remember I went to Boots Upstairs back in 1969, a beach club on St. John Street in Spartanburg. I was on leave from basic training, and on this particular night, they were playing as a three-piece—either under the name Toy Caldwell and Friends, or the Caldwell Brothers, I'm not sure. The band was smoking on the Jimi Hendrix classic "Manic Depression." It was Toy, Tommy, and Steve Smith at the time. They got so loud that Boots pulled the plug on them. It was my only night back home, and the music had died. I didn't even get to hear one whole song. I was devastated.

Rudy Wyatt

Toy and brother Tommy started up a group called the Toy Factory, which included Wayne Casasanta, Ron "Redrock" Edwards, Franklin Wilkie, Toy, and Doug Gray. Jerry Eubanks would join after returning from California.

Franklin Wilkie

I was let out of the service on a hardship discharge because my father had cancer. Word had already gotten to Toy that I was home for good. That night, I dropped by to hear the Toy Factory play. Toy went up to Chris Brawley, a friend of Jerry's who was playing bass and told him his friend that had been in the service was back home, and he'd be playing from now on. He didn't fire him in a mean way, just matter-of-factly. But that was Toy. Friendship was everything to him. Chris went on to start a band called High Cotton, which recorded an excellent record for Mercury Records, produced by Allen Toussaint. I do remember that Chris had a terrible accident with a chainsaw, and lost a couple of fingers on his left hand. He had to quit playing bass, but he took up slide guitar and became one of the best.

Shortly thereafter, Carol Cox joined the band for a while. He came to auditions on Spring Street. He was well trained on piano, so it caused the band to expand its horizons. Doug no longer had to sing all of the songs, and the choice of material was becoming more jazzy. Toy Factory was playing Steve Winwood and Traffic tunes, Elton John, and John Mayall. They were just beginning to play some originals, "Can't You See?" and many early versions of Caldwell's.

Doug Gray

Tommy Caldwell had damaged his leg during basic training in the Marines and was sent home on a medical discharge. He was itching to play, so he bought himself a Telecaster, and a wig—so that he would fit in—and began playing rhythm guitar with the band.

Franklin Wilkie

We were booking through Beach Club Promotions, Cecil Corbet. Cecil heard some of our original material and sent us to record in Muscle Shoals. We did some tapes with Barry Beckett, a keyboard player and engineer. I remember him saying the material was good, but he wanted us to leave Toy down there. [Laughs] After all, that's where Duane Allman got his start. Corbet engineered the opening spot for the Toy Factory on the Allman Brothers Band's eastern tour.

Doug Gray

We had a Tom's Peanut truck that we converted into an equipment truck/sleeper. Joe McConnel was sound engineer. Steve Burgess—we called him "Superchicken"—drove.

Franklin Wilkie

Tommy went to play bass with Pax Parachute for a bit, a band that featured George McCorkle and Paul Riddle. They were doing a lot of that Grand Funk stuff. He went and bought him a new bass. When Tommy left, we hired David Ezell. We did a few rehearsals with me, Ezell, Toy, Ross Hanna, and Doug Gray, but it never did gel. There was just something wrong with the chemistry. For a while, Toy was rehearsing with both Toy Factory and Pax Parachute.

Paul Riddle

Pax Parachute was playing at the Sitar club on Main Street. Tommy had just gotten discharged from the Marines, and on that night, he made a dramatic appearance in the back door of the club, wearing his service trench coat and cowboy hat. It was the same coat he wears on the gatefold photo of the first album. Tommy looked over at me, and asked, "You with me?" I answered back, "Yeah." I was a junior in high school when all that happened.

George McCorkle

There was resistance all over the South when we started. We got thrown out of clubs left and right for playing our own music. We'd play a set and the club owner would raise hell because we weren't playing something by someone else. But we weren't gonna do it! We thought we had something, and we knew the only way we was ever gonna find out was to stick with it.

Jerry Eubanks

Toy called me up and said he was looking for a flute player, and of course, I couldn't play a lick on the flute. I was a sax man, but, of course, I said, "Sure." Then I busted my butt to learn the flute. [Laughs]

18

Toy Factory & the Piano Tuner

The band, now called Toy Factory, was taking form, and decided it was time to record a proper demo tape. In order to finance the studio cost, they booked a few shows around the area, including one at the Ruins in downtown Spartanburg.

Doug Gray

We cut a tape at Mark V Studios in Greenville [South Carolina]. We had booked some dates in order to pay for the tape. One of those dates was in Spartanburg at a place called the Ruins, which used to stand in the lot across from the *Spartanburg Herald-Journal*. We were opening for Wet Willie. It was Jimmy and Jack Hall from Wet Willie. Donna, their sister, also sang with their band. But they took the tape to Phil Walden at Capricorn, and we were invited to come down and play at Grant's Lounge. We played for the weekend and met with Phil Walden. We were all just freaked out, really nervous. We went down there and talked and played and talked some more. We had a big meeting the next day. About two weeks later, we signed a deal with Capricorn.

Jimmy Hall

Wet Willie was playing Spartanburg, South Carolina, at the Ruins. We were booked there as the headliner. We didn't really pay attention to who was opening until we got there. But we sat out front and listened to them. They just knocked us out from the beginning. It was a sound that was totally unique to my ears, and to the other guys in the band as well. It had a lot of the elements that we were into— good Southern music, good rock and roll. But there were so many things that set them apart from the others.

I was pretty close to Doug. We related on the lead vocalist position that we both had with our bands. I can remember talking with those guys when they recorded their first album. My girlfriend at the time worked at Capricorn, and another friend of ours, Carolyn Harris, was an engineer there. During that first recording, my girlfriend was in the studio a lot with them, and I'd come down too.

George McCorkle

Capricorn didn't like the name Toy Factory. They just didn't feel like it was commercial sounding. The band was rehearsing on Spring Street, when we found the name tag that belonged to the former tenant, a local piano tuner now living in Columbia, named Marshall Tucker. It was no big deal. We said, "Hmmm...Marshall Tucker. How's that for a band name?" Everybody shook their heads yes, and Toy said, "Good. Let's go eat."

Moon Mullins

From the beginning, Doug was an exceptional singer. He offered uniqueness to the band. Each segment offered something special to the band. Toy's guitar playing, and Doug's singing. Doug was a strong singer with a wide range, almost an extra instrument, with his vocal abilities. Which is one reason he's managed to carry on this long, the distinction of his voice. He worked hard in the studio, getting his vocals correct. He worked long hours. His vocals were always the longest part of the session. He had a good ability, and he always worked hard at getting it right. I knew him as a friend first and as a member of the band later. We always got along really well. He's full of shit. [Laughs] I never had any problems with him. You just had to realize his ego and work around it. I had a serious case on my hands with Toy, so Doug was a relatively easy project.

Paul Riddle

The MTB started in 1970. George McCorkle had a band called Pax Parachute at the time. Anyway, a friend had told George about this little guy over in Drayton who played jazz drums and practiced all the time. Well, as it happened, I didn't know anything about rock and roll. Most of what I was into was jazz, having taken lessons from

David Haddox, a well-known teacher in Spartanburg, as a teenager. I had played in some beach bands as a kid, with horn sections and all, but other than that I was listening to Miles Davis and Charlie Parker. I was playing light, jazz style. I remember, after I joined Pax Parachute, always hearing George yell, "Play harder, play louder!" He was real good to put up with me. George was like a big brother.

I studied for about three years with David Haddox, and he taught me to read. He was playing at a supper club in town. They had everything from belly dancers to floor shows. The band's regular set was mostly swing music. Dave was really interested in my playing, so eventually he got me to sit in with him. Every now and then, my dad would take me up to the club and I'd sit in on a couple of songs. As I got older, about seventh or eighth grade, I would play there on weekends. Dave would get other gigs and he'd let me fill in. It was an experience! I'm glad I came up playing the old standard swing, cha-chas, rhumbas, and different things.

We had started playing our own stuff, songs like rehearsing songs like "Hillbilly Band," "Take the Highway" and "Can't You See." It was a "make it or break it" kind of deal. I was kind of on the outside looking in. All of them had played together before, with all of the different versions of the New Generation and the Toy Factory. George had been in the Puzzle and the Rants with Toy. It was all those different groups. I was the new kid.

Franklin Wilkie

They went to Mark V Studios in Greenville and cut "Can't You See," "Take the Highway," and "Low Down Ways." They took the tape down to Macon, and Phil signed them on the spot. I remember asking Tommy, "Did you guys get a lawyer when you went down there?" He said no, they had just lined up like ducks and signed on the line that day.

Paul Hornsby

Shortly after the Wet Willie Band was signed to Capricorn, they played with a band in South Carolina that really impressed them. They came back and told Walden about them, and an audition gig was set up at Grant's Lounge for the Marshall Tucker Band. Phil liked what he heard, and a demo session was set up. Actually, Johnny Sandlin did the session. For some reason, he didn't wind up producing the group, so I was asked to take over.

The Marshall Tucker Band had previously cut some demos in Muscle Shoals. Nothing had become of that. Now they had cut more demos at Capricorn with only lukewarm results. When you saw them on stage they presented a freight train full of energy and excitement. There had to be some way to get this across on studio tape.

This was my third attempt at producing. The first was a failure, the second was more promising, this one had to be the one! As far as having a scientific approach, I had none. I had very little producing experience to draw from. What we had going for us was some great songs that Toy Caldwell had written and a band who were the easiest to work with I had ever met. They brought their enthusiasm with them and played their asses off like they had been doing for the last few years. Not much thought was given for an "image." We took each song individually, and added whatever we thought fit that particular cut. On "Hillbilly Band" there was a fiddle added. Toy played steel guitar on several cuts. If you read the musicians' credits, you'll see that Jaimoe played "gitongas" on "Can't You See." Actually, that was just him beating on the back of an acoustic guitar instead of using congas! Wherever there was a "crack" left, I filled it with a keyboard. Everyone got to explore their ideas and try what they wanted. I don't think we left one spot open for anything.

Well, we spent eight weeks in the studio. There were many fifteen-hour days. At the end we came out not knowing what we had. I had been so close to the project and spent so much time on it that I didn't know if it was great or terrible. I don't have any idea of what the band thought.

When we handed the tape over to Capricorn, it wasn't clear what they really thought either at first. The label was brand new, and with the success of the Allman Brothers, maybe they thought this project would be cut from the same mold. Well, it wasn't. It had more country influences—steel guitars, fiddles, etc. The term "Southern rock" was yet to be coined. By the time those two words were used in conjunction, it was perfectly normal to use all of the above ingredients within one band.

Anyhow, Capricorn was somehow convinced to release the LP. It was simply titled *The Marshall Tucker Band*. One of my favorite definitions of "luck" is "being good at the right time." *The Marshall Tucker Band* was that. At the time of the release of that LP, they were opening act on tour with the Allman Brothers. Band. What a perfect audience to showcase a band like that. It allowed thousands of people to get a taste of what the band had to offer on that record. It was practically a hit right out of the chute.

Johnny Sandlin

Of course, I went to see them when they first came to audition with Phil, and they played at Grant's Lounge. They would come in there and say "Mr. Walden" and "Mr. Sandlin" [laughs], and I don't know if anybody had ever called me that before. They were just such nice and decent guys. I did some demos with them and then Paul [Hornsby] did some better demos with them that got them signed. Toy was great. I used to love when we were doing some of the Cowboy albums—and there were several that he played steel on—he was just great to work with. Most of my dealings were with him. I remember going skeet shooting with him one day, and he was right handed and left eyed. They had this weird shotgun that had a cutaway stock and he could put the gun up to his right shoulder and move his head through where he was looking down the barrel with his left eye. It was a weird situation. [Laughs] He was a good player. Great guy.

Doug Gray

Without Phil Walden, the Marshall Tucker Band would have probably been a band without any success at all. We're buddies. Everything in the past was business, and business is business. Now we're all friends again.

George McCorkle

I had a '66 Chevelle. That thing made so many damn trips to Macon! That's how we traveled. It's all we had. We were cutting a record, but we still didn't have anything. We used to have some fun, now. Doug and Jerry and all of us were probably as tight during that time as we were with our own families. We spent more time with each other than we did with our own families.

Paul Riddle

We had the first record ready to go. Toy had written all the songs by the time we were discovered by Wet Willie, who went down to Macon and told Phil Walden about us. That really opened the door for us. They booked us in Grant's Lounge, and Phil came out to see us. Everybody was dancing in the aisles. We were signed immediately.

Charlie Daniels

We first played a show together in 1973. We both opened for the Allman Brothers Band in Nashville, and I walked in their dressing room and said, "Somebody told me you s.o.b.'s used to go to Jenkins Junior High School." Toy jerked around and looked at me like, "Who in the hell are you?" [Laughs] I told him I used to go there too. We just kind of hit it off. We've been doing that way ever since.

Dru Lombar

They were a great bunch of guys—the salt of the earth. Carolina boys, country boys, not pretentious at all. What a unique sound. They gave a hundred percent. They hit the stage, and they'd go out and give the people their money's worth. They were great guys, man. And, once again, there was a relationship there where they were very supportive of us and, you know, it was like a big family with all those bands.

Elvin Bishop

Toy Caldwell. What a guy. *What a guy.* One of my favorite guys in all history. He played with his thumb and fingers at a time when nobody else did hardly. He had his own original sound and he just went for it. A great songwriter. There just wasn't anything to not like about Toy.

Charlie Hayward

Yeah, Tommy and Toy both—man, it was just so amazing to play with them because you could stand over on the side of the stage and watch them. They'd both play with their thumbs. They learned that from their dad. And they'd play so fast sometimes you couldn't hardly even see 'em. Both of those guys were great people. They were both military, too. When people would see Marshall Tucker, a lot of them would be watching Doug sing or Jerry on the flute or Toy playing lead, but I was always watching Tommy and Paul and George. They were always in the pocket. They never relinquished the groove. It was like a stranglehold from beginning to end, you know?

Allen Woody

Toy Caldwell is a personality and a musical presence that we all sadly miss, he and his brother both, for that matter. I thought Tommy had a real Berry Oakley type thing going in his playing. He was obviously influenced by Berry, and then he took it to a whole different place. People like that, like the original Marshall Tucker Band—Paul Riddle is a dear friend of mine, he's a good friend of Warren's and Matt's. That guy is a slammin' player. The whole thing that they had going on with that band was great. The songwriting was great, Toy's guitar playing, with the Wes Montgomery thumb-picking was great. That was a deep, cool thing.

Charlie Daniels

Playing with the MTB was great. It was a natural show. We used to end the night up with three drummers on the stage doing something everybody knew. We probably did more dates with Marshall Tucker than any other band that I know of.

Tommy Crain

On the road, I guess [my favorite band to work with] would have been Marshall Tucker Band. Toy and I were great friends, and once we got to know each other we did everything together. I just loved playing shows with them. I loved Wet Willie, but I guess I enjoyed playing with everyone. My all time heroes are the Allman Brothers, and Duane and Gregg grew up in the same part of

Nashville I grew up in, but at the time I did not know them. When we finally did meet, Gregg was really nice to me and encouraged me to play. We did some great tours with the Outlaws. They were college tours and were lots of fun with no restrictions on the concerts, and we could do whatever we wanted and it was a blast. I used to jump off the bus and ride with the Outlaws because we were just great friends.

Moon Mullins

Toy actually tagged the nickname "Moon" on me. It came from a comic strip that ran up into the fifties. A lot of people named Mullins end up being called Moon. Steve got the nickname "Puff" from a football game at Spartanburg High School years ago, something to do with a powder-puff game. And "Blackie" came from the fact that he always dressed in black—always wore a black t-shirt.

Henry Paul

My first recollection of the Marshall Tucker Band was hearing them on the radio and seeing their records in the store. This was probably around 1974. I loved their country music influences and the image they projected with the artwork on their albums. I knew they were connected to the Capricorn Records scene in Macon, and they represented a version of my dream come true. Just before the release of the Outlaws' first album we got a chance to open for the Tucker band in a small theater somewhere in Georgia. I remember how excited we were to be working with a band of their caliber and musical character. After the show that night Tommy Caldwell came to our dressing room to say hello and introduce himself. He complimented us on our performance and asked us if there was anything we needed. We told him we were running low on beer, so he gave us two cases of ice cold Coors. This was before Coors was sold in the east, and it was a much-sought-after rarity. Well, needless to say this made quite an impression on me. Tommy's kindness and outgoingness that night defined him as a person, and it became clear to me that he was the band leader and that he ran the organization from a position of strength and generosity.

Fred Edwards

We [the Charlie Daniels Band] met the Marshall Tucker Band for the first time in Kansas. John Hammond opened the show, just him and his guitar. Playing his blues. He kicked ass. Then it was us, and we kicked ass. Then it was time for Tucker. Wow. After they played, it became a new era for us. They wanted to tour with us because they liked us so much. So we did thirty days with them, back to back. Paul Riddle, their drummer, and I became buddies. This was when we had the Fire on the Mountain band, so, Gary Allen and I used to stand behind Paul Riddle every night to watch him play. When Paul got off the drum stool he would always say "I sucked tonight." And we would always say, "No, you were great." Tommy and Toy Caldwell were always hanging out with Charlie and David Corlew, our road manager, so we all partied every night. You come to my room, I'll meet you in your room, whatever. Then the shit hit the fan. We got a hit called "The Devil Went Down to Georgia." After this we started doing gigs with Lynyrd Skynyrd headlining.

Taz DiGregorio

Toy and Tommy were just incredible people. They were great musicians. As far as Toy is concerned, the only other guitar player that I ever saw in my entire life that played—and I won't say the same style but with the same technique—it is B. B. King. Toy was so close to B. B. King, and I did not understand it until he had passed away. Toy played with more of a country feel, but they played with the same intensity, which is really something. Tommy Caldwell—I had never in my life seen a bass player like Tommy. Tommy would stomp with his feet just scoot up towards Paul Riddle and then the whole thing would come up. They were very good to us. Let us open shows for them, and they helped us out and really helped us out a lot. They were one of the premiere Southern rock bands because they touched on all types of music; they were good people and they were GIs in the Marines. Artimus Pyle was, I think, Toy's buddy in the Marines. They were real Americans that played real American music. I don't know anyone who plays like that anymore, not with that intensity. It just doesn't happen anymore.

Moon Mullins

Well, I roomed with Toy so I got to see a lot more of how he went about writing songs. Generally, the way a song would appear was Toy had a hook line or a riff he'd worked out on his guitar. He'd sit around and play and come up with these great ideas. That's when you realized how funny he was. He'd be doing this serious song and go off onto this silly shit, lyric-wise. But as he wrote all this either me or somebody else would be jotting down notes for him. He'd come in to the show early the next day, usually at the steel guitar or on his other guitar. He'd start messing around, putting things in order. As soon as that was done the band would usually take an hour in the dressing room before the show and that's when songs were usually worked up. They'd usually have songs worked up before studio time although they could go through some dramatic changes. A country song could become a lot more than a country song. Everybody would come in and record their parts with Doug and Jerry being the last ones on that process.

Billy Bob Thornton

I saw Marshall Tucker in Memphis at the Mid-south Coliseum back in—it must have been '73 or '74. They were the headliners, and the other two acts were the Outlaws and the Charlie Daniels Band. Of course you know the show was about five hours long. [Laughs] 'Cause you know Marshall Tucker would start playing something like "24 Hours at a Time." But man I loved that band. I just remember watching Toy play with his thumb like that, playing all of that crazy shit. I thought, if I could play guitar like that...but I'm not really a guitar player. I just play well enough to write my songs. I don't dare play it next to the guys I play with.

19

Together Forever

The Marshall Tucker Band had arrived. They had gold records, fame, and all the trappings that go along with it. It was beginning to look like everything they touched turned to gold. The band was a major contributor to the success of Capricorn Records, and one of the top three Southern rock bands performing.

Charlie Daniels

In the early seventies the hottest bunch of pickers in the country was the Marshall Tucker Band. I know because we traveled with them and opened for them night after night after night. I marveled at just how incredibly hot this band could play. There were a lot of unique things about the Tucker band. For one thing, Jerry Eubanks's flute put a whole different spin on a guitar-heavy sound, topping it off and riding just above the controlled chaos that was the Tucker sound. Tommy Caldwell's thumb-picked bass and Paul Riddle's drums laid down a beat and a bottom that was just pure-t fun to jam with.

Taz DiGregorio

Marshall Tucker Band's Tommy Caldwell came to Charlie and said he knew we were broke and gave us a thousand bucks and told us to take it and pay him back when we could. What a nice gesture of brotherhood. They really took care of us. We all worked together. We toured with Skynyrd a lot and would finish the shows and all pile into one room both bands and both crews in one hotel room and you cannot get a better brotherhood than that. It was really something. [Laughs]

Brad Lesley

I met Toy Caldwell for the first time at the Walnut Grove Opry House in Spartanburg, South Carolina, in the late seventies. Did my first shot/sip of moonshine that night as well—what a shock. I was playing with the Greensboro Hornets in the Western Carolina League, and the Phillies had a team in Spartanburg that played at Duncan Park. Nice old ball field, but the locker rooms were tiny.

Chuck Leavell

Toy and Tommy were the greatest. I suggested Stu Levine as a producer for them after Paul Hornsby stopped working with them and played on a few tracks on a couple of albums with them. I would always sit in with them if they asked. They were all good guys, and I had wonderful times playing and just hanging out with those boys. Toy was *sooo* funny. He could crack me up. They were both good joke tellers. Toy definitely had the fastest thumb in the world, as far as guitar players go, and was a great songwriter. Tommy was a little more serious, sort of the bandleader, as far as I could tell. It's so sad how it all happened, Tommy's accident, and after that Toy was never really the same. Then Toy's death, and their other brother died as well. [Tim died a month before Tommy.] I know that had to be tough on their parents. So sad. But I'll always remember them fondly, with a big smile on my face.

Moon Mullins

I was the production manager, stage manager—there are a lot of different names for it. I was with the band through 1984. But the job just rolled along. It expanded as the band got bigger and the crews got bigger. Somebody had to take charge and do all that advance work along with the other. At the time, Puff and Blackie, neither one wanted the job so it just kind of fell in my hands quite by accident. After the Tucker Band it all helped because when you drop back into the club level, it's good to be able to mix sound or call lights. It all became handy after that. Like I said before, Toy was never hung up on where he played, and I was out with him after the Tucker Band for about a year and a half or two years.

Butch Trucks

Paul [Riddle] is one of my best buds. We've been touring together for decades, and Paul has been one of the solid, feet-on-the-ground guys when all of the rest of us were losing touch with reality. I am proud to call him my friend.

George McCorkle

When you went out there to play with Toy, Tommy, and Paul, you just planted your foot in one place and rode it out, until you got there—especially on songs like "24 Hours" and "Ramblin.'" I don't think you could run a damn and get that kind of workout. You should have been up there when Tommy was playing bass. You'd go, "Holy shit, I've got to keep up with that." He was driving the song. As it wore on, the intensity just kept getting stronger. It never let up. I get out of breath every time I think about it. [Laughs]

Paul Riddle

We would go out on a limb every night. It would be just rocking out loud like a thunderstorm, and Toy would bring it all down to a whisper. He had a sense of magic, and his guitar would take us places where we didn't even know we were going.

Chris Hicks

I heard them in 1976 at the Macon Coliseum and saw them again in 1978 two years later in the same place and again in 1980. I believe that was shortly before Tommy passed away. I saw the original band three times. What I remember about the first time was going with my cousin, and he got me hip to the vibe, kind of Fillmore East thing, long guitar solos, and the band breaks down with Toy playing for however long he wants to play with the spotlight on him. It was very good ensemble type stuff. It's almost like orchestra music when the bands get to doing that. Even at that young age I remember a couple of moments in my mind that this was just really, really good. I never dreamed at that time I would play with the Marshall Tucker Band. It's kind of funny how my life has worked out that way. But I definitely understood the energy that they were going for and had already been exposed to it from the Brothers thing. A couple of other bands from here that never made it were Capricorn wannabe artists. One of those bands was Burhham Wood. I never met anybody that knew them but I loved the sound. They had that vibe going.

Brad Lesley

I have considered Doug Gray, Toy, and the MTB boys family for some thirty-plus years. You take away baseball. I would have never met the Tucker boys that night at the Walnut Grove, nor would my life experiences have been as plentiful as they have been. Like I said— I owe this game.

Elvin Bishop

We used to have a lot of fun just hangin' out and carrying on and going crazy, especially with Toy [Caldwell] [big laughs]. We got known just minutes before the Tuckers did. The Capricorn thing was rolling. We had a gig in Sacramento sometime during the early seventies and Marshall Tucker was opening for us. They got into town a day early, and Toy and George went to some club downtown, and they told them that Toy was Elvin Bishop and George was Johnny V, and they rolled out the red carpet for them, and they drank free all night long. They had a great time. [Laughs]

We went fishing the next day, me and Toy. We hit it pretty hard back then, and we had a hangover. It got to be a little past noon, and we're out in the boat. Toy kept on saying, "Boy, I'm hot. It's just too goddam hot." I looked over at him and I could tell he was doing it on purpose. He just started slowly leaning over and just fell out of the boat. He let himself fall in the water. [Laughs] He paddled around a little bit and then got back in the boat and said, "Man I feel a lot better."

George McCorkle

I love *Searchin' for a Rainbow*. I just think that was the turning point for us that opened a lot of doors. And I like *Tenth*. It was one of my favorite sounding albums. And I love the live album. I think that Toy and Tommy and Doug did some monumental things on that record that set the pace for the future. Doug's voice, like on "Ramblin,'" was amazing. He delivered the songs as good as a writer would deliver his own work. That was a big plus for us. As a writer, you have to consider that you have a singer that can deliver that song just like you hear it in your head. Tommy's bass and Toy's lead, ain't nobody else could do that.

Justin McCorkle

I was born and raised just outside of Spartanburg; it'll always be home. Well, I guess some of the earliest memories that stick out to me are the times over at Creative Arts studio in Moore, and earlier than that the bus they had. I was just amazed at that stuff in there man.

I can remember just about all of them recording at some point there. I remember I always liked to watch Paul play drums. I was used to Daddy playing a guitar all the time around me, so I suppose the drum kit with Paul T. beating the heck out of them was a different experience for me. I was too little to really know what exactly what was going on, but I do remember I had to be quiet when they were listening and recording. I used to go out there on the floor when nobody was around and play Daddy's guitar, or try to play it. I thought it was the coolest thing that I could watch them play something and hear it all together in the board room. I can still remember the smell of that studio. I'm not sure what it was, but reflecting back it kind of smelled like new carpet or something of that sort.

I also remember the bus that they rode. Man that thing would put me to sleep. I used to crawl up in Daddy's bunk and cover up with his goose-down sleeping bag. I remember the sound of that motor inside the bus, and I remember watching Buddy drive it, and I even remember Daddy driving some. I rode up to the venue at Red Rocks one time with Daddy and Johnny Lawson in the MTB 18-wheeler. I was flying high man; it was awesome.

Daddy was a really normal down-to-earth guy as far back as I can remember him. He taught me how to fish and hunt, gun safety, how to play golf, ride a bicycle, all the things that most American fathers do with their children. He had race cars, and that was one of my favorite things. I loved going over to the racecar shops with him and seeing other cars and listening to them run. To this day a good ol' loping small block Chevrolet gets my blood pumping! I bet I drove

100,000 miles in his '67 Chevy II drag car while it was either sitting in the garage or on the trailer. The other guys in the band and their families were all so very kind and loving to us "kids." It was literally like a big family looking back at it now.

Henry Paul

With the Outlaws' rise to stardom the following year [1975] we had the opportunity to work with the Tucker boys a lot. I was always impressed by the band's power and unique musical personality. I think Tucker commanded more respect than any other band short of the Allman Brothers, and it was clear when you were in the presence that you were in the company of grown men! From the Marine Corps tattoos on their arms to the close-knit group of professionals they hired to help them in their work, these were serious people doing great work without the bullshit trappings of excessive rock and roll stars who pretend to be badasses.

Some of my fondest recollections of the Tucker Band were Tommy's boots with golf spikes in the bottom that he wore with shorts to play golf in; Toy's incredible talent as a player and a songwriter; Doug Gray's seemingly effortless range and vocal power; Paul Riddle's energy and intensity as a drummer; George McCorkle's song "Fire on the Mountain"; Jerry's jazz influence; and their Silver Eagle bus all decorated inside with western-style hardware and leather. This was a band of intense professionals who dominated the rock and roll world for a moment. To this day I respect them more than any other band of the time.

Paul Hornsby

Something I might comment on was the attempt to get a hit single out of the band. Well, they were famous for long extended "jam" songs, sometimes over six or seven minutes. The record label would ultimately come up and ask me to hand them a three-and-a-half-minute version that the radio would play. No mean feat! I got a lot of practice with razor blades—cutting tape—trying to get a verse, a chorus, a bit of guitar work, and finishing off with the chorus, then fade, all within the constraints of three-and-a-half-minutes.

Well, just before we started the *Carolina Dreams* album, I was in a
gig dressing room somewhere with the band. I had not yet heard any
of the new material for the upcoming album. I asked Toy if he had
anything ready for the next project due to begin in about a month. He
said, "Listen to this and see what you think." He had a
practice/tuning amp in the dressing room. He started to play and
sing a new song. Doug and Jerry chimed in on the harmony. I was
blown away. I told him right there, "That will be your first hit single!"
It was "Heard It in a Love Song." From the first day in the studio, we
approached that song as being the single. We purposely kept it short,
with just the required guitar, flute, piano licks added. This was such a
melodic song. I wanted every note, whether played or sung, to stick
in every listener's head. From the opening flute lines to the final
guitar licks, I think everybody who was around to hear music in the
seventies can hum it. And that was indeed the band's biggest selling
record. It went to number 10 on the pop charts in *Billboard* magazine.
The group and I continued to work successfully together through
1976, completing the LP *Carolina Dreams*, which was released in early
1977.

George McCorkle

There are three songs that I have written that I am very proud of.
I am extremely proud of the "Last of the Singing Cowboys" that I
wrote by myself when I was with the Tucker Band. That was a
landmark for me—I am a story-writer—if you listen to them I write
stories. "Last of the Singing Cowboys," "Fire on the Mountain," and
"American Street" are all three blessings and gifts. These are gifts that
came to me, and I do not know how I got them. They just came and I
accept them. It is a blessing that a man can write a few songs in his
life that he is proud of. There was so much thought that went into it.
The story is just awesome. Back in those days if you looked at all of
the people we were playing with and hanging out with, this was just
a story of what happened to one of us, maybe in the long run, maybe
the one of us that might have lasted through the century. This was the
one that that guy in the story ran into. He'll be there yet. To be
honest, I always thought it would be Toy. I could just see him an old
man, sitting in a chair, playing an old beat up guitar and singing old

cowboy songs. He was so prolific it was scary. I always accepted him as a friend, not really for all the ability he had. I just didn't think about it at the time but he was real, real good.

I will always think that the fourteen years of the Tucker Band was something great that I got to do. I will live with that knowledge of who I was in that situation because of the impact that band made on the average person, you know what I mean? That band made such an impact on the average man that all of us, the six that started the band, will always be remembered for that—you cannot outrun it. I respect so highly that aspect of my life, and at times it is hard to stand on my own. I accept it, and I accept the challenge and I make that very plain every time I stand in front of a mic.

Justin McCorkle

Us rug rats got to go along on the road sometimes. I can remember being backstage and everyone was so kind and laughing and just having a great time. They always paid attention to us and made sure we were well taken care of. Our mamas were always with us as far as anytime I can remember being at a concert. So you know that we were all taken care of and being spoiled rotten, I'm sure. Cassady [Toy's oldest] dragged us all around most of the time and kept us in line. [Laughs] So she was the big sister that kept us little tykes straight. I guess I was the closest to Cassady in age until Amber. Jeff and Geneal were the same age I think and Helena and Gabriele were a little younger than they were. I hope Cassady doesn't see this and get onto me for telling that she's a couple years older than me. [Laughs]

George McCorkle

That song ["Fire on the Mountain"] was written as a metaphor. Every line in it pertains to that time on the road with the band. I used to get tons of letters from people telling me what they thought the song meant. You wouldn't believe it. I used to love reading those letters.

Rusty Milner

Together Forever is one of my favorite MTB records. It had so many flavors in it. It's just such a great fusion of so many kinds of music. Just that whole album; they were into a really cool fusion. *Together Forever* just kind of sums it up. I guess being a musician I just like fusion. I'm a big fan of Larry Carlton, and I'm a Jeff Beck fan, too. Another favorite is *Tenth*. Just recently a friend of mine happened to have it on when I walked into his shop, and I caught that. It brings back a lot of memories. You could tell they were evolving into something else. Songs like "Last of the Singing Cowboys" from *Running Like the Wind*, which was sort of in that direction. I just enjoyed that jazzy, funky spirit. That was an era of the band I just really liked.

Paul Riddle

I had many opportunities to jam with my heroes, like Carlos Santana and B. B. King. There were so many others. But we played four shows with Santana. He played before we did. I don't know how they came up with that, but they suit up. They come out there ready to play. Carlos loved Toy. And he loved "Running Like the Wind," and we were opening with that tune. He would come out and jam on it every night. George bought Carlos a nice cowboy hat like they wore, and he'd wear it.

Playing with Little Feat was great too. Sam Clayton would play congas with me, and Toy would come out and play steel on "Sailin' Shoes." Lowell George would always come out and sing and play some slide with us.

With B. B. King, we were lined up for ten shows together. The first gig was at West Point. They were great. They were like a jazz audience. They came in their uniforms with their dates, and they'd clap after every song. They were real loud and appreciative. The whole band went into B. B.'s dressing room to meet him. So on the last night, we asked B. B. to come out and jam with us.

Moon Mullins

I suppose the high point for me came in the late seventies, Madison Square Garden, doing those big shows right before Tommy died. We did some big shows. I remember in Madison Square Garden when the lights went down, and all of those lighters went up, and there were thousands of straw cowboy hats out there. The electricity in the air made the hair on your arms stand up. That left a serious impression on me. The band didn't have that many bad nights. On their worst nights they were good. They were strong on stage.

George McCorkle

I think Tommy was far more technical than Toy. He probably knew more about the instrument than Toy. But Toy just knew enough to get by. The rest of it was straight from the heart. Now Tommy was a hard player, he was a solid bass player. He would never let up on you. He had a tremendous drive. Tommy's great feature in life was that he was a leader. A *born leader*. He served in his best capacity as a human being as a leader. But that band was full of drivers. Anybody in that band had the potential on any given night to make that band work. But Tommy was the driving force. Musically, on some nights, I believe Toy Caldwell was one of the best guitar players who ever lived. All great guitar players have their moments, but having stood up there beside him for all those thousands of shows we did together just proved to me that no matter who came up on stage to play with us, he always held his own with that style. I mean, I've seen him onstage with Carlos Santana, Dickey Betts, Elvin Bishop, B. B. King, Freddie King—I've seen him and Freddie just beat each other to death. They'd just be head to head, playing as hard as they could, screamin' in each other's face and just having a ball, tryin' to blow the other one away. There was no harm intended. It's just a friendly competition. When you're a guitar player of that magnitude, you just want to be the best.

Tommy Crain

Those guys were great musicians, as well as great human beings. That band was meant to work. I'll say it again about that band: money was never a factor. Nobody ever sat down and said, hey, if we put this record out, we'll be millionaires. That was never a thought. I mean, hell, we all dreamed about owning a new Les Paul, or cars and stuff, but it never got into that millionaire dream. In Nashville and in the music world, money is a driving force. And when you cease to have that driving force, usually that's when you make it. If money is the key, you lose. You have to play it from the heart first, and then it will sell.

In 1975, Phil Walden and the powers that be at Capricorn decided to hop across the pond for a short tour of Europe. The Marshall Tucker Band headlined, along with Bonnie Bramlett and Grinderswitch. A special release LP called Straight Southern Rock *came out of the tour, and some tracks recorded live in England appear on the Capricorn album* Hotels, Motels and Road Shows.

Moon Mullins

We'd gotten to the point where we had gotten a little spoiled here. Going over to Europe kind of dropped it back down to a family level where everybody had to get along. We were traveling in close quarters. It all went well as far as I remember. Johnny Lawson and I went over first. We were there for about ten days before they came. That was my gig throughout. I did a lot of advance work. Over there, we set up the rehearsal hall and set up transportation, got truck drivers and stuff. I was always involved in all of that.

Johnny Lawson

One thing I remember about that trip is that during rehearsals, we would drink a lot. There was a guy across from the theatre that sold Blue Nun wine. We bought every bit of Blue Nun he had. After a while, he would see us coming and hang a sign on the door that said "Closed."

Paul Riddle

Dog, [a nickname for Doug] bless his heart, when we were in Europe, he had a bad foot—he had a paw go out on him. [Laughs] He was limping around. We kidded him a lot because Ruth, his ex-wife, was there at the time, and she walked him around so much. So he'd be laying around at the hotel eating ice cream. He loved to eat ice cream.

Johnny Lawson

We all went to the Louvre. How many people can say they have seen the Mona Lisa? This painting had an infrared security system all around it. It was set up on a mound, back against the wall, and you could only get so close to it. You couldn't take flash pictures either. And of course they had a guard posted there, too. But there were all sorts of priceless artworks in there.

Bonnie Bramlett

The tour to Europe is quite a memory. Toy and the Marshall Tucker Band and Grinderswitch—Joe Dan, Dru, and the boys backed me up for a set as well. We had a blast.

Peter Cross [A fan in Great Britain]

When Capricorn sent the Marshall Tucker Band, Bonnie Bramlett, and Grinderswitch on a "Straight Southern Rock" tour of Europe in late 1976, I knew I had to be there. Grinderswitch kicked things off with their good-time boogie before backing Bonnie's passionately delivered and nicely varied set. Toy Caldwell's virtuosity was at the heart of the climax from the MTB, with his pedal steel and smoking lead guitar work. The cowboy attire filled the room. I journeyed south for the London and Manchester shows, before heading off into the snow for a slow overnight hitch home, repeatedly listening to the recording we'd just made on a big fat recorder under the seat. I'm still kicking myself for not taking better care of that tape.

George McCorkle

That trip to Europe was a lot of fun. I guess that's the only time back then that any of the Capricorn bands played overseas. The audiences were great. Besides Charlie's [Daniels] Volunteer Jams, that may have been the most fun I had with the band. Oh, and playing at the White House.

Not only did the Tuckers attract huge amounts of fans worldwide, they were deeply loved and respected by their fellow brothers and sisters of the road.

Henry Paul

Skynyrd was more punk. A little bit more rock and roll with all the fixin's. The fighting and the swagger. The Tucker band didn't play that game. They were men. They were fuckin' men. They wore United States Marine Corps tattoos. It wasn't like "We're in a rock band, fuck you." It was, "We're grown men who play the shit out of music." I don't know how much older Tommy was than me, but I was not as grown up as he was. I had not done as much as he had, not only professionally, but his stint in Southeast Asia, I mean, the boy had been all up in it. Grinderswitch was the perennial opening band on all these tours. It was just a cultural extravaganza. Southern rock was sort of born from what all of that was, and the Outlaws were probably the last band to get in on that. I mean, you can say Molly Hatchet, but they were a totally different thing. We didn't share with them what we shared with Tommy and Toy and Charlie. At least I didn't. They came along and enjoyed significant success, and I was respectful of their success. You learn to appreciate someone else's success. But I didn't embrace it musically and culturally like I did Charlie and Tucker.

Paul Riddle

It was kind of surreal. [Performing at the White House for Jimmy Carter and family] Thousands of people all dressed up in black tie, drinking champagne, and this hillbilly band from Spartanburg is up on stage wailing. My mother got to meet President and Mrs. Carter. It was neat.

Johnny Lawson

We did the album in Miami in '79 [*Running Like the Wind*, their first for Warner Brothers]. And we all stayed in this huge home that was owned by the Bee Gees. It was out on the Biscayne Bay. Indoor pool, everything. The studio was in Coconut Grove. I mean, you'd think we were a part of the mafia or something. Here we were, from Spartanburg, South Carolina, in this mansion where everything is provided for you—food, maids, it was great. I can't complain at all about that. Stewart Levine was the producer. Buddy Thornton was the sound engineer, the man that worked for the Allman Brothers. It was comfortable—I'll say that. It was real good for the band, to come back to that house after recording. On Saturday and Sunday we wouldn't even go into the studio. We would just kick back.

Paul Riddle

My favorite track is George's "Last of the Singing Cowboys" from the *Running Like the Wind* album. That song was my kind of song. It's so hip. I'm as proud of that track as anything we ever did. That's typical Tucker at it's best to me, a pretty melody with a funky rhythm section underneath. I still feel that was one of our best albums. There are a lot of good memories surrounding that one, like sitting at Tommy's feet while he sang "Melody Ann." Great memories. And I loved working with Stewart Levine—he was a genius.

Doug Gray

We recorded it at Bayshore Studios in Coconut Grove, Florida. I didn't want to stand on that little mound in the studio that the Bee Gees stood on, so I went to New York and recorded my parts at the Hit Factory.

20

Another Band Loses a Brother

The band's next album, Tenth, *would be the last album to feature bassist Tommy Caldwell. The Marshall Tucker Band played to a packed house on Long Island on April 18, 1980. The concert was broadcast live on the* King Biscuit Flour Hour *[and would be re-mastered and released on CD twenty-six years later.]*

This near perfect show would be the final performance by Tommy. He was hospitalized following a Jeep wreck in downtown Spartanburg on April 22, 1980, and passed away at Spartanburg General Hospital on April 28, just one month after a his younger brother, Tim, was killed in a collision with a county maintenance vehicle. After Tommy's death, the Marshall Tucker Band was really considering calling it quits. The band had not only lost a brother and a friend, but they had also lost their number one cheerleader and businessman.

Moon Mullins

I spoke to Tommy right before it happened that Monday morning. He was going to the YMCA to work out. He was coming by here to pick up something. He was in that old Land Cruiser. He had sold that thing and bought it back. It had a full roll-cage, racing seats, and everything. He hit the left side of the car with his right-side tire, it went up on the side and his head hit the pavement. It was just a freak accident.

Doug Gray

It was really hard. Every morning you get up and take a shower and go down to the hospital. Inside, you knew that he wasn't going to make it, but you still wished that he would, you know? It got to the point where I couldn't go back and see him. I wanted to keep my memory of him onstage smiling with that white shirt on, holding that bass. He was really the driving force.

When he passed, it was the most devastating time in my life. I had lost friends in Vietnam, but this just floored me—it floored everybody in the band. It caused a major change, like an earthquake.

George McCorkle

I felt really, really weird. But it's an acceptance thing. You have to accept the situation, you know. We went out and played the Warehouse in New Orleans that first show. You have to overcome that first hurdle of actually playing a show without Tommy, because he was such a strong leader. But we all joined together and said, "We have got to get through this if we are going to continue." It was really hard. I know personally, for me it was.

Paul Riddle

It was Toy's call. He felt very strongly that Tommy would want us to continue.

Doug Gray

We knew we would go on. And Franklin Wilkie was the natural choice. We let Toy make the choice as to when we would hire Frank and when we would go out to play again. I took over as spokesman for the band after Tommy died. I purposely listened to everybody I could to learn how to talk to people. Because I really had never given it any thought. Hell, somebody had to do it. Toy wasn't going to do it; his whole purpose was to stand back there with the guitar and play his ass off, just like he always had, and to sing the songs he felt comfortable singing. Toy told me many times, I wrote these songs for you to sing, not me. But I went back and listened to every live record I could get my hands on, so I could learn to talk to an audience. Tommy knew how to jack people up and get them excited, and I wanted to try to do the same thing. I went through six months of hell, trying to get people up and excited—not just because Tommy was gone, but because I was trying to copy everyone else. So now, I've decided that when I walk up to the microphone, I'll just say what I feel. It's never the same. Sometimes it's funny, but it's always from the heart. So what I learned from that was to just speak and sing from the heart.

Paul Riddle

The band might have dissolved had it not been for Franklin. He was already a friend. We had known him for years. He was hurting just like we were, and he worked extra hard to overcome the pain just like we did. He and I are definitely soul mates. He is family. Together, we all made it work. Musically it was very different—we knew it would be.

Franklin Wilkie

It was probably a lot harder on the other guys than it was on me. I guess I was the choice because I knew the material, and I was a friend of the band. I had been playing at a club called Cassidy's, and Toy called. He was a little apprehensive, because things had been going pretty good for Garfeel Ruff. We had one album on Capitol Records and we were looking for a new deal with another label. He told me they had decided to continue, and then he said, "If I'm going to have to go up there and play, I can't think of anyone I'd rather look over to my left and see than you." I told him I'd be honored, and he said, "Well, we'll be starting rehearsals in about two weeks. We want to have you up and running in three weeks."

We began rehearsals at Memorial Auditorium two weeks later. I could tell it was real hard on Toy. It was hard on all of them. Songs they had been playing for years and years, and now they were having to rehearse them. They didn't want to rehearse "Fire on the Mountain" or "Can't You See." So they'd get about half-way through one song and stop.

My first show was at the Warehouse in New Orleans, and it was packed wall to wall. With no air conditioning, the temperature hovered around the ninety-degree mark. The band was drenched by the end of the first song. I didn't move a lot, I remained very stationary. But I could feel Tommy there with me.

The second show was at the Astrodome in Houston. I remember Doug coming up behind me shaking his tambourine, and George would come over and play beside me, all making me feel more comfortable. Then I looked behind me and saw this 100 x 100 foot screen with the back of my head and my bass on this closed circuit TV screen. I froze in my tracks and wasn't moving. George came dancing over beside me and said, "C'mon baby, you gotta move!"

Paul T. made sure that me and him had connecting rooms. He really helped me through. He'd have a stereo and we'd listen to tunes. He was really an anchor. He reached out to me, and we've become very close over the years because of that.

Paul Riddle

Tommy Caldwell would always instill so much confidence in all of us. These high stress gigs, like TV shows and things, he'd just say, "Oh, this is going to be fun." He just took the edge off. He knew how to talk with Doug, and he knew how to talk with George, and he knew how to talk to everybody collectively. I think that kind of spilled over to us after he died. I remember Tom Ross, our agent, shaking my hand when we were doing [the television show] *Fridays*, and he said, "Gosh, there's no sweaty palms in this crowd!" I mean, you rehearse all day, and it works into a dress rehearsal, where you run through the whole show, and you watch it and change whatever needs to be changed. Then it goes on live. It's a little nerve wracking, but if you channel that nervous energy toward the music, you're fine.

Franklin Wilkie

We had completely finished the *Dedicated* album when Warner Brothers told us they wanted something more pop-oriented to go on the record. They said they were going to push the album to a pop audience, as opposed to the new country that was forming in Nashville. Bad decision. We did the beachy "This Time I Believe." We could have slid right into that movement that was forming where Alabama was breaking ground.

Not long after I joined, we did the *Born to Play* concert at Spartanburg Memorial Auditorium. I'd been with Marshall Tucker about a year at the time. Garfeel Ruff still owed the bank a lot of money for loans we had taken to buy equipment. So we did that concert to pay off the loan. We made just enough to pay them off, with the help of MTB, whose rumored appearance packed the house.

The Marshall Tucker Band played "This Time I Believe" and "Tell the Blues to Take off the Night" from the new record.

George McCorkle

I think my high point came when we reached a goal that I thought was out of reach—getting a gold record. Our first record went gold, and that was a highlight for the Marshall Tucker Band. And playing Madison Square Garden was a highlight. When we headlined the Garden, that just seemed to be the ultimate in making it. Hell, that whole thing was just a ride. Lots of high points, lots of low points—a lot more highs than lows. But it was a helluva ride.

Franklin Wilkie

We'd go out for ten days and home for ten, but sometimes we'd go out to the West Coast and stay for forty days. We were on one tour where we were just hitting city after city. Charlie Daniels would open one night, and we'd open the next. We had gone through California, Seattle, and wound up in Portland, Oregon. That night, Toy comes walking through the front door, half asleep and says, "Where in the hell are we?" Somebody said, "Portland." Toy says, "Maine?" We said, "No, Toy, the other side." And it was like that. It got kind of hard to remember what state or city you were in, we were moving so quickly.

George McCorkle

That band [the original Marshall Tucker Band] loved to play, man. There was one thing about us; it was hard to keep us off the bus. We really did love to play. That was the highlight in all of our lives, I think. Every show we played.

Doug Gray

When Tommy died, we asked the record company not to go overboard on publicizing it. When Toy died, we had not been playing together for eleven years. But we will always be connected to these guys. I do Toy's songs every night. You can't disallow the fact that without Toy and Tommy Caldwell, there would have never been a Marshall Tucker Band. Toy was the backbone. Tommy was the driving force. The rest of the guys from the original band, including Jerry and myself, were just guys who happened to be good enough to play with Toy and Tommy.

21

The Tommy Bond

Paul Riddle told me about the "Tommy Bond" during my first sit-down with him back in 1994. He explained that the true, close friends of Tommy Caldwell shared a unique bond, much like blood brothers. Over the years, it has become quite obvious just how much this ol' boy was loved.

Moon Mullins

From the formation through his death, Tommy [Caldwell] was the leader. Everything was a democratic process and put to a vote, but Tommy had the hands-on control. He was a dreamer, and he had a way of making you believe his dreams. I think everybody in the band always gave the crew lots of credit. The crew was a necessary and important part of the organization. The promoters would take lots of shows because they knew they were going to have an event with no problems. We were there on time, the show closed down on time. The efficiency of the crew had a lot to do with it.

Tony Heatherly

I'll tell you what a great friend Tommy Caldwell was. I was playing with Mickey Fowler and the Variation Band back in the seventies. We were Toy's favorite jam band. When he was off the road, he was with us. Toy was always coming in and jamming with us. He loved to play his steel guitar with us because we did a lot of the old classic country stuff a lot too. Anyhow, I met Tommy, and we just hit it off like we'd known each other forever. Naturally, I tried to copy every lick he ever played, because he was one of the greatest bass players ever. His tone and everything was so good, I just tried to carbon copy it. Toy told me one time that I was a champion at that, and that I could copy Tommy as well as anyone he knew. You don't know how good that made me feel. Tommy, bless his heart, would send me like a gross of Rotosound bass strings. And you know how expensive those are. He'd send me about twelve packs at a time. He kept me in bass strings for years, up until his death. And one night I was playing at Big Daddy's here in Greenville, and I blew a speaker. Toy got on the phone and called Moon and some of the guys from the crew. It wasn't but about an hour before they were all over there with these drills, taking my speaker out, and put a new one in. I said, "Wait a minute, man. Who do I owe for this?" And they said, "No, man. Tommy told us to go get a speaker out of the warehouse and put it on for you." They looked like a crew for Richard Petty. It was things like that that really blew me away. But nobody had a freer heart than Toy or Tommy. I saw Toy give a kid from Spartanburg a Les Paul guitar, because he wanted to learn to play. He also gave Mickey Fowler one. He gave Jimmy Westmoreland a guitar. I kidded him about it, I said, "Toy, you've given everybody else a guitar but me." He looked at me and said, "Yeah, but Smoke, I gave *you* a job!"

Henry Paul

It was learning by example. If you were embraced by someone like Tommy Caldwell—and of course Toy was the creative core of the band, but Toy was always in fast forward, you had to watch that movie in fast forward—but Tommy was the voice of reason, the methodical calm. I went to Tommy's funeral, and they took this guitar strap of his and laid it over the casket before they lowered it into the ground, and it was the end of an era right then and there.

Paul Riddle

A lot of people knew each other through Tommy. I call it "the Tommy bond." If you knew Tommy, you will understand. If not, it's real hard to explain. His personality was so dynamic. He was such an unspoken leader. It wasn't an arrogant thing at all. It was just confidence. It never was, "How are we gonna climb this mountain?" It was "How are we gonna go through this mountain?" You could feel his presence when he walked into a room. A very positive force. When you were around him, you could do anything. And he had so much love in his heart for the music. He was just driven. He saw it a long time before any of us did. He was connected to that universal energy. He just made it happen. Grab this arm and hold on, brother, we're about to take off.

George McCorkle

Tommy was like a little brother to me. He was younger than me. Some of my earliest successful music was related to Tommy. We did talent shows together in high school and had so much fun together. He was a born leader, a great human being and a great bass player, and I loved him like a brother.

Doug Gray

Tommy was my inspiration. Not as a singer or a player, but because of the fact that he wanted it to be the best band in the world. When Tommy left, we lost probably sixty percent of the band. As a friend, you couldn't ask for a better person. When I think of Tommy, I think of him going into western stores. He finally found something he really liked to wear on stage, and he'd stand up there and look so proud. He'd make you feel proud by the way he acted. He didn't have to say nothing.

Charlie Daniels

There was a time there in the seventies when we were touring with the Marshall Tucker Band. It was a good package, but we weren't making a whole lot of money at the time. It was taking everything we had just to get by. One night Tommy came up to me in the dressing room and asked, "Why aren't you guys staying in the same hotel as we are?" We told him we were trying to watch our pennies, and we were staying in a smaller, less expensive place. The next night, Tommy came up to me in the dressing room, reached down in his boot and handed me a big ol' sheath of money. He said, "Here's a thousand dollars. I want you guys staying in the same hotel we do. If you get to where you can pay it back, pay it back. If you can't, forget it." That was Tommy Caldwell about as well as I know how to describe him. He really cared about people—he especially cared about his friends. Tommy kind of had the helm of the band. He was the guy that everybody looked to for saying what was gonna happen. He was a good business guy. After he passed away, it was never quite certain as to who was handling things. Toy didn't care about business. He just wanted to play his guitar. The business end of things really went down after Tommy died. He was really missed, and certainly his bass playing was missed too. He was an authority figure in that band. Of course, Toy was too. Nobody went against Toy. But Tommy was the business end.

Paul Riddle

He was always the leader of the band. Tommy could deal with all of us. I mean, he and I were inseparable. Nobody other than my parents influenced me more in my life than Tommy. It's that "Tommy bond" again. There are people I haven't seen in years and years, and we'll talk and it's just like old times, because we have that bond. It's real dear. There's a reverence about it.

In the early days, when it was just a couple of road guys and the band, he put some pennies in an envelope, and gave each one of us a penny—and Puff and Blackie (the road crew) had to split their penny—and gave it to us, and told us, one day we're gonna have a road manager and we're gonna do fine. He'd always make sure we had money to eat. He would always look after the band.

Toy Caldwell, Sr.

I never had any trouble at all with any of my boys. There were all three good boys. [*Speaking of Toy, Tommy, and younger brother, Tim. Tim was not in the music business, but handled horses on a pro level. Sadly, he died in an auto wreck just a month before Tommy in Spartanburg.*]

Paul Riddle

Tommy and the band went down to the bank in Spartanburg. We had just received our first royalty check, and everybody needed their money. The teller told Tommy that it wasn't a check, but a draft, and would take three days to clear. Tommy was real nice at first: "You don't understand, these are my people, and they need their money."

Well, the teller wouldn't budge, and Tommy let loose on him.

"Get him out here! Get him out here!"

"Mr. Caldwell, you're gonna have to calm down." The teller was beginning to panic.

"I'm not calming down," Tommy said. "I am calm. Get him out here!"

"Who, Mr. Caldwell?"

"The president. I want to talk to the president."

Thirty minutes later we had our money.

Mark Burrell

Toy didn't have much stuff at his house that he kept of Tommy's; he had given a lot of it away. But he had this old silk shirt that was the last one Tommy wore on stage. He asked me to wear it on the *Toy Caldwell* album cover. It was really an honor. Tommy was a skinny guy.

Paul Riddle

Toy was so nice to me after Tommy died. I had a horrible time with that. My mother helped me get through it, month after month after month. I would say I wanted to quit and go home. Every night after the show, I would tell Toy I was gonna quit. And I'd call her every night, and then I'd get over it for one more day. I just missed him, man. I just missed him.

22

This Ol' Cowboy Goes Home: Toy Caldwell

On February 25, 1993, Toy Caldwell died at home, in his sleep, of respiratory failure. The founding father of the Marshall Tucker Band, the man who wrote the largest part of their hit songs, was gone. The thumb had stopped, his Les Paul silenced forever. He had just released his first solo album on the Cabin Fever label, and there was a major buzz going on in the music industry regarding the release. With guest shots from Gregg Allman, Charlie Daniels, and Willie Nelson, and featuring his band, Tony Heatherly, Pick Pickens, and Mark Burrell, the recording was a surefire hit.

Charlie Daniels

I have the greatest respect for talented people who can take nothing and make something out of it. Such is the case of the songwriter. He pulls thoughts out of thin air and molds them into a song that never existed before. And when that same songwriter is capable of coming up with a great melody, it's an even bigger accomplishment. But when that same person writes the lyrics, composes the music, and then interprets it on a musical instrument, that person is something special. Such a man was my friend Toy Caldwell. He came with his own melodies and wrote down to earth, straight-ahead, beans-and-cornbread-type lyrics that us common folk can identify with.

With the Marshall Tucker Band, he was up in front, sweating and straining Toy Caldwell, with his guitar turned up to ten and the speakers in his amp pushed to the limit with every note, playing what only he could play. To say Toy was unique is a gross understatement. He played his own style and his own riffs, and you could have listened to him alongside fifty other guitar players and have no trouble picking him out. He was just that different.

I can still see Toy now, standing onstage next to Tommy, with his eyes closed and that thumb fanning the strings of his Gibson, and the most incredible sound coming out, sounds that could turn a crowd of people upside down.

George McCorkle
Toy was a great influence on me. He was a great guitar player and a great songwriter. He was a world-class songwriter and guitar player. I'll never forget him.

Joe Bennett
Now, I'll be honest with you—Toy Caldwell, playing with that thumb—that was totally original. Nobody else did that. Wes Montgomery was the closest anyone came. But that was how he got his own sound.

Moon Mullins
Toy was an absolute clown, with lots of two- or three-line jokes. So funny. But he was such a poet. Many nights I saw him write notes on toilet paper, Gideon Bibles, anywhere he could just to have something to work off of the next day. His jokes were kind of the same way—you had to kind of just be there. Toy would give you anything. He took care of everybody. He took care of his family and he wanted to share all his wealth and all his fun with everyone.

Elvin Bishop
He had those one-liners for all occasions. He wouldn't just say, "I'm hot." He'd say, "I'm hotter than a fresh fucked fox in a forest fire." [Laughs] That's him ain't it?

Artimus Pyle
I was in the Marine Corps with Toy Caldwell. I had heard about this big guy they called "Toy." And they were messing with me because I was a Pyle. So they were calling us Gomer Pyle and Toy. Boy, did they mess with us in boot camp. But we all hooked up, and they turned me on to Charlie Daniels, who, in turn, turned me on to Lynyrd Skynyrd and the rest, as they say, is history.

Gregg Allman

Toy Caldwell was a good ol' guy. I played on his last record, and I never got to see him after that. I really enjoyed it. "Midnight Promises." We recorded down at Mud Island in Memphis. In that old firehouse they made into a studio. They had a B-3 set up and hell, I was out of there in two hours. I was in the moooood!

Chris Hicks

I have thought about putting a spot on my website called "walking with the dinosaurs," and in a way that is what it felt like to me. After working with Hughie [Thomasson] all those years, I met people that were not necessarily my peers but a good ten to fifteen years older than I was, and this has always been the case with me. Even when I was younger, the black musicians like Bobby O'Day that I have met in Macon kind of took me in, and I was honored to have played with those guys because I do play from the heart. To be accepted by those guys was important. Then another whole level was when you get to the rock and roll thing that got me into the big time with Hughie and that got me into playing with Tucker and Toy. We did a lot of gigs with the Toy Caldwell Band. Toy had just started to get back into playing, and he and I had met a couple of times, and I had sat in a time or two when Alan Walden had introduced us. He was very nice. Then we started having a friendship, and when we played dates with him he would always play with us. Sometimes he would not even take his band, and we would sit in and do songs with Toy. That's how much respect Hughie had for him. It was like family.

We spent many late nights together in hotel rooms playing together and spent more time like that than playing onstage. We got to be real musical buddies. We loved to exchange chords that we had learned. I loved songs and so did he, and we would play any song that we enjoyed together. Those were precious times for me to get to know someone like that on that level. I don't think he or Hughie knew the shadow that they cast in the music world. I think that they just did what they did and to be not just accepted but very close to those two cats in both a personal and musical way was a blessing. I learned that your personality and your music are two different things, but both of those guys shared a cowboy theme. There was definitely a Western feel to their musical styles when they played an E-minor and both were Southern-influenced but very similar and quite different at the same time. They both loved me and accepted me, and it meant so much to me. Now that it has been years ago and they are both gone, I have an appreciation of being in that family circle. I am looking at a big, mounted bass on my wall that Toy passed down to me...and it means a lot to me.

Tony Heatherly

I had first met Toy somewhere around 1973. I was with a group called Mickey Fowler and the Variation Band, and we were playing down in Spartanburg. We were playing a lot of Waylon Jennings and Outlaw music, some Marshall Tucker too. Well, as much as we could, with Mickey and me singing. I mean, who can copy Doug Gray? I don't even think Michael Bolton could copy Doug Gray. We had just certain songs that we could play by them. But Toy came out to a little club on the Frontage Road off of I-85 that Moon Mullins was running. I remember Moon wanted us to come down there and jam. I kept hearing this sound in the kitchen, and I went in there, and it was Toy playing the steel guitar. You know how he was always on fast forward—he jumped up and shook my hand and said, "I'm Toy Caldwell." Later, he came out to jam and he wanted us to play some old Hank Williams songs, because he wanted to get feel of that pedal steel guitar. From then on, when they were off the road, we were Toy's chosen band to jam with, and that went on for several years, on up until I left Mickey's band in 1980. We used to play at Big Daddy's here in Greenville. In fact, the first time I met Charlie Daniels, it was at Big Daddy's. They were in town, and Toy brought Charlie over. There we were in this club in Greenville with Toy Caldwell and Charlie Daniels onstage. We had a fiddle player that was really good at the time, from Lyman, named Jimmy Rumsey, and he was up there playing twin fiddles. The Skynyrd boys would come over and jam when they were in town, and bring those backup singers. They were great.

Tim Lawter

I knew Toy the last couple or three years he was alive. When he played that gig at Shooters [the show recorded and released under the title *Can't You See*] in Spartanburg he invited me and I went. I went to the dressing room to talk to him, and he said, "Man, I want you to sing on this thing so bad." But I was so sick, my throat was so sore, I couldn't even talk. Toy also played on the original version of "Daddy's Eyes," in the old little studio that me and Barri Smith had. But Toy was a real solid individual and a great player. I bought the first record when I was about fourteen, I think. Paul Riddle and I are about the same age—Toy's playing was so great. And one of the songs that didn't get much air play, but it blew me away was "I Just Tell Them My Jesus Told Me So." Toy Caldwell with those hands and that tone, and the way he played—he was brilliant. You didn't see that when you walked right up on him. It was in his hands and his talent. I always said these guys are from Spartanburg. That was a source of pride.

Tony Heatherly

Before we got into a bus type of thing, we'd be up late at night driving, and Toy didn't trust anybody driving but me, and I didn't trust anybody but him. I guess it was a Vietnam buddy thing. But, I've always been a history buff; I am really into the Civil War. We'd be going through the Shenandoah Valley, and we'd always go 81, through Gettysburg. I'd get to talking about it, and I'd say, "Man, Toy. This was a great battle that was fought here in 1863. I think if we had not been so much on the offensive, we may have won this thing." He'd say, "Really? I don't remember too much about the Civil War, Smoke. Tell me some more." I'd tell him. "Wouldn't it be something if we'd be riding down through here and see a ghost cavalry coming through?" I really think I inspired a lot of his songs. He didn't forget a thing. Anything you told him, he remembered, and drew off of it later. He was the type of fella that, if he knew you were into something, it wouldn't take him but about two or three weeks, and he'd be an authority on it. He read all the time. Then he read all these books on the Civil War, and he was telling me things I didn't know. It was amazing. If he knew you liked something, he wanted to learn about it so he could talk with you about it.

Tom Dowd

Oh, yes. Toy had a wicked sense of humor. Oh God, he was so funny. I only had short contact with him for about one or two months, but he would say and do things, and then when I went back to the room to reflect on the day, I would realize what he was doing and think, "That son of a gun, now I just realized what he was saying or doing!" He was hilarious.

Charlie Daniels

Toy was just ol' Toy. He was generous. I've had him give me stuff you wouldn't believe. Back in that same time when we weren't making a lot of money, he gave me four brand new speakers, and he wouldn't let me pay him for 'em. He said, "I can't use 'em. I play with my thumb, and they're Celestions, they don't have enough highs on 'em for me." He said, "You take 'em. Keep 'em." He loved playing that dad-blamed guitar. He had a totally unique style. Toy was about half hillbilly, and about a quarter jazz, and about a quarter rock and blues and stuff. But no matter how far out he'd get jamming, you could always hear those country licks in there. He was just my friend—my buddy. I couldn't go to his funeral. At the time, my mother had cancer, terminal cancer, and the end was getting pretty close. We were playing up in New York, and I had taken my wife and my son just to spend a couple of days, and get away from it all. And it just floored me when they called me and said that Toy had died. I said, "I just can't go. I just ain't ready for this." Even to this day—I don't know. There's a hole in the world since Toy Caldwell died. There's a place in the world that nobody else can fill that's uniquely shaped like Toy. And that's in my heart, and certainly in the music business.

George McCorkle

Me and Toy hooked playing guitars together. But we were real good friends from many, many years ago. I think that cat was one of the most talented people who ever lived, and he never got the credit for it. I loved him like a brother, too.

Doug Gray

Without Toy Caldwell, there would have never been a Marshall Tucker Band. There would have never been any of these great songs that are out there that have been played over two million times on the radio. When he did something, he did it right. If he didn't play a song just right, it would piss him off so bad, that he would be mad at himself. And you don't find too many people like that, a lot of them will blame somebody else, and then all of the sudden, you're mad at your wife or something. Toy was always there, and he always made me feel good because he always had confidence in me. He was one of the main people who came up to me after we bought 'em out—he wanted to stay at home since Tommy and Tim were both gone—he came up to me and shook my hand and said good luck. He was the only one who did that.

Warren Haynes

Toy was a writer who had the ability to put into words what the common man felt and, as a guitarist, he had influences from country to jazz to B. B. King that he brought together in a uniquely melodic, soulful way. He always played from the heart.

Doug Gray

Toy was the most complex man I ever knew, the most complex friend I ever *had*. On one side, he had that jar-head Marine attitude, and on the other side was the most tender, soft, person that he really didn't want you to see. He was a complex person, but a joy to know and work with through the years.

Toy Caldwell, Sr.

Toy used to keep a guitar with him at all times. He even carried the guitar when he'd go into the bathroom. We'd knock and knock to get in, but he just kept on playing. He'd sit down and put his foot up against the bathtub and push back. I never will forget, one time he broke the tank loose from the bowl doing that.

Paul Riddle

When Tommy was in the hospital, Toy was so gracious. He had just lost one brother, and another one was dying, but he always had time to comfort me. Especially after Tommy died, when everybody was waiting on Paul to fall apart—well, I didn't. After we brought Franklin into the band and went back and played that first gig in New Orleans, that's when I mourned. It was so much harder on the road. When we were at home, I was okay; I was healing and coping. But on the road—I thank God Toy was there. And no one knows this, just how much more precious can a person be? How much more compassionate? His brother was dead, and he was consoling me. To allow me to come to his room night after night to cry on his shoulder…what more can I say? And not many people saw that side of Toy. But I'll always love him for that.

Toy Caldwell, Sr.

Toy was in the Marines, and he got orders to go to Vietnam. He came home on a furlough first. So he got his plane ticket to fly out to California. We went out to the Greenville-Spartanburg Airport, and the plane didn't land. It just flew right over. And he had to be in California the next morning. So this neighbor of mine who had a pilot's license flew Toy to Atlanta. Toy said every red light on that little ol' plane was a flashing, cause he was trying to get him there in time. When they got there, the doors to the jet were closed, and they wouldn't let him on. They had to pull Toy off of that guy. But he called me from Atlanta. He had no money. It was pretty late at night, and Western Union won't take a check. But Iris had been saving these silver dollars. So I went down to Western Union with 2 pockets full of silver dollars and wired those to him. He got an excuse from the airline for arriving late in Camp Pendleton.

Paul Riddle

Toy's talent has always amazed me. We were on the road for like thirty days straight, and he was always a compulsive songwriter. And he'd always call me back to ask me what I thought of his choruses. Well, he had just written the chorus to "Searchin' for a Rainbow," and I said, "Hey, Toy, this is beautiful." Well, we stopped at a gas station to get some drinks and all, and when I got back on the bus—it must have been ten minutes later—he had finished writing the song.

Mark Burrell

He [Toy] had been to the top, but he didn't mind playing in the clubs. He was the same guy. He didn't have to have somebody up there wiping his damned forehead for him.

Gary Rossington

He offered moral support to us in our time of loss. We were all great friends and musical companions throughout the years. He was a close friend from the earliest years of our [Lynyrd Skynyrd's] existence.

Paul Riddle

Sometimes Toy was so musically intense that he would blow me away to the point of breaking my concentration. Tommy and the others would sometimes do that to me, but Toy was especially prone to giving me that reaction. Toy would come to a climax three times in a song, and he would take it to another step. He always had a magic.

Doug Gray

Toy was one of the best guys there will ever be. He had so much good feeling and good will in his songs. We all miss Toy Caldwell very much.

George McCorkle

The great thing about the band was we always traveled by bus everywhere we went, so we had to be close friends. We traveled in one bus, and the crew traveled in the other. Toy gave me a rifle once for my birthday. He gave it to me after the gig, and on the road the next morning, I was itching to shoot it. I mean I really wanted to shoot it. Toy said, well, there's some old road signs over there. We pulled the bus over to the side of the road and took out the rifle and just let loose on these signs. Just having fun. That was Toy.

Paul Riddle

For a while we toured with Little Feat. It was a lot of fun, cause Toy would go out and play steel with them on something like "Sailin' Shoes," and Lowell George would sit in with us and Sam Clayton, whom I love; he is the sweetest guy. He was so modest. But Toy and Lowell were something else together.

Tony Heatherly

It was February 25, 1993, and it was devastating. I was alone. I was running a store down in Anderson, Jimmy Rogers House of Music. I didn't have many customers, so I was alone. I just locked the doors and pulled the blinds. I didn't want to see anybody. I watched it snow for a while. It seemed like it just started snowing when I got the word he was gone. My wife called and asked me if I was alright, and I said, "Yeah. I just don't want to talk to anybody right now. I want to be left alone." I went and got my favorite guitar off of the rack and sat there and played "Can't You See." I couldn't hardly play for the tears, but it's something you have to get out of your system. I was over at Mark Burrell's house the other night, and he was playing some of the stuff we were getting set to release when he died. I was remembering how excited Toy was about getting the next project going. But it was completely devastating. Charlie Daniels said it best when he said, "There's a great big hole in the world that Toy used to fill."

23

Marshal Tucker's Second Wind: 1984

In 1984, the Marshall Tucker Band decided to call it quits. Doug Gray and Jerry Eubanks struck an agreement with the band to continue, hiring Nashville studio musicians before coming back home to mine the wealth of great players in their hometown of Spartanburg, South Carolina.

George McCorkle

It's like a divorce, in a way. It's sad to say, but if a band stays together long enough, they might eventually get tired of each other. When you've been on the road for that long a period of time, you tend to not get mad at each other, but to drift away from each other.

Paul Riddle

Any time you're in a relationship with somebody for twenty-five years, it's going to be hard. On a serious note, there have been a couple of times recently when I was going through some very tough personal times, and Doug was right here for me. And one thing I'll never forget about Doug was, right after Tommy's accident, when I was just staying at the hospital, Doug would call me up and talk to me, and he'd make me go home and rest. There are a lot of people who have never seen that side of "the pup." I know it sounds trite, but if I needed him right now, I could pick up the phone and give him a call, and he'd catch a plane home. He's just that way.

Tony Heatherly

Basically, what Toy told me was that they had been together for like fourteen years, and they had known each other for longer than that. He just felt like he wanted to do something on his own. I think the feeling was mutual. He never told me anything about any animosity. He said they had gone as far as they wanted to go. I don't think they realized that they could have latched onto the new country thing at that time like Alabama did. They wanted to remain rockers. But I don't think they had any idea of how big the young country thing was going to be. But Toy, even up until the time he died, didn't have much faith in Nashville. So I think they all just decided to go their separate ways. I don't believe there was any big blow-up or anything.

Doug Gray

What it was, Toy Caldwell was the best songwriter and player that I've ever played with in my entire life, and the rest of the guys were all good, too. But it's like I said in a meeting not too long ago, without Toy Caldwell none of us would be sitting in a meeting today. And Toy Caldwell was the one who came up to me after I had bought out the band name, and shook my hand and said, "good luck." I see the band as a company, like the Ford Motor Company, or a good baseball team. When someone leaves, you bring someone in that you feel can do the job well, and the company just keeps on going. People say we're kicking a dead horse, but it's not true. As long as there are MTB fans out there, we'll keep on playing the music they want to hear.

The first thing we did was to go to Nashville and hire the very best Nashville musicians like James Stroud and Bobby Ogdin. People said, who are these people? What's going on? I kept them a summer and showed people that I wasn't going to pull their leg and that Marshall Tucker wasn't going to pull their leg. I tell them every night: I will always be here for you. I will carry on with this band until the day I die.

Rusty Milner

It all started in the winter of '83. Doug called and asked if I'd be interested in playing in the band because he said something was getting ready to go down. I didn't really take it to heart, but he called back in January and said it happened, and we'd start rehearsing in January of '84. I never imagined I'd be playing in Tucker. I guess you could say I considered myself more of a pop/rock player in those days. And I considered Tucker more of a country/Southern band, which I really wasn't interested in at the time. But you get a chance to play and at that level. I was willing to play anything. But it fits my style real well and I fit into it real well, I guess. I've managed to hang around this long anyway. When I first got in this band I really made a special effort to copy Toy's licks because it was his sound, it *is* his sound, always has been. He wrote it, he played it. It's always been giant boots to fill. I was lucky enough that the fans pretty much just always took it in. They liked it, and I've put myself into it, added a few solos here and there, and added some of my own licks.

Stuart Swanlund
I was asked to join in 1985 and played for eight years. I left in October 1993 the first time. I just wanted to stay at home and play around Chicagoland and all that good stuff. The second time I was out because of the hand. Dupitrin's Contracture. It's a bunch of scar tissue that starts building up in your hands and fingers and starts pulling your fingers down. It's an inherited disease, and I just happened to get it. [Stuart would return, and remained in the band until his death on August 4, 2012.]

Tim Lawter
They had never even heard me play. I guess they were going on what Rusty and Stuart told them about my playing, and that I was a songwriter. But Doug just hired me, and we were off and running.

Stuart Swanlund
I don't have any problems with that [being accepted post-Toy]. Tucker fans are dedicated—they always have been. And we're getting new people coming in all the time. It's just lots of fun.

Tim Lawter
I never felt worthy of stepping into the shoes of the ones who came before me. We were always getting folks saying, "You are no Tommy" or "You sure ain't Toy," but I think we stepped up and proved ourselves, you know. It bothered Rusty [Milner] and me at

first, but we just said, we've got to be who we are but at the same time, we didn't want to get too far away from the original tone.

Rusty Milner

I remember going over to Stuart's house when we were young and watching him play the Allman Brothers and Marshall Tucker note for note on his guitar. I don't think he even remembers this; we were probably barely high school age, but a buddy of mine told me about this hot guitar player so we went over to his house. Stuart had a little band and they practiced in the storage room of their garage. That was a big inspiration because I wasn't a big Southern rock fan at the time. But I thought that was some cool guitar stuff, and he was really good. He was influenced a lot by Little Feat too—and Duane Allman. He kind of got pushed into playing slide in the band. They hired him to be a rhythm guitar player, and I told them, hey, this guy's been playing longer than I have. So his slide playing became the thing. If we both played lead we'd sound a lot alike. I wanted him to play slide on "Fire on the Mountain" and "Searching for a Rainbow," to make up for the lack of a steel guitar. It's a little more rocking, with a little more edge, which suits the band now more than a steel.

Doug Gray

Audiences are getting younger. It's really surprising because some of them don't know that you have even one record out. When I go to the message board or the guest book, it is amazing to read someone saying, "I'm seventeen and this was my first concert," or "That was the best concert I've ever seen." I don't know if we'll ever be anything more than what we are today, but we never knew a long time ago we'd ever be around for thirty-something years. The most important thing is to see everybody happy. It's always been my goal that whoever was playing in the band leave that stage with a big smile. We found out that a big part of it was knowing each other so well, and having laughs about one guy having to wear a shirt he didn't like onstage because he didn't have anything clean, and he had to wear a shirt that had not been washed in five weeks. Laughing and happiness makes you keep on going. Not just the band, but the fans of Marshall Tucker come to have fun. They don't come just to get drunk.

Rusty Milner

When Doug got sick in 1989, I had already been talking to him a good bit. I remember sitting up one night on the way from L. A. to San Francisco. I'd say, "Doug, let's start working on some of our own stuff." They were still in that mode of pulling in other people's songs, or just not doing a record at all. But at that time, Doug wasn't in any shape to be very judgmental anyway. It was like a month after that in Harrisburg, Pennsylvania, when he got sick. After that he developed a new lease on life. After that we started doing some things. It was then that we contacted Sisapa Records. They were interested in signing some groups. I talked to them and told them they needed to talk to Doug and Jerry. So they went up there and met with them and it took off from there.

Doug Gray

Don Cameron had already been singing with us and playing keyboards. He went out as lead singer for a few shows while I was recuperating.

I wrote the lyrics to "May We Be Closer Today" a couple of weeks after my second round of surgery. All of that happened for a reason, I'm sure of it.

Rusty Milner

Every time we did a record, we hoped for the best. You always do. So we cut two records at Sisapa, *Southern Spirit* and *Still Smokin'*, but the second record actually came out on Cabin Fever's label. But it was done at Sisapa studios. It was a big, nice studio. I really believe we could take songs from the albums we've done over the past few years and put together a really good *Greatest Hits* record. I'd love to go back in and remix them too. I helped out a little bit with the engineering all along, but I'm just now getting to where I really understand it all. I was one of these kids that goes in there and starts just turning knobs. [Laughs] I'd think I heard something different, and I'd start turning knobs. Now I've got a whole different attitude toward recording. I've learned a lot since then.

And hearing your song on the radio is pretty cool. I remember when they played "Tan Yard Road" on the radio. I had others I'd written played before, but for some reason, I really was proud of that one because it sounded good on the radio.

Tim Lawter

The *Southern Spirit* tour was probably one of the best tours I've ever done in my life. It was big, there were lots of people, it sold good. It was us, 38 Special, the Outlaws were on some of it, Charlie Daniels was on some of it, and I think Lynyrd Skynyrd was on some of it. But it was a strong lineup.

Stuart Swanlund

I really enjoyed that tour with Hank Williams, Jr. The "Southern Thunder" tour in '96 with Charlie Daniels and everybody. That was probably the most fun year I've had with the band. He only did like fifty shows a year, but we were on most of them. It was a big production. That was probably one of the high points, I guess. Another high point was when we sang the National Anthem at Wrigley Field before a Cubs game. That was in 1993.

Rusty Milner

I watched the band go from playing large stadiums to playing clubs. The first year I played with them, we would fly everywhere and get picked up by limos. We went to gigs in limos. Of course, they finally found out that was costing too much. But that was the air around the whole thing. It was exciting. But I watched it go downhill from there. We kept hoping something would pull it back up. I developed an attitude where I didn't think anything was going to happen. The best thing that ever happened to us was Doug getting sick. He had a new birth. When he first got sick, I was ready to leave the band, and Jerry [Eubanks] asked me not to. I was working on some projects on my own and writing songs. I was working with some people in Nashville. We'd put some promo shots together and done some paperwork. But we put the thing back together with Don singing, and it was a lot of fun. We did about eight shows with Don singing three-quarters of the set. We took it on as a fun way to do it. We went back out and did some different songs. I was singing "Hoping I'll Find You," that I did with the Artimus Pyle Band, and a couple of other songs. Tim was singing a few songs. Jerry even sang "This Ol' Cowboy."

Tim Lawter

Just being a part of all that [the 1995 South Carolina Music Hall of Fame induction and jam at Spartanburg Memorial Auditorium] was great. Getting to stand there and look out on all of that, it was history being made. I got to play bass between two great drummers, Butch Trucks and Paul Riddle. You can't ask for more than that. Jamming with Charlie Daniels was awesome. Dave Muse was there, and Hughie Thomasson, Chris Hicks, Ronald Radford. It was great.

Chris Hicks

I started playing with them when I was with the Outlaws because we toured with them a lot, so it kind of turned into one of those things where Hughie and I would jam with Tucker just about every night. So when I was called to fill in for Stuart [Swanlund] I had already been playing with the band for six or seven years although was not a member. I would play the whole set with them and play "Midnight Promises" or "Everyday I Have the Blues." I would sit in for the whole set, and then I got called to play for Stuart until his hand got better. I was asked to stick around for a couple of more years. Then I left and did the Chris Hicks Band thing again, and then out of the blue Doug Gray called in for me to fill in for two weeks. Then Doug said he wanted me to sing and co-write with them and help him do some Marshall Tucker Band stuff. Doug has always been a supporter of mine and wanted to help me get my music out there, and that's what we spoke of and that's what we have done. We have learned how to record better each time. Then it cametime to do my thing and Doug and Ron Rainey were in total support. I had a vision and they had suggestions and they supported my vision. This has really helped me along the way.

Doug Gray

Chris had already worked on a lot of projects himself and played on his own and other people's stuff, so we just decided it was time for him to do his thing. He has dedicated so much to Marshall Tucker. He gave his whole life to the Marshall Tucker Band. Chris is one hell of a songwriter, and I never met a person who didn't like Chris. He's got the songs. Paul Hornsby is helping him with it [*Dog Eat Dog*]. It's going to be great.

Everything always comes back around. In 1979 everyone said Southern rock was dead and gone. Now, thirty years later, it is back strong as ever. But I don't believe it will ever go huge and mainstream again because the companies are not marketing Southern music. They are concentrating on rap, hip-hop, and pop. The big companies, and I am part owner of one of them, have a tendency to want to make money, and they make money that way. But still, Southern rock will always have its audience, and when I am on that stage it's not about making money; it's about expressing yourself and entertaining. And the money is an afterthought.

24

George McCorkle Joins Toy and Tommy

George McCorkle of the original Marshall Tucker Band passed away on Friday, June 29th, 2007, at 11:30 in a Nashville Hospital at the age of sixty. Prior to his illness, he had recorded an excellent solo album, American Street, and was working on a follow up. He had recently sat in and jammed with Doug and the MTB a few times, and had several of his songs recorded for their The Next Adventure release.

Justin McCorkle
Daddy had quite a few songs in his catalogue of course. I couldn't tell you exactly which songs he had picked out for the G=MC2 album that he was working on. He had all of the songs that were possible for that album demo'd already. A couple of guys in Nashville mentioned some further plans for Daddy's music and possibly a tribute album. Unfortunately I haven't heard anything else about it.

Charlie Daniels
I don't think the world understands what a big part of the Marshall Tucker Band sound should be attributed to the wild rhythm guitar playing of George McCorkle. George took no prisoners and let it all hang out with a ringing open string bang-slam rhythm that pushed the song along and held all the parts together.

Tommy Crain
Oh, I love George. It's not easy to stand beside Toy Caldwell every night and be compared as a guitarist, but George could handle it, and he always, I mean *always*, brought it. One of the greatest rhythm guitarists in Southern rock, and while Toy was in the

spotlight as lead guitarist, George had some pretty mad skills on lead as well. And as a man, well, they don't come no better.

Justin McCorkle

Jam 4 George [November 2, 2007, in Spartanburg, South Carolina] was an amazing, God-sent show. That's about all you can say. All of you that helped plan and pull that show off are the ones that made it happen. Everybody showed an absolute amazing outpouring of love for my Dad and what he was about on that day. Everyone that was there was just so happy to be there and smiling and just having a great time in honor and in memory of a great person. I was really shocked that we actually pulled it off like we did [laughs]. It would be impossible for me to sit here and name how many people did absolutely crucial things to make that show happen, and it all came together perfectly. Everyone that was there was really happy and honored to be there. And in the end we paid for the show and got to start a foundation in Daddy's memory that will hopefully help in the fight against cancer. It was just an amazing time. Old friends reunited, new friends made, families joining together, and of course some great Southern rock music.

Update 2014: The Marshall Tucker Band continues to play hundreds of concerts yearly, record and issue classic material from their vast archives. The band today consists of Doug Gray, with guitarists Chris Hicks and Rick Willis; bassist Pat Ellwood; drummer BB Borden; and sax/flute/keyboard man Marcus Henderson.

Jerry Eubanks is retired, and Paul Riddle still teaches drum lessons and performs in a jazz band called Watson's Riddle. He occasionally sits in for his friend Jaimoe in the Allman Brothers Band.

Gregory Lenoir Allman
© Kirk West, kirkwestphotography.com

The Allman Brothers Band press photo for *At Fillmore East*
Capricorn Archives Photo

The Marshall Tucker Band, the early years. *(clockwise from upper left)*
Toy Caldwell, George McCorkle, Jerry Eubanks, Tommy Caldwell,
Paul T. Riddle, and Doug Gray.
© *Bradford Photography*

Duane Allman, Dickey Betts, and Berry Oakley burn white hot
in Chapel Hill, NC, May 1, 1971.
© *John Gellman, jgphoto.com*

Scott Boyer and Tommy Talton of Cowboy.
Courtesy of Tommy Talton

Toy Caldwell rips it up. San Diego, 1975.
© *John Gellman, jgphoto.com*

Toy and Tommy Caldwell in the pocket. Chicago, 1978.
© Kirk West, kirkwestphotography.com

Elvin Bishop jams with George McCorkle, Toy Caldwell, and the rest of
the Marshall Tucker Band. Bayfront Center, St. Petersberg, Florida, 1974.
© John Gellman, jgphoto.com

Phil Walden *(front)*, Frank Fenter *(in helmet)*, and the rest of the
Capricorn gang pose for a Creem Magazine picture.
Courtesy of Georgia Music Hall of Fame

Brothers of the Southland. The Marshall Tucker Band with Monte Yoho
and Hughie Thomasson of The Outlaws. Backstage in San Diego, 1975.
© John Gellman, jgphoto.com

Sweet Bonnie Bramlett.
Capricorn Archives Photo

Dickey Betts hangs out with Frank Fenter at one of the star-studded
Capricorn Picnics in Macon, Georgia.
Photo Courtesy of Robin Duner-Fenter

Tommy Crain of The Charlie Daniels Band backstage, 1976.
Photo Courtesy of Tommy Crain

Charlie Daniels, backstage in Chicago, 1978.
© Kirk West, kirkwestphotography.com

Lynyrd Skynyrd rocks Great Britain, February 5, 1977.
Pictured, Allen Collins.
© Peter Cross

Same show, February 5, 1977. Billy Powell on piano.
© Peter Cross Photo

Lynyrd Skynyrd 1977, with Steve Gaines.
MCA Records Photo

Lynyrd Skynyrd *(left to right)* Leon Wilkeson, Billy Powell, Ronnie Van
Zant, Gary Rossington, Bob Burns, Allen Collins, Ed King.
MCA Records Photo

Molly Hatchet. *(seated)* Banner Thomas, Dave Hlubek, Duane Roland. *(standing)* Bruce Crump, Steve Holland, Danny Joe Brown.
Epic Records Photo

Blackfoot. *(left to right)* Charlie Hargrett, Jakson Spires, Rickey Medlocke and Greg T. Walker.
Atco Records Photo

Molly Hatchet rocks the stage at Greenville *(South Carolina)*
Memorial Auditorium, 1980.

© Lynn Armonaitis

Hughie Thomasson and Frank O'Keefe, October, 1975
in a diner down the block from Clover Recorders in L.A.,
where the Outlaws recorded most of their first album.

© John Gellman, jgphoto.com

Outlaws Wedding: 1975, Clearwater, Florida. *L to R:* Frank O'Keefe,
Henry Paul, Billy Jones, Hughie Thomasson, Monte Yoho,
Charlie Brusco, Fred Cularo, Alan Walden—
At Hughie's wedding to Judy, his second wife.
© John Gellman, jgphoto.com

The Outlaws, 1975. In front of Alan Walden's cabin in Macon, Georgia.
L to R: Monte Yoho, John Gellman *(photographer)*, Jeanne Paul, Henry
Paul, Frank O'Keefe, Billy Jones, Becky Jones, Alan Walden,
Beppie Walden. Shot on a tripod with self timer.
© John Gellman, jgphoto.com

Toy Caldwell in Brewerton, New York. 1992.
© *Tom Bell*

The Allman Brothers Band, 1992.
© *Kirk West, kirkwestphotography.com*

Gov't Mule in Macon, Georgia, 1994
© Kirk West, kirkwestphotography.com

Henry Paul *(and his very cool T-shirt)* rocks the Simple Man Cruise 2012
with Monte Yoho and the rest of the Outlaws.
© Tom Bell Photo

Jimmy Hall of Wet Willie, 2010.
© *Bill Thames, billthamesphotography.com*

Scott Boyer and Tommy Talton's Cowboy reunion, 2011.
© *Bill Thames, billthamesphotography.com*

Blackfoot's Jakson Spires, playing with The Southern Rock Allstars in Virginia.
Author Photo

Johnny Sandlin, playing bass with the Capricorn Rhythm Section.
© Bill Thames, billthamesphotography.com

Donnie Winters *(Winters Bros. Band)* performs at the legendary
Grant's Lounge in Macon during the Hearts of the South show in 2012.
Author Photo

Both of Lynyrd Skynyrd's Rock and Roll Hall of Fame member
drummers—Bob Burns and Artimus Pyle—jammed together onboard
the Rock Legends Cruise II in January, 2013.
© *Tom Bell*

Matt Abts of Gov't Mule.
© Bill Thames, billthamesphotography.com

Charlie Daniels entertains at the annual Angelus event
in Tampa, Florida. December, 2012.
© Tom Bell

Alan Walden and Bob Burns *(Lynyrd Skynyrd)* at a benefit show
held at Grant's Lounge in Macon, 2012.
© *Roxanne Lark*

Larry Howard of Grinderswitch and Paul Hornsby
at Grant's Lounge in Macon, 2012.
© *John Charles Griffin*

Chuck Leavell performs, 2012.
© *Bill Thames, billthamesphotography.com*

Charlie Daniels and Doug Gray backstage in Florence, South Carolina, 2013.
© *Tom Bell*

Dickey Betts, 2013.
© Tom Bell

The author with Charlie Daniels at the annual
Angelus event in Tampa, Florida, 2011.
© Tom Bell

Part 4

The Charlie Daniels Band

Whiskey & Guitars

Before he assembled the first incarnation of the Charlie Daniels Band, Charlie Daniels had been working as a producer and session guitarist, performing on classic albums like Bob Dylan's Nashville Skyline, *and LPs by Leonard Cohen, the Youngbloods, and Ringo Starr. Since the first lineup of the CDB, many great players have been counted among the ranks, but only one player remained beside Charlie from the beginning until his accidental death in a car wreck at the age of sixty-seven on October 12, 2011; that was Joel "Taz" DiGregorio.*

Taz DiGregorio

It was 1964, and I was in Orlando, Florida, staying in a place called the Palomino Motel on Orange Blossom Trail. I was working in a lounge band that did just a variety of music. I sang and we did not use a bass player, I played bass pedals on the organ and the sax player, Jerry Kaskie was his name, well, he got drafted, and then we hired a guitar player and *he* got drafted. Well, I was out of work for about four or five months, and finally I got a job in a place called La Flame that was out near the air force base in Orlando. I worked there with just the drums and organ, and I could do a five-piece band with drums and organ, playing bass, and singing. He [Charlie Daniels] came into the club as the main attraction one night, and I was playing the breaks. His guitar player quit, and he was playing bass at the time. He went back to playing guitar, and the funny thing is when I met the man he said that he was looking for someone to start all over again with a band, and he said let's have lunch. So, we had lunch, and he told me that if I would cut off my long hair and beard he would hire me to be in his band. It was very funny. That was 1963 and 1964. I played for a couple of years with him in a band called the

Jaguars, and I got drafted and he went to Nashville and played with Bob Dylan. We were playing—not really writing—and trying to figure out how to do it. By the time I got out of the army he had the flip side of "Kissin' Cousins" called "It Hurts Me," and he was on his way.

Basically the original band was Charlie, Jerry Corbitt from the Youngbloods, Billy Cox from Band of Gypsys, Jeffrey Meyer, and myself. That band did not stay together but about six months—then it just dissolved. Then it was me and Charlie and Jeffrey and a guy named Earl Grigsby. The original Charlie Daniels Band still can be heard if you can find it. It is a bootleg and it is called *Corbitt and Daniels, Live at Carnegie Hall*.

We opened in 1970 for Delaney and Bonnie, and it was a showcase and they brought Atlantic Records and all of these companies came, and basically they wanted me and Charlie and did not want anyone else. We decided we would all stay together.

Charlie Daniels

I had a great time recording with Bob Dylan. They were great sessions. It was real loose, and there was no pressure to do this or that or the other. He wanted everybody to play their own thing. And that's basically how his music is. He writes the song and everybody just sits around and plays whatever they feel fits. It was a lot of fun. I enjoyed playing with Leonard Cohen. A lot of the country artists were just straight-ahead sessions. And as much fun as the session work was, I knew that I wanted to have my band and play out live.

And to answer your question, yes, I recorded with George Harrison, but it wasn't released. It was George and a drummer named Russ Kunkel and myself. And I recorded with Ringo Starr, but it was pretty much a straight-ahead country session.

Fred Edwards

I first met Charlie in Berkley, California, in 1970. I sat in with the band at the New Monk. They liked my drumming, and of course the look—my hair was down to my ass. [Laughing] So, three months later Charlie calls me and says, "You have a ticket waiting at the San Francisco airport to Nashville." That was August 12, 1971.

Taz DiGregorio

The first album was supposed to be called *Corbitt and Daniels*, but what had happened in Carnegie Hall, Delaney and Bonnie's sound man, whom we knew recorded our show also and after the show—I am not sure what happened, but something happened with Corbitt and he quit the band. Charlie was really very upset, and they were supposed to go in and do an album called *Corbitt and Daniels*; the contracts had been signed and the money had been put up and Corbitt quit. So, I took Corbitt's place on the first album. He sang half and I sang half and from that point on we just kept working at it until we finally hit on it. That album was *Te John, Grease and Wolfman*.

Te John was the bass player, and Wolfman was the drummer, and since I am half Italian and half French-Canadian, I was Grease. It was one of those things where Charlie loves to give people nicknames. That was one of those Southern rock cultural things. "Grease" never stuck, but "Taz" did! He hit that one right one the nose.

That day that they took that picture [the inside gatefold of *Te John, Grease and Wolfman*], we had forgotten that they were coming. [Laughs] We were having the after-recording party—just the four of us on Long Island about a hundred miles out of New York City. We were pretty partied out by the time they got there, and we did not even know that they were coming. The guy just looked at all of us and said, "What ever you do, please don't look at the camera." [Laughs]

Fred Edwards

I was with Charlie from August 12, 1971, until October 1985. This was right after the *Te John, Grease and Wolfman* album. I learned all of that album and was ready to play the songs, but when I got to Nashville, we only played three of the songs from that one. Charlie was starting a new band with myself and Buddy Davis, a friend of Charlie's from the clubbing days before he did his Nashville session career with Bob Dylan. Then there was Earl Grigsby on bass, Taz DiGregorio, and Charlie. We played all around. Locally at first. We used to travel in vans back then. After six months of this, from the

East to the West coast, It was time to do *Honey in the Rock*, my first recording session. Seems like back then Neil Wilburn was the engineer. An old friend of Charlie's from the Dylan sessions.

Out of these sessions came our first regional hit called "Uneasy Rider." After we toured this record for a year, Earl Grigsby left the band. Charlie called Billy Cox, the former Jimi Hendrix band member. Billy had played on Charlie's first solo album. When Billy came, everything was hunky dory as far as I was concerned. Billy liked my drumming. To me he was a legendary fellow. I asked him a lot of questions about Jimi. He was delighted to answer. After Billy left, Buddy Davis split. Then Charlie had to form a new band.

A guitar player named Barry King was with us during the Cox era. Barry King was a friend of Buddy Davis, from Louisville, Kentucky. I think those two were with us for about a year. After all three of them left, we had a session player out of Nashville, Ted Reynolds. Ted was with us just a few months. Then Charlie had to hire three new players. Still loving the sound of two drummers, he hired three guys that played together for a time. Taz and I found this guy that lived down the street from us when we all lived in a house in Donaldson, Tennessee, Barry Barns. Barry brought in his drummer friend Gary Allen, also from Nashville, then Mark Fitzgerald from Salisbury, Maryland. We rehearsed six hours a day until we were ready to go on the road. This band was together for two records, *Fire on the Mountain* and *Way Down Yonder*. That was when Charlie got his first bus—a Scenic Cruiser. That old bus left us on the side of the road more than got us to gigs. [Laughs] With this band we had our first gold album. "The South's Gonna Do It Again" and "Long-haired Country Boy" were hits. Well, these guys left and I was still there, waiting to see what was going to happen next. At this point, Charlie, Taz, and I were very tight brothers. Charlie told Taz and me to go out and find a new band, so we did. We went to a bar called Mickey Finn's and that's where we saw Tommy Crain playing in a band with his brother Billy. They were playing all of the Allman Brothers material. They were so good! They had all of the licks down, man. Taz looked at me and said, "These are the ones we need in our band." Well, Billy was only sixteen at the time, but he played just like Duane Allman. So we took Tommy. He was delighted to join us. Out of the previous band came Don Murray, the drummer. A friend of the previous band. Don and I clicked good for a few albums, *Night Rider* and *High Lonesome*. We didn't have a bass player, and Charlie brought in Charlie Hayward. Now we had a band!

Charlie Hayward

After playing with Dr. John for three months, we were still in Macon. It was that fall, in October, when Duane [Allman] got killed and then Chuck [Leavell] hooked up with the Brothers and got to be with them. Then we played on the *Laid Back* album with Gregg. Me and Chuck and Jimmy Nalls played on some of it. He had lots of different great players. We had Johnny Sandlin produce it, and he also played bass on a couple of tunes. [David] Fathead Newman played saxophone on it. and Buzzy Feiten played guitar lead on "Queen of Hearts." Tommy Talton and Scott Boyer, they were right in there, too. To this day, that was one of the most fun records that I remember playing on. The way Johnny did things, he knew just what he wanted and just went in and did it. If you listen to it with a metronome, it is up and down and all over the place. It was a great feel. He did a great job of producing and mixing it. After that was done, I wanted to get away from Macon. Lou, our drummer, passed away and I went back to Tuscaloosa and played in a band called Foxfire. We just played frat parties and stuff like that for a couple of years. Then, finally, I hooked up with Charlie through Paul Hornsby. Paul was one of those guys from Tuscaloosa that I had played with and I had known him from years before. He had been in a couple of those bands I had played with. He had produced *Fire on the Mountain* and I think that was the first album he had done on Charlie and I think all of his musicians, drummer, guitarist and bass player had all quit on him at the same time. Then I got a call from Charlie, who had gotten my number from Paul who had recommended me, and he basically just hired me over the phone without hearing me play a note. They played in Tuscaloosa the next night and opened for Lynyrd Skynryd, and I took my bass and played a couple of songs with him in the dressing room. I got on the bus and have been going ever since.

Tommy Crain

I had a band here in Nashville that was pretty successful locally called the Flat Creek Band. My brother Billy and I both wrote some original music with this band, and after that band broke up I formed a band called Buckeye that played in the southeast region. Then when I got the offer to play with the Charlie Daniels Band in 1975, Billy took my place in Buckeye. Then Billy went on to play with Bobby Whitlock, after the "Layla" and Eric Clapton thing for several years. Then after that, he moved to Florida and played with the Henry Paul Band for about nine years, and then when Henry went back to the Outlaws and broke that band up, he played with the Bellamy Brothers for about nine years.

The band I mentioned called Flat Creek had a road manager named David Corlew, who is Charlie's personal manager now. When the band broke up, David went on to road-manage Charlie Daniels, and in 1974, my band Buckeye opened the very first Volunteer Jam, and I actually played the first musical note of any Volunteer Jam ever because it started with a guitar riff. But I had met Charlie that night, and he told me that he was losing both his guitar players and drummer and asked me if I would be interested. Well, to be honest with him I told him that I was still playing with my brother Billy and I didn't want to leave him. I thought it over for about one week and turned him down because of that, and in retrospect that was a stupid thing to do, but I was naive back then and didn't know what was going on. One year later we played at another Volunteer Jam, and at that time my band had broken up. He asked me again and I gladly accepted. Charlie said that we would be going on tour the first of the year in 1975, so my wife and I drove down to Knoxville and saw a show and she left me at the hotel and went home and Charlie and I went up to the hotel room, and I roomed with him for six years after that. I learned all the songs from the *Fire on the Mountain* album, and he and I just sat up in the room with two electric guitars and no amps and just played the whole thing, and it was just magical. I had never experienced anything like it.

Paul Hornsby

One of the great groups that the Marshall Tucker Band began touring with was the Charlie Daniels Band. They had become friends, so now that we were allowed to put fiddles on rock 'n' roll records, we had Charlie come in as a guest on all the Tucker albums that I had a part in.

Charlie approached me after the first Tucker LP and said he liked what we had done, and asked if I would be interested in working with his group. Up until this time, Charlie had one hit— "Uneasy Rider." I liked Charlie a lot and agreed to go and catch some of his shows and get a feel for what he was doing.

If I had one criticism of his band, it would be that he was doing a lot of stuff that sounded like the Allmans. He did it great, but it wasn't anything new. At the end of a show in Tuscaloosa, I remember that for an encore he brought out his fiddle and did "Orange Blossom Special." After a set of guitar-oriented-Allman-Brothers-influenced material, that fiddle during his encore made the fans go crazy! I could see an obvious direction taking place here. We did several albums together, and that fiddle sound remained prominent on all of them.

I think the easiest and one of the biggest records I ever cut, was the first Charlie Daniels Band we did together called *Fire On the Mountain*. From pre-production rehearsal, to tracking, overdubbing, and final mix took eleven days straight.

Oh yeah! I always remember this—during this album we had sort of a deadline to meet. The band had to get back out on the road for some dates. Also, I think the budget was pretty low, so we didn't have a lot of studio time to waste. We had some pretty good tunes cut as we went along on this project. One was an instrumental, which we called "Fiddle Boogie." Well, it was pretty good, but I didn't think it was strong enough to stand alone as an instrumental. Charlie assured me he would stick some lyrics into it eventually. Well, "eventually" was limited to eleven days. Every day when we came in to start the session, I'd ask him if he had finished writing any lyrics for that "fiddle thing." He would always reassure me not to worry. I'm a naturally born worrier, and I knew I didn't want that thing on the album like it was. Every day it was the same story—"Have you finished the lyrics?" "Don't worry," etc.

It got right down to the last day for mixes, and we had no lyrics for "Fiddle Boogie." I said, "Charlie, this is it. We got to have something." He said, "Just give me a few minutes. I'm going up here to a quiet place in the front office [of the studio]. I've got a few ideas. I'll be back shortly." We took a break. He came back in about fifteen minutes and said, "I got something I want to run by you fellows." We put the track on, and he went out to the microphone and began to sing something about "Dickey Betts playing on that red guitar," and "ol' Lynyrd Skynyrd's playin' down in Jacksonville." We all fell out. That obviously was "The South's Gonna Do It Again." No more worries here.

Well, again this was in my early days, so to speak, of producing [1974]. I thought there were several pretty strong cuts on that album. However, when they informed me that the first single to be pulled would be "The South's Gonna Do It Again," I thought they were crazy. Then they told me to tune in to WLS in Chicago, of all places. They were playing the hell out of it! We followed the jock's lead and that was indeed a hit single.

Today that album *Fire on the Mountain* is one of the musical high points that I'm proudest of. There have been many other moments, but that one is very strong. After twenty-six years it still hangs right in there and keeps selling. I suppose among all the records I did, the rival to that one would have to be the Tucker's *Where We All Belong*. I thought that was really a classy collection of music. Incidentally, both albums were done back-to-back in 1974. I think just as I was finishing the Tucker LP, we overlapped the beginning of Charlie's album.

Fred Edwards

I guess my favorite CDB memories are playing at the White House for Jimmy Carter's Inaugural Ball. This was with the Marshall Tucker Band—quite an experience. Then later we were invited back for his daughter Amy's pool party. I'll never forget all the security standing around. Then Tommy Crain jumps into the pool with her. We all stood back and said, "Damn, Tommy!" Anyway, we all got photos with Jimmy and wife in cowboy hats. I display them in my house still today. Also, playing Carnegie Hall—the best sounding hall I can remember. All of the East coast fans, from New Jersey up to

Cape Cod, they were our best man...those people loved us. Thank you, guys.

Tommy Crain

We had lunch with President Carter and Rosalynn at the White House. I got to be good friends with Chip Carter, the president's son, while we were campaigning for him and playing shows, and he played a joke on me one time. We had lunch by the pool and they had an oompah-Marine band playing in the corner. Chip says, "Does anyone want to go for a swim?" I had brought my trunks, and little Amy was playing in the pool at the time. I jumped into the pool big time and made a huge splash, and when I came back up there were four Secret Service men there saying, "Son, you just don't do that." Well, I got out and asked Chip where I could go change back into my clothes, and he said to go through this pink door and change. I went through the pink door, and I am standing there naked, getting my clothes on, bent over, and the door opened and it was Rosalynn's mom standing there. I mooned the first mother-in-law. [Laughs] Chip was laughing his brains out when I came out of there.

Jimmy Hall

I remember first seeing him [Charlie] in Tennessee—of course! I was very impressed. He had elements of both the Allman Brothers and Marshall Tucker, and I like that territory. Two drummers and two guitar players. He forged his own way playing country, rock and roll, and rhythm and blues. He's always been a gentleman and a fine friend. We were managed by the same guy for a while. We toured with him in 1981 and 1982 with my solo group, and of course, Wet Willie played with him a lot. I'm happy to say we're still friends, and I want to say that Charlie did a great thing with the Volunteer Jams. I participated in most of those.

Tommy Crain

I guess I co-wrote about sixty songs. Charlie is a super guy, and he takes very good care of his band members and treats them as front men rather than side men. When I first joined the band, like Taz said in his interview with you, Charlie would let us have a song on every record. Taz and I got to do one song per record, and no other artist lets you do that. As far as the writing goes, we would go out to Charlie's and put all our ideas together and start rehearsing, and this would all gel and get put together. He would give us 50 percent and he took the other 50 percent, and this was so nice of him because he wrote most of the stuff and we all just added to it. He was super-cool to let everyone be a part of the music. That was really big of him and there is no other man like him alive.

Charlie Hayward

We were all a little wild and crazy when we were younger, and Charlie would tell you the same thing. There are a lot of things we are not proud of about our past. But nonetheless, they are a part of who we are and we are mighty fortunate to still be around. But with Charlie, what you see is what you get, pretty much. He's a guy who believes in treating people fair. There have been times—many times over—when he could have fired a lot of us. But I think he holds to seniority and for sticking with him through the rough times. Maybe it was that more than talent sometimes. I'm not saying he hasn't had good musicians all the time, but probably there have been times in his career when he could have gotten some aged musicians, but it wouldn't have been the kind of band concept that he likes to have. He's just a solid person. Very dependable, too. I've seen others in the business that get chewed up and spit out, but he just kind of grabbed the bull by the horns and rode it on out. Through the big years and through the lean years, he always maintained his focus on what he wanted to do in music. He never gave up. I think Charlie has just been a great guy to work with. I hear about all these other guys that are hired by the tour, and they come up to you and fire you at Christmastime because they don't want to pay you or whatever. Charlie's like an abnormality in the music business, he really is. And I'd like to add that Charlie has probably been a Christian all his life, but I came to know the Lord back in 1984. And since then we have even more of a closeness because of our similar beliefs. And just having a handle on life. He is not just a music guy. Family is real important. He likes to go home and ride horses or go fishing or go to the mountains. That's the way I am, too. I like to spend time with my family. You have to have some kind of balance. You can't be just all music. I don't know about cats like that. There are some guys like that, all they do is live and breathe music, but me, I've got to get away from it sometimes.

Tommy Crain

We had cut our last track [for *Million Mile Reflections*, 1979] and then Charlie's eyes got real wide, and he said to Taz and me, "Boys, we don't have a fiddle song on this album. We have to have a fiddle song." Then he asked Taz and me to come out into the studio room, and he said that he had this idea about the Devil and this kid having a fiddling contest. I immediately came up with the beginning lick, and Taz and I and Charlie sat down and we put the music together in about thirty minutes. We went home that night, and overnight Charlie had written the lyrics out. He came in, and we recorded it the next day and then won a Grammy award for it.

In 1990, Tommy Crain made the decision to leave the Charlie Daniels Band. He would sit with bands but would not form his own group until 2005 when he joined forces with an Atlanta blues band to become Tommy Crain and the Crosstown Allstars.

There were many, many reasons I left the band. I was getting burned out traveling on the road. When I first joined the band we were doing about three hundred dates per year. I was getting older, and my daughter was fixing to become a teenager, and my wife's career in endurance riding was blooming, and my brother and I had made a pact that if he had come off the road and wanted to do a band that I would do it with him. I had told Charlie years earlier that there may come a time when I would have to leave the band to play with my brother again. He said that all I had to do was let him know when that happened, so I went to him and told him how I felt. Six months later I was at home working with my brother Billy.

26

Redneck Fiddlin' Man

Over the years, Charlie Daniels would become only more of a living legend. Fellow Southern rockers, band mates, and fans across the world watched as Charlie moved seamlessly into country music, becoming a member of the Grand Ole Opry.

Taz DiGregorio

My friend Charlie—let me tell you what. No one has ever heard this story before. When I came to the Charlie Daniels Band, I had no earthly idea of what the basic fundamentals of how to write songs were and this man came and got me in Huntsville, Alabama, in a hay wagon and put my B-3 on it. We came to Nashville, and I lived with him for a couple of years. He taught me how to write songs and about life, and this man has a heart like no other man I have ever met. This man cannot only write songs, but he is the most talented man I have ever met in my life. He does it all. In the studio he did what they call head arrangements, and he is a totally brilliant man. This is how good of a friend he is—I believe it was 1980, not really sure of the year but I think it was, we had an album called *Full Moon*. I had a song on that album called "No Potion for the Pain." He allowed me to write, sing, and just about produce one song on every album. No other artist would ever give anyone, another writer that opportunity. The record company said, "Absolutely not," and he went to New York City on a plane and said, "Absolutely yes," and we are going to do this whether you like it or not. He is about as much of a friend as you can have; it doesn't get any better than that. He is a very understanding man, and you cannot do anything that he hasn't already done. He understands where you are coming from because he has already been there. There have been times over thirty-one years that it is not always the best of relationships because you are always going to have some disagreements, but we have always transcended that, and the main goal has always been the band. A guy asked me the other day, what have I been waiting on to do the [solo] album? Well, I have been busy with the band; and as long as there is a Charlie Daniels Band there will always be a Taz in the band—and that would be me!

Bobby Ingram

In spring of 1999, we [Molly Hatchet] were asked to join Charlie Daniels in the history making Volunteer Jam tour. It was history making because it was never taken out of the state of Tennessee. We went from coast to coast, playing some of the largest venues in the United States. We were on the bill with Charlie Daniels, Marshall Tucker, and Hank Williams, Jr. The entire band had a blast. We saw many of our friends on the tour and covered a lot of different material in the set. The tour also corresponded with the tail end of our *Silent Reign of Heroes* release.

I must say that Charlie Daniels is a true gentleman, and his Southern hospitality is unequaled. For the second year, Molly Hatchet has proudly participated in a most special event that takes place in Clearwater, Florida. It is the eleventh annual Charlie Daniels / Angelus Concert and Celebrity Golf Tournament to help all of the handicapped children and adults that live at the Angelus home located in Hudson, Florida. It is very rewarding for us, and we will continue as long as Charlie wants us to. We would want everyone who is able to be a part of this experience. It is held in January in Clearwater, Florida.

Gregg Allman

Charlie's a wonderful guy. He sent me this quadruple-X sized Beaver Stetson hat; it must have been like a really expensive cowboy hat. I mean, you could use this hat for a parachute. [Laughs] I've still got the damn thing.

Tommy Crain

He is a super guy to work with. You don't cross him because he is a disciplined man and has his values and issues, and he knows what he wants. He didn't get there by being stupid, but by being smart. He has been through lots in his career, with managers, people that were not quite honest. But he has handled it, and he is still out there and going for it.

George McCorkle

I hold him in high praise. He has been doing it for a long time, and he is still doing it. Even living up here, I don't see Charlie that often because he's out working all the time. Me and his son see each other a lot. He is the president of Charlie's Wooley Swamp Publishing company.

Dru Lombar

The godfather, man. He's the one. All of his band were great guys. Always supportive, talented, always in your corner. Always willing to give you a shot.

27

Volunteer Jam

If there was one single event that summed up the whole feeling of brotherhood during the early days of Southern rock, it was Charlie's Volunteer Jam. Beginning with a concert in Nashville's War Memorial Auditorium on October 4, 1974, the jam became a yearly tradition. The second concert in 1975 was filmed and released to theatres and is now available on DVD. Beginning in 2000, Charlie began Volunteer Jam tours, the first of which featured the Marshall Tucker Band and Molly Hatchet touring with the CDB.

Charlie Daniels

Volunteer Jam was a live recording session. We were doing the *Fire on the Mountain* album, and we wanted to do two live cuts, so we figured the best place to do it was in Nashville, which was about the only place we could draw a crowd at that time. We got some recording equipment and asked some of our friends to come up and jam with us. That first year, Toy Caldwell, Jerry Eubanks, and Doug Gray from the Marshall Tucker Band and Dickey Betts from the Allman Brothers were in town, and we invited them up. It was called Volunteer Jam, naturally, after the state of Tennessee. After the first time, we decided we needed to do this again.

Fred Edwards

Our first Volunteer Jam was at the old Nashville War Memorial Building. Our special guest was Dickey Betts. We jammed until the cows came home. We did a few gigs with the Allman Brothers. The one I'll never forget was in San Francisco at the Fillmore West on New Year's Eve. I stood onstage to watch the Brothers play after we played. The energy was so much fun; they liked us a lot and we liked them. We met all of their road crew, a good bunch of fellas, Red Dog and Joe Dan Petty, to name a few. Later we would find out Joe Dan Petty had a band called Grinderswitch. We played quite a few gigs with them. There are ten Volunteer Jams under my belt, so, how can I explain all of them? Let's see—I backed up a lot of artists, because it was a three-day event. In 1975 we had Chuck Leavell, Jimmy Hall, the Marshall Tucker Band, Dickey Betts. Volunteer Jam 3, there was Wet Willie, Sea Level, Willie Nelson, the Winters Brothers, Toy Caldwell and Paul Riddle, Bonnie Bramlett, Papa John Creach, and Mylon LeFevre. It was one of my favorite Jams because I made a lot of new friends. But all of the Jams were just great.

I really liked Jam number 7 too. This was while we were doing the *Full Moon* tour, so we had a 5-piece horn section, four female singers, the Stony Mountain Cloggers—then all of the artists to back up. Well, it was a hoot. Since there were so many bands, we could not do a set change for everyone, so, the artists without their musicians we backed up. What a great opportunity for the CDB. Ted Nugent, Crystal Gayle, Mylon LeFevre—hell, even Gary Busey was backstage hangin' out. Willie Nelson, John Prine, Gregg Allman, Dobie Gray, Ray Price, Papa John Creach, Delbert McClinton. Gee...Johnny Gimble, Bonnie Bramlett, and Dickey Betts.

Doug Gray

The Volunteer Jams are always a great time for everyone. I have so many happy memories of watching Toy Caldwell rocking out up there on stage with Charlie and the Outlaws, all those great bands. I just stood over to the side until it was my turn to sing. A lot of that was recorded. Those two CDs on Blue Hat with Volunteer Jam tracks are great. I still wish Charlie would release "It's My Life," where I sang with him. I really liked that one.

Tommy Crain

I played on every Volunteer Jam, even after I left the band. The first Volunteer Jam I opened the show with my band. The second one I was with Charlie in Murfreesboro. When we had the Volunteer Jam in Nashville, we always had it at the Municipal Auditorium, and Charlie always got us rooms at the Hyatt House, a few blocks away, because we would have some beers after the show and would not have to drive home. Just another way he took care of us. So after the show was over one night I go back—and my Mom was such a great fan and she and Dad always came to the shows—one night I went in after the show and there was my mom and Dickey Betts arm and arm having a nice time talking. It was a sight. [Laughs] Doing the Volunteer Jam was always such a pleasure, and there were so many great performers that I can't even mention all of them. For the first seven or eight Volunteer Jams, we would back up all the performers. We learned all their songs, and I was the bandleader at that time.

Dennis Winters

The Winters Brothers Band played ten to twelve Volunteer Jams when they were held in Nashville. We were featured on two of the Volunteer Jam albums, *Volunteer Jam III & IV* and *Volunteer Jam VI* on Epic Records. Great memories.

Charlie Daniels

I don't look at myself as having a role; I feel like I am just an entertainer. I don't see myself as an influence or having a certain image to live up to. I am just an entertainer that goes and plays shows and makes records and tries to entertain people. I have much more of a mature look at my career per se than what I had when I was younger. I have kids come up to me and say I have been listening to you for a long time and you have had an effect on my music, but I really don't look at myself in that way. They say it, and I just don't look at myself that way. I am just a picker, man.

Part 5

The Capricorn Records Family

28

The Goat

Phil Walden, Alan Walden, and Frank Fenter started Capricorn Records in 1969 in Macon, Georgia, after Phil lost his primary R&B artist, Otis Redding, in a tragic accident. Both Phil and his brother Alan had dearly loved Redding, and the death hit them both hard. Phil decided to move away from his longtime specialty, sweet soul music, and work with rock bands. He met with Jerry Wexler from Atlantic Records and they struck a deal to open a Southern record company, publishing company, and studio. After hearing Duane Allman play on several records recorded at Rick Hall's FAME Studios—including sides by Wilson Pickett and Aretha Franklin—Walden met with Hall and bought Allman's contract. Duane proceeded to assemble the Allman Brothers Band.

Tom Dowd

The whole thing called "Southern rock" began back in 1969 when Phil and Alan Walden and Frank Fenter launched Capricorn Records in Macon, Georgia. The Allman Brothers Band were undoubtedly the first Southern rock band, followed very closely by Lynyrd Skynyrd down in Jacksonville, Florida.

Tommy Talton

You can call it that, a brotherhood. But it is something that will never exist again…. It *was* a brotherhood. Capricorn studios was a house that we could go to. It was someone's living room that we were fortunate enough that Phil had put that together. He had had success with Otis Redding and had the money to have that establishment built.

Tom Wynn

The studio was just plain funky. It was housed in an old storefront building right in the middle of downtown. There was no sign; and, walking up to it, it looked like just another dust-crusted vacant building. The front was vacant; the studio area was a big room with a control booth in the back of the building. That area must have been used as the warehousing for the retail store that originally used the building.

Most of the other buildings in the neighborhood were vacant. Seemed like they probably had been vacant for a long time. I remember the Heart of Georgia Diner was across the street, and I never worked up the nerve to actually eat there. I remember the red neon lights on the mission building's cross that said "Jesus Saves" would glow huge in the fog. We could see it from several blocks away coming out of the studio late at night. It was the heart of old Georgia.

The studio sounded good. We didn't bother much with instrument isolation back then. We were playing the tracks live, and the room was large with a high ceiling—and we didn't play too loud so it wasn't too much of an issue. I think there was an eight-track recorder at the time, if memory serves. It was a decent machine at the time, and later it was changed to a 24-track Studer, I'm pretty sure. The control room was large enough for the whole band to be in for playback. Johnny [Sandlin] had a number of different speakers he could choose for that. Some were audiophile quality, "as-good-as-you-could-get" type, and some were half-blown automobile speakers so we could hear what it would sound like coming out of the radio driving home from school or work. We could hear either one by flipping a switch.

I think one of the most interesting, and possibly instructive, memories I have of the place had to do with Chuck Leavell. Chuck was hanging around a lot. He was playing with anyone who needed a keyboard player; and according to his discography, Cowboy's *5'll Getcha Ten* was the fourth album he ever played on. But the amazing thing I found out was that Chuck had a set of keys to the studio, and every day he'd go down there and practice, all by himself for at least six or eight hours. Nobody else around, Chuck would be at the grand piano practicing. Totally focused, totally straight, he would just practice his instrument—not too amazingly, people noticed.

Johnny Sandlin

Well, before I was at Capricorn I had a job in Miami, and there was this studio there owned by Henry Stone. It was just a small—*very small* four-track studio upstairs above one of the warehouses. Tone was a huge record distributor in Miami. They were extremely large. That was where the record stores got their albums. I played drums on demos, and Eddie helped me get that job. He introduced me to Steve Alamo, who was one of the people in charge along with Henry Stone and Brad Shapiro, the producer. I think that my very first session was playing on a single that was Betty Wright and Steve Alamo doing a duet. And at that time was a risky thing, black and white artists performing together. It was a neat thing. Anyway, while I was down there Phil had meanwhile started his studio in Georgia. That was in late 1969. He wanted to hire a studio band and do a Stax thing. That was my whole idea, you put a rhythm section together and work every day and get tight and put a distinctive sound together for your studio and your artists. That is exactly what I wanted to do, and Phil called me while I was working at Tone and asked if I was interested in working up there. I thought about it, but I felt like I was doing okay and I liked my job there. In the meantime, the Allman Brothers had gone up there and signed a contract, and Duane called and asked me to come up and said that we could all do music together again. I took a trip up there, and when I was going home through Macon it just felt right. I loved the town, and it is one of the few towns I get around in easily without getting lost. So I came home and went from being out of work for six months to being offered about three or four jobs at one time. I was fortunate. I went back to Tone and put in my notice and moved up to Macon.

Randall Bramblett

Johnny [Sandlin] is a great producer. He's a real easy, laid back guy. He always gets those great sounds he's always gotten, you know? He's always consistent and really easy to work with.

Bonnie Bramlett

Oh, I love Johnny Sandlin. He's my brother, and one of the greatest producers of all time. He really respects the music.

Paul Hornsby

After I had been back in Tuscaloosa for nine months, Duane Allman called me from Muscle Shoals where he had been playing sessions during this time. He had come to the attention of some Atlantic people, who had heard his work on the Wilson Pickett's cut "Hey Jude." After finding out who this guitar player was, they—I think it was Jerry Wexler—expressed an interest in forming a band around Duane and had brought Phil Walden aboard as Duane's manager. In the phone conversation with Duane, he asked me if I would come up to Shoals and play on some cuts with him and see what would happen.

I did go up there, and while I was there over the next few days, Phil Walden came in. Johnny Sandlin and Pete Carr were also called in for the sessions. Duane also brought in Jaimoe and Berry Oakley, with whom he had recently been jamming down in Florida. Out of these sessions came some well known cuts that later appeared on the *Duane Allman Anthology* LPs.

Basically, Phil wanted to put the Hour Glass band back together, in a sense. Well, for me, Sandlin, and Carr, we had been on a virtual roller coaster for the last two years and were in the middle of looking into other musical interests. A rehash of what we had just gotten out of seemed to be walking backwards.

Walden suggested that if the three of us wouldn't be a part of this group, maybe we would consider coming to work as the rhythm section for a new recording studio he was building in Macon. At that time I had never heard of Macon. I remember asking him what state it was in.

Over the next couple of months, he called a lot, and each time the deal got a little sweeter. I think what really clinched it for me, though, was that Johnny Sandlin and Pete Carr had decided to accept the offer. We had always sort of stuck together. I was finally convinced though, and on July 4, 1969, I moved over to Macon to become a full time studio musician.

Phil Walden had, until this time, had most of his success with R&B acts like Otis Redding, whom he had managed. Also, he had a booking agency that had booked most of the major R&B acts in the nation, for instance Sam & Dave and countless others. Many of these acts had been recorded at the Stax studio in Memphis. At the core of Stax studio was the rhythm section, which really was Booker T. & the M.G.s. Having drawn from these experiences, he wanted to put together a recording studio staffed by musicians along the lines of the Stax group.

So, presto—Johnny Sandlin, Pete Carr, and myself, along with Robert Popwell became the staff musicians at the new studio in Macon called Capricorn Sound Studios. Popwell later went on to play bass with the Jazz Crusaders, of well-known fame. We literally glued acoustical tile, built baffles, and added hands-on construction to this studio.

At this time we recorded behind such acts as Arthur Conley [of "Sweet Soul Music" fame], Eddie Floyd, Livingston Taylor, and others.

Johnny Sandlin

My deal with Phil was that I wanted to produce and play on records, and we had agreed that I could produce and play the drums. I reserved the right to produce at a future date. Some of the first things that we worked on were demos with Jackie Avery. We did that for a while, and then Phil wanted to cut a record with Johnny Jenkins. Before that I guess the first thing that I played on was some Swamp Dogg stuff that I love to this day. Then I got to do a couple of singles with Arthur Conley, who was someone that Phil managed at the time. Another reason that Macon appealed to me was I was a huge Otis Redding fan, and I loved everything he did. I had every record and even had worn them out. I knew that Phil had managed him and a lot of the acts. Phil was involved heavily with acts from Muscle Shoals.

29

Ol' Brother Willie

Wet Willie was formed under the moniker "Fox" in Mobile, Alabama, in 1969, changing their name to Wet Willie a year later and became one of Capricorn's early success stories. They recorded a series of powerful records, lead by the charismatic front man and lead singer Jimmy Hall. The band cracked the Top 10 national chart in 1974 with "Keep on Smilin.'"

Jimmy Hall

I wouldn't take any amount of money for the time in which I was born, and the time in which I grew up. I wouldn't take anything for the situation I was in. Doing what we did with Wet Willie—rocking in the seventies—it was the best of all worlds. It was like being indestructible. I was in a rock band; we had records, and we were on the road playing with everyone we'd ever idolized. How can you beat that?

Dru Lombar

Wet Willie. One word comes to mind—soulful—band full of soul. Nice cats. Jimmy Hall, the best-kept secret in the South. That guy can sing and play. And showmanship—he should have been a big, big, big, big star. But he's a real humble, laid back guy and not a pusher—a beautiful cat. They wrote some great songs, uplifting stuff, like "Keep on Smilin.'" They were the funk side of Capricorn, I thought.

Doug Gray

Jimmy Hall is my favorite singer. We always had great times with Jimmy and his brother Jack and sister Donna. Oh yeah, Donna.

Every man at Capricorn was in love with Donna. She's so beautiful, a great singer, and sweet as sugar.

Paul Hornsby

Another group that I was a real fan of, were my old Alabama compatriots Wet Willie. I did two albums with them—*The Wetter the Better* and a live thing called *Left Coast Live*. I would have liked to have continued with them, but after *Wetter the Better*, the group made a label change to CBS. CBS wanted to take the group into a more of a disco direction, and that left me out entirely! So ended that musical relationship.

Bonnie Bramlett

Wet Willie is a fantastic band. My sister Donna [Hall] rocks, and you know how much I adore Jimmy Hall.

30

Sweet Bonnie Bramlett

Bonnie Bramlett came into Capricorn with a reputation for greatness, having spent many years performing with her husband in Delaney & Bonnie and Friends. It was a group that at times featured everyone from Eric Clapton and Bobby Whitlock [later Derek & the Dominos], George Harrison, Dave Mason, and Duane Allman. She recorded several solo albums including a duets record called Ladies Choice.

Dru Lombar
Bonnie Bramlett just showed up in Macon and immediately became one of us. Not only is she one of the best female singers of all time, she is also a real honest, down-to-earth person. She is number one in my book!

Bonnie Bramlett
"Superstar." That's my baby. "Oncoming Traffic" is probably my favorite, but I did not write that, Gregg Allman did. I think my favorite performance as far as reality in the studio is "Oncoming Traffic," with Gregg Allman performing on the piano—it is special.

Randall Bramblett
Bonnie Bramlett is one of the classic great soul voices. She's got such a spirit and energy about her when she sings. She's a winner. She is a survivor. And she's got that voice that nobody else has. She's unique. I always enjoy working with her. She's a great spirit—a kindred spirit.

Dickey Betts

Oh, I love Bonnie. That's the singingest son of a bitch. [Laughing] She taught me how to sing. I'd be a great singer if I had a voice, you know? [Laughs] 'Cause I can really sing, I just don't have a voice! But what little I have I got from her. She told me, "You can't try to control it. You just got to open up and let it go!"

Johnny Sandlin

She is the best white female singer out there, and the best that there ever was. The first time I saw her live was at that thing at A&R Studios in New York where Duane was playing with Bonnie and Delaney. That was such a great performance for them. When that was over I went back there and told Phil to *please sign* Bonnie Bramlett because I wanted to produce her and work with her. Finally, it came about that he did. I thought the world of her then, and she has gotten even better today. I can't say enough about her. I love her to death.

Billy Bob Thornton

Oh, I know Bonnie Bramlett. She's amazing. What a singer. You know, I started hanging out with that whole set in the eighties. I knew Phil Walden real well. He was actually my manager for a time. He managed two actors, Jim Varney and me. This is when Capricorn had folded, and he went into management. And then Capricorn came back with 311 and Widespread Panic. Phil ended up getting me to direct the first thing I ever directed, which was a documentary on Athens and Widespread Panic called *Widespread Panic Live at the Georgia Theatre*. That's where I got to know all those guys, Col. Bruce Hampton and Vic Chesnutt, the guys in Widespread and all of that. As a matter of fact, Dave Schools was at my house a couple of years ago—and Warren Haynes.

Dickey Betts

Oh, you know, anytime we're around each other we just wail it up. She and I have created more good music when we get together. It's like lightning between us, you know? In a good way. I knew her and Delaney. I can't sing like Delaney and I don't pretend to, but when I get around her I always try to. I get my gospel voice out.

[Laughs] She gets a kick out of that, and it fires her up. We got a kick out of that whole thing.

31

Cowboy

Another excellent Capricorn band was called Cowboy, lead by Scott Boyer and Tommy Talton. The band had a sound reminiscent of the Eagles, but before the Eagles. Originally formed in Florida, the band became a huge success, and when Gregg Allman did his On Tour '74 *album, Cowboy joined him as his backing band. They were even given two tracks of their own on the double-album. One of the great success stories of Cowboy is "Please Be with Me," written by Scott Boyer and recorded with Duane Allman playing Dobro.*

Tommy Talton

When Scott and I met it was through a mutual friend named Becky. I don't know what she said to him, but she told me that there was this guy I needed to meet that she had met from Jacksonville, and he writes his own songs like you and plays guitar and sings really well. At that time it was hard to find someone that wrote their own songs. It was not like it is today, because everybody now writes their own songs.

I had just come back from California in late 1969 and had been living in L. A. for a year, and I was writing a lot. I was doing solo gigs in coffee houses and folk clubs. I was doing some Dylan songs and then my own stuff. Becky says that there was this guy I needed to meet. She introduced us and we both had our guitars. I know this sounds made up, but this is exactly what happened.... We sat down and pulled our guitars out, and Scott played me "Livin' in the Country," which was a song we did on the first Cowboy album. I felt it was so neat to find someone else that also wrote their own music and that the music was good. I forget what I played for him, but after

I showed him a song, we just sat down and asked each other who could we get in the band.

We got together with a friend of mine, Tom Wynn, a drummer for We the People, and I had grown up with him. He was also in a band called the Non-Chalants and the Offbeats that I joined that turned into We the People, and he was the original drummer in Cowboy. And George Clark, a friend of mine from Orlando was playing bass, and Scott knew a piano player named Bill Pillmore from Jacksonville. We all met up and literally within the next three months of our meeting we were all living together in a house in Jacksonville and doing nothing but working up original songs and playing all day and all night long.

We were throwing newspapers at 2:00 a.m. to pay the rent, and young kids would come by our rehearsals. These thirteen or fourteen-year-old kids with some name like Van Zant or something. [Laughs]

They would come in and listen to us and we would just constantly play. Then a guy named Duane Allman came through while we were living there, and he was with Capricorn Records and Phil Walden at that time. We stayed up until early in the morning a couple of times and played together. Duane went back to Macon, and I don't know what he said to Phil, but we had all those contracts back in the mail. Phil had never met us or heard us but he knew that Duane knew what he was talking about. It must have been something fairly acceptable. [Laughs] It was pretty neat.

Tom Wynn

I had stayed in touch with Tommy while he was in California after We the People had broken up. When I heard he was moving back to form a band with Scott Boyer in Jacksonville, I knew I wanted to be a part of that band just based on my history with Tommy. Somehow we agreed I should move to Jacksonville to be part of what was to become Cowboy.

Crazy when I think back—I left a solid gig at the Wreck Bar to move to Jacksonville to start a band with no intention of doing covers or anything else that might indicate we could make a living. But, as I mentioned, hippie-dom was getting started—we had to do it. So, Tommy Talton, Scott Boyer, Bill Pillmore, George Clark, and I all moved into this big old house together—played eight or ten hours a day—*every* day. We did that for months. We learned a bunch of original songs...life was good.

We had no money—only one running vehicle between us—Scott had a job delivering newspapers, and we'd take turns helping him on the route. On payday, we'd go to the farmers' market and buy dozens of eggs. Fried eggs on peanut-butter sandwiches were a delicacy. We were all very thin.

Scott Boyer

Well, I think it was seven or eight years that we were together. We got together in '69 and broke up in '75 but ran until '77 with a last rendition. The highlights were many. One was the first time we played at the Fillmore East. It was Cowboy's first time in New York, and our road manager was driving our Ford station wagon like a maniac on the way to the Fillmore to the hotel. And I remember him making a comment about "That's how everyone drives up there." We got into a wreck, just a fender bender but we were late by five minutes, and we ran in to get our instruments. Bill Graham is yelling his brains out at us, and we were running to get to the stage and play. I remember running down the stairs to the stage with Bill right on my trail, cussing me out. "How dare you be late for a gig at my club!" [Laughs] That is a very vivid memory, and we had a great show, thank God. Another memory of the Fillmore was the next time when we went there, and I can't remember the name of the headliner, but maybe it will come to me in a minute. It was some large act that had been booked there a couple of times and not shown up—so many of these fans had been holding their tickets for some time to see whoever it was. So we walked out onstage to a chorus of boos from the audience. Then Bill Graham came out from backstage and stepped up to my microphone and said that the people that did not like the music that he presented could go up to the front door, get your money back, and go home and listen to your 45s. Some guy in about the third row yelled, "Fuck you" and Bill Graham jumped off the stage to get the guy, but about the time he got there, the security had grabbed him and dragged him out of his seat and pulled him up the aisle with Bill kicking him in the ass as he was being dragged. We

only played Fillmore East two times and then Winterland with
Gregg. Many years went by, and I ran into Bill Graham when he was
having lunch with Phil Walden and he remembered me. I was
amazed at his ability to remember people. We played a pretty good
show that second night, and I think we were billed with BloodRock
and Spirit.

Tommy Talton

The way Cowboy was entered into the situation, if you can
imagine that two people would meet and within six months after
meeting be in the studio recording and doing all original songs and
having free reign over what you do musically. Not having business-
men in suits coming in telling us that it won't work. Johnny Sandlin
was at the helm, producing. Like one night we would be recording a
Cowboy record, and then Chuck Leavell might walk in and put a
piano on a tune. It was literally that loose. There was no request to
have him booked to put a piano on two songs at 4:00 p.m. for
Cowboy. It happened because it was all a spirit of camaraderie, and
as Dickey said, a brotherhood. That word was not used until after the
fact, after you had been through it. We didn't call it anything.
Someone would just have a new song to do and it was fun.

Tom Wynn

As I recall, Scott had played in bands with Duane and Gregg
Allman when they were all in high school five or six years earlier. The
newly formed Allman Brothers Band had just been signed with Phil
Walden's Capricorn Records in Macon, and they were starting to gain
a little altitude. Capricorn was looking for new groups to bring
forward, and Duane told Phil Walden about us because of his history
with Scott. Duane had never heard the band at the time—actually, no
one had heard the group yet as we had never played out.

At some point, Phil asked Johnny Sandlin to come to Jacksonville to hear the band. He did. And when he went back to Macon, he
apparently told Phil Walden he thought we had something worth
hearing. So that was it—Duane told Phil; Phil sent Johnny. Phil
signed the band, Johnny was our producer, and Duane got famous.
The lesson must be—always help your friends.

Pete Kowalke

Back to school. Actually, Tommy Talton and I went to the same high school. I just knew of him and occasionally maybe would say hello. He was a year or so younger and ran in a different crowd than I. But we were there at the same time. I knew Tom Wynn and George Clark in kind of the same ways, as they had the same situation as Tommy as far as me knowing them went.

After college, when I was in Daytona and other towns in Florida kicking around, I ran into Tommy a bit again, and of course I already knew about Scott. And I am gonna have to say here that the idea of Tommy and Scott being great musical players together kind of first spawned in my head, cause I knew Tommy from Winter Park and Scott from FSU and Jacksonville—no one else did—and I put the idea out somewhere to someone, maybe one of Tommy's friends, that he and Scott should get together. I don't know who I told this to, maybe even possibly someone on Scott's end. Maybe even Scott. It is all a haze, but I do know I originally had the idea of those two, and then someone got a party together and they finally met and there you go. Yep, I did have that original "flash" in my head. And then when Tommy brought George and Tom along and Scott brought Bill, and I was asked to also be in the group, but I was hung up on a girl and went to New York chasing her and playing with this other fella. It was a low time of my life, sleeping on the floor of a friend ['s apartment] in NYC and pining away over this girl, while the others were in Macon making their first album.

At some point I realized I was fading up there in New York, and I called Tommy up and wondered if there was still a place for me in the group. He was so cool, and said, "Come on down." When I got there it was like warmth and love to the max—friends, Southern charm and hospitality, music, recording in the studio. Man, I was so much better off immediately! The guys were all great, and so was everything. I got in on the first album, not every tune, but definitely a good portion. And I wrote a song with Billy that got to be the first tune on the album, "Opening." I wrote the first part, he did the second.

So then there we were. I always felt I was the crazier one who wanted to hard rock it, and here we were doing this great new country rock, which I loved and enjoyed. Still, I was a little nuts, and I think that they consciously or unconsciously wrote some of their songs about me. My guess, of course, but the influence in there definitely. In songs like "Everything Here" and "Right on Friend."

Anyway you know the rest of that story, a bit more than two years later the original band broke up, and Scott and Tommy continued on with other players. We were young and had a lot to learn, but I still feel that for the most part the original band had the greatest feel of any players they played with after us. Although they did do some really cool stuff of course 'cause them boys is talented and brought some great players in. Also, they did the Gregg Allman tour and album. They probably did more than that but I can't recall at this point—it's the Reagan syndrome. [Laughs]

Scott Boyer
We went up there and got there late at night and we were taken to this grey house that had cots, similar to army cots, and we all fell asleep on them. At 3 a.m. we were awakened by the police, who wanted to know what we were doing in there. We explained to them that we were musicians for Capricorn Records and had been put up there. Nevertheless, it was a harrowing experience.

After that, the band moved to Cochran, Georgia, and we had this huge farmhouse. There were only three bedrooms but they were fifty feet by fifty feet. There was someone living in the corner of each bedroom. We had the band, which was six people; Tommy, myself, Tom Wynn on drums, George Clark on bass, Pete Kowalke on guitar, and Bill Pillmore on guitar and keyboard. Those are the original six fellows. We lived in Cochran for a while, and the neighbors down there would come out and sit on the hoods of their cars on the weekend and just watch us because we had long hair. These were just good old country folks and they had not ever seen hippies before, and they would just sit out there and watch.

There was a junior college in Cochran, and you couldn't hold hands there—and males were constrained from carrying females' books. That's how conservative it was there. The landlady came over and said that we had to go after about three or four months, and by that time a lot of our friends from Florida had come over—about twenty-five or thirty—and never left. [Laughs] I remember us driving back from New York one night, about a fifteen-hour drive, and we were all exhausted. I went into my room, and there were about three people sleeping in my bed. I woke one of them up and the guy made the mistake of asking me who I was, and I went on a tirade about how that was my bed and he wouldn't live long if he didn't get out. The landlady said that we all had to go, and we went to get some apartments in Macon.

Tom Wynn

We went into the studio and did what we had been rehearsing in our little practice room for months. We played everything live, and my memory is that it didn't take long at all. I don't think the basic tracks could have taken more than a week or so. Some of the vocals were overdubbed here and there, maybe a guitar part or two, but mostly just went down live—all of us playing at the same time— usually two or three takes. Johnny has a way of keeping things drama-free, and I'm sure that helped a lot. In retrospect, seems kind of like a dreamscape—did I mention hippie-dom was just starting? I think we actually captured some of it on tape. Breathe deep.

Pete Kowalke

Ah yes, memories of recording the first album. Nice ones indeed. Once I got to Macon with the guys it was like night and day, so comfortable and so cool. Great weather, great friends, great music, food, the H&H [restaurant]—yeah it was cool. Very friendly and you know, really Southern. I was definitely soaking in it. Going down into the basement into the reverb chambers. We would crawl in and smoke a joint together. They were concrete boxes with tile on the inside for natural reverberation, microphones and such down there hooking up upstairs. So that was a good time. Then we toured and had lots of other good times, oftentimes with the Brothers, and then the "New Jersey chicks," a group of women who were our good, good friends who always met up with us when we were there and hung out and took us places and all.

Tom Wynn

It [the Fillmore] was definitely the real deal. The theater was an old, probably 1870s opera-house theater. I'm not sure, but my guess is the room would hold about 3,000 people. It had very ornate Victorian-style plaster carvings and moldings in the lobby and public spaces. Heavy, high theater curtains, the old recessed footlights at the front of the stage. And it had all been taken over by us—the Hippies laid claim. We created a major commotion, and it was wonderful!

The sound system was enormous and all tube-type amplifiers and folded-horn speakers. The sound was physical; it would shake your core, but it was clean—no distortion, no over-exaggerated bass. The sound was huge and clear. I had heard "loud" before, but this was more than just loud. It was better than the best stereo I had ever heard and a lot bigger.

The first time we played there, Black Sabbath opened for us. They weren't my cup of tea. Still, an interesting bill—Black Sabbath and Cowboy. What a concept! And I think Jethro Tull headlined that night, and that seemed a more reasonable fit.

I think Bill Graham was only present at one of our shows there—my memory is of a very busy guy who was focused on putting on the best show he could. I remember thinking that he was seeing everything. He was at the helm of a pretty unwieldy ship, and he made it work week after week. He and his crew developed a system to make sure hundreds of groups like ours got in and out with a minimum of fuss. My guess is they would do shows for twenty or thirty acts every month; it was an efficient operation. I believe it was sold out every time we were there—that speaks to customer confidence. Even if the audience didn't know every act on the bill, they would come. When a show was booked, the house would fill because the audience knew Bill Graham wouldn't let them down. It was the Fillmore.

Pete Kowalke

The whole thing was just a dream. [Playing the Fillmore] A really fun one. I remember Jethro Tull, how Ian Anderson would run backstage in the middle of his show and just walk around and chat, run back out, wiggle his foot at the spotlight—really fun.

Tom Wynn

We did the second album in Muscle Shoals—Muscle Shoals Sound—home studio of the baddest musicians in the world. And we got to be there. That studio was popping out hits at the time. The rhythm-section players—Barry Beckett, Roger Hawkins, Jimmy Johnson, and David Hood—owned the studio, and they were playing on everybody's records. Paul Simon, the Staple Singers, Aretha Franklin are just a few. Say what you will about musicians, but those were some pretty smart guys.

The studio was usually booked twenty-four hours a day. When we did our record, we had the day shift and Leon Russell had the night shift, so we'd cross paths sometimes at the shift change. That was cool for me because Leon had Jim Keltner playing drums for him on that session. Jim is kind of the gold standard of drumming for me, so to be in proximity to him really impressed me. The guy is so solid and steady and still creative within that steadiness; it's no wonder he's played on so many hits for the last forty years.

I guess the most memorable moment from that session was when Duane came to sit in. He played slide acoustic Dobro on Scott's song, "Please Be with Me." I think the tag work he did at the end of that song ranks right up with some of the best licks in rock 'n' roll history. Those final notes could slice through stone. He had heard the song for the first time thirty minutes earlier, played it through two or three times, and then he did that. His game could not have been any higher.

Scott Boyer

Oh, yeah, we were doing the second Cowboy album, recording *5'll Getcha Ten*, and the studio was being redone at that time in Macon. Johnny wanted to finish the album. He convinced Phil Walden to let us come here to Muscle Shoals Sound Studios. At one point they came in, and we did a few tracks and I was done for the day. The other guys still had parts to do, and our road manager—who is another story entirely—took me back to my room. They were supposed to come and get me for dinner, and they forgot me and left me there. Suffice it to say that I grabbed a pen and started writing. I was doing free association in my head, and then I looked at all the verses and started putting the verses in order the way they rhymed, just sort of a Zen way to write a song. This was just busy work because I got left at the hotel. I was not trying to write the next classic tune. Duane came in the next day and wanted to play. Well, we had three guys on guitars already. He wanted to know if we had something new, and we tossed out a few tunes. Finally I played "Please Be with Me." Duane said, "Yeah, that's the one I want to play on," and I remember that Johnny Sandlin looked at him and said that he felt that it was a beautiful song.

So I was a little puzzled; I didn't think I had written any masterpiece. I didn't really care that much about it, but have over the years grown quite fond of it. [Laughs] It has treated me well, and I am grateful to have written it. The motel over here where I wrote the song is now run by folks from India, and they live in that particular room, so I can't go back over there to try and write another song and see if history repeats itself.

Tommy Talton

That was one of those songs that just came out. ["Please Be with Me"] It came out of Scott. I believe the level of honesty that you live your life in will open up the tube that connects you to the muses and to the other side. Any information that wants to be communicated to those of us who are still here in the physical world comes through that tube if you open it up. It's called creativity, but in actuality it's just copying what someone's telling you through the tube. That is how "Please Be with Me" came through. That's how my song on the first album called "Josephine beyond Compare" happened. I got up at 2:00 a.m. and wrote the entire song immediately and then went back to sleep. When I woke up, first of all I was thinking, "Josephine? Where did that come from?" The writing was not mine, very female, with that feminine look. I never edited that song, never changed a word of it from what I wrote at 2:00 a.m. out of a deep dream. Many people have come up to me and said that song meant a lot to them and that it was real strong. I credit it to the fact that I didn't mess with it.

Pete Kowalke

On the second album, *5'll Getcha Ten*, I had a bit more influence. The songs were a bit more advanced. Still, just great fun. At times I was probably a pain in the butt because sometimes I would think I wanted to do harder rock. But in the end, I really enjoyed and benefitted from the country rock sound we had.

I thought the album was just great, still do. Certainly magical things happened. Like Tommy's lead guitar on my song "What I Want Is You." Like the ending of "Looking for You," where very subtly me, Duane, and Chuck Leavell did some stuff that just blended into one thing—really, really special stuff. And Pete Carr gave me the idea to use a volume pedal and fade notes in and out during the end of "Looking for You." And there were a host of other great spots.

Tom Wynn [on the late George Clark]

George was one of the steadiest, most consistently excellent guys I've ever known. George constantly humbled me. Never with words or judgments, but with his willingness to work hard at whatever he was doing with zero fanfare or arrogance. He was extremely competitive, rarely with others—but unendingly competitive with himself in the things he found important.

Whatever interested George, he did well. He was an excellent musician, fisherman, golfer, and woodworker. He was patient except with those who had no patience, and he wasted no energy debating them. He would simply be somewhere else, doing what he thought was important.

George and I worked together for a long time, both playing music, which continued until the week before he passed—he played great that night, as usual—and in the custom-woodworking shop we shared for a number of years.

Pete Kowalke

Cowboy was just great. I loved it. Living together, playing together, going on the road and having a ball. Creating beautiful albums full of great music. Hanging out with the Allman Brothers and all the other incredible musicians who came through. Living out in the country was great. We had lots of friends—maybe too many [Laughs]—hanging out with us. Walks in the pine forest behind the house in Macon—fantastic; going out in the corn field and smashin' down a spot and then getting nekkid and laying in the sun. The Brothers actually came out one time and jammed in our front yard!

32

The Train to Grinderswitch

Formed in Jacksonville by Allman Brothers Band roadie Joe Dan Petty and a mix of some of Jacksonville's finest players, Grinderswitch recorded a series of smokin' blues-based Southern rock LPs for Capricorn Records. The band toured with all of Capricorn's finest, including the now legendary European jaunt with Marshall Tucker and Bonnie Bramlett.

Dru Lombar

I went to Macon in December of 1972. I had heard that Joe Dan Petty, who was working with the Allman Brothers Band, was going to put together a band. So, I went up there to see about that and I hooked up with him. Larry Howard and Rick Burnett had come up from Aburndale—they were friends of Les Dudek. We ended up living in this house in the country where we lived and rehearsed and wrote and played twenty-four hours a day. We lived off of $25 a week Joe Dan would pay us. He was the only guy working, as a crewman for the Brothers, so he was keeping us in cigarettes, beer, and food money. We did that until Paul Hornsby came along and listened to the tunes, and he got Phil Walden interested. Then we went into the studio and off we went.

Larry Howard

We had a group together in Florida. Of course we all grew up playing the same circuit in Florida. Dickey's band, the Jokers, and Gregg and Duane and the Allman Joys. We all played the pier in Daytona and all the same places in the mid-sixties. We all knew each other and played together at times. When Duane got killed, Dickey started a band called Solo—he actually recruited the keyboard player that we had at the time, Peter Celeste; he is from Sarasota. He and a couple of other guys left Florida to come to Macon and play in Dickey's band.

Then, after the band had been together for a short period of time and all these guys had moved up to Macon to play in the band, then they decided that they would continue the Allman Brothers Band. The record company and the people in the band did not want Dickey to do a solo project at the same time he was trying to keep the band going without Duane. Berry was still alive at this time, but he had brought these guys to Macon, moved these guys up there and he did not want to just break the group up after just having moved them up there. He contacted Les, and Les came to Macon to take Dickey's place in the band Solo, and this was to go on to become its own entity. So, Les took Dickey's place in Dickey's own band. That is how Les ended up playing on *Brothers and Sisters* because he took Dickey's place in Dickey's band. So, Les was here in town with the band that Dickey put together when Duane died. Les went into the studio and played on "Ramblin' Man" and "Jessica." That's where the connection between Dickey and Les came in. During that period of time, Joe Dan Petty was a roadie for the brothers. Joe Dan had been the drummer for Dickey's band in Florida, the Jokers.

Joe Dan was up here in Macon and just working for them and not playing with anyone. He told Les that he would like to start playing again and put together a band. Les said he had just left a band in Florida, and the drummer and guitar player are still down there, and Danny Roberts had taken Les's place. Danny was in a band when we left to come to Macon, and Danny went with a band called Mudcrutch. Me and Danny and Rick [Burnette] were playing with a band when Les left to come up here. We kept the band together, and then Les called and said we should come up and meet with Joe Dan and jam and play with him and see what would happen. Me and Ricky came up and met Joe Dan, and the day we got here we were out at the Brothers' farm and Joe Dan fell off a horse and broke his collarbone. We were up here to play with Joe Dan, but after the accident we couldn't play with him. So, we sat down and had a long talk about what we wanted to accomplish musically and what our musical philosophies were. Then we went back home and packed all our stuff and moved to Macon and started a band called

Grinderswitch without ever having played with Joe Dan. The band was formed on the basis of similar philosophies and ideals. The band Mudcrutch went with Danny and moved to Colorado and tried to get something going and began recording with Shelter. That band is where Tom Petty came from. He was the lead singer in Mudcrutch. They did some recordings and demos but could never get a deal. The band split up, and the next group that formed was Tom Petty and the Heartbreakers. Tom is from Gainesville, and he was in Gainesville at the time, and this whole crew was playing together in different formations in different bands at that time.

I moved into a house in Macon was Dr. John's Band's—Alex Taylor's Band's—that was Chuck Leavell and Lou Mullinax and all those guys were in that house. Lou Mullinax was the drummer that played with Alex Taylor and also Dr. John. But he OD'ed there and that broke the band up and that house was available. So, me, and Joe Dan and Ricky moved into that house. Then I was at Grant's Lounge here in Macon one night and heard a guitar player and singer playing in a band called the King James Version. I liked them, and when it was over with I went to the Carousel, a barbeque place, and here is this guy standing there from the band. I went up to him and told him how much I liked his guitar and singing, and he asked what I was doing. I told him that me and Joe Dan and Ricky were in this band together, and I said that it was too bad he was in that band because he should come and jam with us. He told me that was his final performance with the band. That band went separate ways, and Dru came to our house and played together for about six days, and he went home and got his stuff and came to live at our house.

That is where Grinderswitch was formed, two doors down from where I am living now. When Ricky and I decided to live in Macon and go home and get our stuff and move we had been at the Big House hanging out for a month, and when we went home to Florida Berry got killed. We left town to get our stuff and when we got back Berry was gone.

Paul Hornsby
Grinderswitch were a great bunch of guys. They had been friends of Dickey Betts whom he had persuaded to come up to

Macon. Joe Dan Petty had been an ABB roadie off and on. We had become friends and began to jam a little, so back in 1974 I began to go out to their band house in Perry, Georgia, outside Macon, and kick around a few tunes. They consisted of two guitars, bass, and drums. I would throw my Wurlitzer in the trunk of the car and go out there and jam to all hours.

We finally got around to putting some things down in the studio. The record label [Capricorn] liked what we were doing, so we churned out an LP of some of the finest boogie stuff I had every heard. They could play a "shuffle" better than anyone I knew. After several LPs, the group just never took off. I think of Grinderswitch as the "trench soldiers" of the Capricorn roster. They never got the push a lot of other groups got. But they had heart and never slowed down from touring-gigging. Through all of the hard times a group like them endures, they kept the best sense of humor of all to keep them going. There isn't a day that goes by that I don't think of some hilarious line quoted by their bassist, the late Joe Dan Petty.

Dru Lombar

When you're twenty-one years old and you're out there playing for ten or twenty thousand people a night, you know, you're just loving it, man. And people loving it—getting off on what you do—it was just a good, high-energy, positive situation. It was work, I mean. Like when we toured with the Brothers, they might have a day in between each gig. We'd spend that day driving. Say they were in Greensboro one night, and the next night they might be in New York or Atlanta. They'd get on their plane, they had a jet they chartered, and they'd pop right up. Us, we'd get in the van and hit the road, but we didn't care, you know? We spent most of our time on the road. When we weren't playing with the Brothers, we were playing with Skynyrd or the Tuckers or Charlie. We did a lot of dates with Charlie Daniels and Marshall Tucker—I mean *a lot* of dates. And we did the stuff with Wet Willie and the clubs, of course, where we'd get to headline our own rooms.

Larry Howard

The biggest high point of that band was the fact that all the members of the band were together for about eight years, with me in the band, and after I left they did a couple of albums. During that period of time, Gregg would kid us about never coming home. We worked, realistically, all the time. We would go on the road with the Allman Brothers, and then we toured for several years with Charlie Daniels and Marshall Tucker Band. We would go out for forty or forty-five days at a time and come home for three or four days and then do it again. Then we booked clubs and everything we could between that.

This is the only band I was ever in where we literally worked every night we possibly could. Through all of that the four original members—and then later on Steve—I think the high point of that band to me was the fact that it was really a family. We went through unbelievable good times and bad times, and everyone to this day is very respectful of each other. We are brothers and more in the real sense than blood brothers. We had incredible highs and lows together. Ricky and I started playing in a jazz, Dixieland band together when we were about thirteen years old. We had been playing music since 1963.

I had never played in a permanent fixed band with anyone but Ricky. This was since the age of thirteen years. But, the first band I played guitar in, Ricky was the drummer, and up until 1980 he was the only drummer I had ever played with. Joe Dan was an incredible person, he and I were very much alike and very strong personalities. We butted heads over the years and were very protective of the other guys in the band over the years. You couldn't call this a love/hate relationship—it was a love relationship—just like a marriage. We fought sometimes, and everyone in the band did. I did not know any of the Southern bands that did not fight. Joe Dan and I did not ever get physical, but Dru and I did a couple of times. There were nights when we went onstage and literally fought with our guitars, literally in a battle with the guitars and then in to the dressing room continue it there. The next morning we would hit the road again and I think the band—more so than any of the other bands—we were close; we were able to rebound from whatever our problems or differences were then. I can cite you personal things that we went through in the band that were incredible as far as some of the relationships with other people, in particular in the area of females, we went through some incredible changes, but the next morning we were on the road and everyone was smiling.

Dru Lombar

Charlotte Speedway was great—the August Jam. We played with the Brothers and Emerson, Lake and Palmer, in front of 300,000 people. I've never seen so many people in one place at the same time. We flew in on a helicopter and said, "My God, look at this!" It looked like a sea of people. It was an incredible experience. And the Brothers shows, especially Madison Square Garden and Long Island, they were just really great shows. And doing Central Park with the Tuckers. That was real cool, man. Right in the middle of New York City, all these guys in cowboy hats. I loved it. And when we went over to Europe with the Tuckers, and we took Bonnie Bramlett with us. We were her band as well as being Grinderswitch. That was real cool because she is the queen of soul, man. I mean, she is probably the very best white woman soul singer on earth. It was great! It was crazy, you know? We were over in Europe, all these cowboys drinking that German beer in the beer garden and listening to the oompah band, you know, and Bonnie gets up there and starts jamming with this polka band. We were just whacked, man. It was fun.

Larry Howard

Well, I had such a great time I hardly remember it. [Laughs] It was one of those tours. When we got into London on the first day we had been playing at the Starlight Amphitheatre right before. Actually, we had been on that tour that culminated at the end of Europe. Grinderswitch had been on the road for about 120 days straight. We had done a whole tour of the U.S. starting in the northeast, across the U.S. and all the way down through California and Texas and through the Midwest, back down into Louisiana and Alabama, and that whole area and then into Macon for three days of rehearsal with Bonnie and straight to Europe for one month. I do not think I had a day off for

120 days. When we got over there we had been at the Starlight, and some people we had known from a motorcycle group came to the Starlight to see me and Toy [Caldwell] and said, "When you get to London, go to the Hard Rock Cafe; someone will meet you and be there to go with you throughout Europe." When we got there Toy and I got a taxi and went to the Hard Rock cafe and had no idea who would meet us. Toy and I were in our usual form—which was pretty shaky—and we got this taxi and the driver took off like a New York taxi driver, and Toy started yelling and got down in the floorboard of the taxi. [Laughs] Toy was screaming at the guy and hollering at me wanting out of the taxi. We went to the Hard Rock Cafe and went into the bathroom, and this guy came in and said he was supposed to meet us. Toy and I both did not know how he knew we were from America, but we were standing there with cowboy boots and hats on, and no one else looked like that. [Laughs] We were so naive we didn't stop to consider we looked so different from everyone else. I can tell you for sure that I know all these people, and no one is going to tell the true story of what happened between 1971 and 1980. It will never be told. No one will ever tell it.

Red Dog Campbell
Oh man. That's a tough one [the death of Joe Dan]. Me and Joe Dan were truly the odd couple. It was like people used to say, they're just like a married couple, leave 'em alone. Joe Dan would want the room cold, I'd want the room hot. He'd want to watch Discovery, and I'd want to watch the news. We had all of those things like that back and forth, but yet we had a big bond between us. We were roommates for twenty-eight years, so obviously we had something there. He was just a great person, though. Joe Dan was a little more subdued than I am. He was a little slower; I'm a little more hyper. We were just a great match. One kept the other in check. Probably more so Joe Dan keeping me in check. [Laughs]

33

Macon Magic

Macon, Georgia, was the undeniable hub of the Southern rock universe. In the U.S., Don Kirshner presented a special episode of Rock Concert *called "Saturday Night in Macon, Georgia," featuring the Allman Brothers Band, the Marshall Tucker Band, Wet Willie, and Martin Mull. In England, the Old Grey Whistle Test sent their crew to Georgia to film* Macon Whoopie, *an excellent documentary featuring live footage of Marshall Tucker, Wet Willie, Dickey Betts, Bonnie Bramlett, Stillwater, and more. Macon was world famous.*

Johnny Sandlin
Every day you never knew what would happen, and it was usually something wonderful. It seemed like as the days passed, more and more people were getting interested in the music and it was getting more recognition. One of my favorite things was when Jeff Beck came in there and he was looking to put a band together, and I think that was where he hooked up with Jimmy Hall. Jimmy ended up on some of Jeff's records. I was down there to record the rehearsals for several days. We would go see bands at night. When the Brothers were home, they would be at Grant's Lounge or sitting in somewhere, or there would be a bunch of us going out to jam. Boz Scaggs lived there for a while. I would go out and jam at clubs. There was always something happening and we could get into all kinds of trouble.

Eddie Stone
During the mid-seventies, there was a club in Macon called Uncle Sam's that Phil Walden owned. They had a lot of big bands in there, but it was also a playground for Capricorn artists. We were the

house band out there. [Roundhouse, the band that would later become Doc Holliday] Stillwater was the house band, and we were the house band. We rotated out. That's one thing that made the music scene in Macon so hard to do. They could go out to Uncle Sam's and pay a dollar or two cover charge, and see $300,000 worth of entertainment on stage. They'd all come out to have their beverage of choice and party. The equipment was there. I called it the Wet Tucker Brothers. You'd see Jimmy Hall jamming with Toy and Tommy Caldwell. Or Jaimoe or Gregg or whoever. One night on my B-3, there was Gregg Allman on one manual and Bobby Whitlock on the next manual. And Toy and Dickey and Martin Mull up there playing. My brother was Bobby Whitlock's road manager during the Capricorn years. So I got to go in and witness some of the sessions. Bobby had great people playing with him. Dru Lombar from Grinderswitch was a man who influenced me. They were so good. They took us out on the road with them. Great guys, Joe Dan, Dru, Larry Howard, Ricky [Burnette], Steven Miller—they showed us how to be something better than a bar cover band. I'd go down to the studio, and the Brothers would be finishing at night and Bobby would be starting in the daytime. Or Skynyrd was doing *Gimme Back My Bullets*, and Bobby Whitlock was recording during the daytime. I saw some incredible things happen in this city. We took it for granted back then. Everybody played on everybody else's album. If you'll notice, my new CD was done that way. It was done in that building, so the vibe was there. I tried hard to capture the Macon thing on my CD. Everybody I called up was so gracious, and they all agreed to play. Jimmy Hall wanted to play, but we had scheduling problems. Same with Larry Howard.

Billy Bob Thornton

I was a huge Marshall Tucker fan. I never knew those guys— that's the only bunch I never really knew. But I was a big Southern rock fan and such a fan of Capricorn Records that I could mention people that were on the label that nobody had ever heard of. I was obviously a Wet Willie fan, but also a huge Grinderswitch fan.

Paul Hornsby

Within the first year, the Allman Brothers Band had sort of taken off. The Capricorn record label was established. The move was made toward signing more rock and roll acts. Livingston Taylor had his first success, recording in the Capricorn studio with the rhythm section. We also began seeing more self-contained groups coming into the studio who didn't need studio musicians on their recordings. Coming to work every day in the studio was a natural progression to experiment with all the recording gear. I guess what started my producing career was when Phil asked me to produce some sides on a local Macon group called Boogie Chillun.

Well, for me this was really an experimental project. I could see the handwriting on the wall as far as a limited future as strictly a studio musician. We recorded this group for nearly a year, with the group breaking up and reforming probably five times during that project. Near the end of it, I think we were down to maybe one or two members of the original group. I then called some of my old buddies I had played with in Tuscaloosa.

We had a unique situation here in reverse. Usually, you form a group, play for a while, then cut some demos, then if you are lucky, get signed to a label. Here we had already started the record with no group to finish it off. So, I convinced Chuck Leavell, Lou Mullinax, and Court Pickett to move over and step into a ready-made record deal. We did get to finish the project, though piece-meal, with some pretty good stuff thrown in by these new members. Capricorn didn't release it but sold the rights to the short-lived Ampex record label. It came out with the group renamed Sundown.

That was my first attempt at producing, although I had been doing studio session work for a number of years. A pretty good experiment really. The next project had better results. Not that it was a hit, but that it got good reviews and was noticed. That was a group from Texas called Eric Quincy Tate. They were probably the best "bar band" I ever heard. They played a lot in Macon at a place called Grant's Lounge. There was a tremendous following here for the group as well as in Atlanta, where they relocated. The LP was titled *Drinking Man's Friend.*

David Cantonwine

In 1967, I was having the time of my life; it was like—wow! Joe Rogers and I played together in a band named the American Way. We were still in high school at that time. Dyke McCarty, our drummer, had this brother Allen who was the host of an *American Bandstand*-type TV dance show on Saturday mornings called *Teen Time*. We were on TV every other week. Our manager owned the biggest rock venue in town, the Stardust Rollercade, so we played there every other week. I was seventeen and in high school. The band, the girls, sex in the parking lot during lunch—we were local rock stars. I really can't remember why our band broke up. But Joe and I parted after that and played with other bands. Somehow I wound up in Austin, Texas, jamming with all those acid freaks—remember, this was still '67. Anyway, I got a record deal with International Artists out of Houston—more acid. I think that was on a Friday. I was suppose to start recording an album on Monday, so I decided to go down to see my parents that weekend who lived in Corpus Christi. Long story short, while I was there I went out to a club called the Muddy Turtle, and that's where the birth of Eric Quincy Tate took place.

Donnie McCormick was a true friend and mentor. He taught me how to be a real musician. I guess I can say that about all the guys in the band. We spent a lot of time together, touring and playing club dates. Donnie was a one of a kind. He didn't act like, sing like, or talk like anyone else. And he was great at making you watch him while he was singing or playing the drums. Hell, I used to have a blast watching Donnie perform—and I was in the band! Best seat in the house.

Wayne "Bear" Sauls was another true friend who would do anything for you. We were playing down at Grant's Lounge one weekend, I think it was Saturday. We all got up and wandered around Macon and found this fresh meat market, and Bear said, "I bet they got pigs feet in there." So we go in and Bear told the lady that he wanted four pigs' feet. She said, "Honey, these all for you?" Bear said, "Yeah." She says, "Okay, I'll give you four pigs' feet. You gonna eat them all at one time?" Bear said, "Just four pigs' feet please, %#$*&!!" The lady hollered out, "Junior! Give the man sixteen of them pig feet!" I guess you had to be there but we all laughed our asses off. But yeah, Bear was a friend and damn good guitar player— sorry, *great* guitar player.

Jimmy Nalls

When I first met Chuck [Leavell], he was seventeen years old and he was already Alex's [Alex Taylor's] band leader. He was so focused for such a young man. See, I left Virginia and moved to New York City and started getting session work when I was nineteen. I was real lucky. And through Peter, Paul and Mary—I met Paul Stookey up there and played on his first solo album—and he knew Tommy Talton from Cowboy. I heard that Alex was looking for a guitar player because Joe Rudd was quitting, so that's how I got the gig and met all those guys. When I met them, they were rehearsing up on Martha's Vineyard 'cause that's where Alex and all the Taylors lived. But when I met Chuck, he was such a mature, focused, schooled, street-wise player at such a young age, it was incredible. We became fast friends very quickly. In fact, we became roommates. He was a vegetarian, and he talked me into being a vegetarian. They used to call us "the Omelet Brothers" because that's all we'd order. Cheese omelets. So anyway, Chuck has just grown into one of the most sought after, respected players in the business. You can hear his influence everywhere. All the playing he did with the Allmans, and of course with Sea Level. He's just a phenomenal player. And what a human being. He's got a heart as big as Georgia. He's a genuinely nice guy. Like we talked about earlier, meeting people that you admire, I think he's one of the ones who doesn't disappoint somebody when they meet him, if they like his playing and have been following his career. When he speaks to you, he is genuinely interested in what you have to say. He's been a real friend through this Parkinson's thing. Somebody that I could talk to. Shoot man, I just can't say enough good things about him.

Chuck Leavell

We had some great shows playing theaters with Jan Hammer being the opening act, and then he would sit in with us. Sea Level was a great band. We had a hard time with the record company and the retail stores, because we were so hard to tag. We did instrumentals, but we sang, and we played rock 'n' roll, but we played R&B, and we had tinges of jazz. I felt for the label and the stores, because they couldn't figure out where to put us—rock? instrumental? jazz? But we didn't really care. We just played and had fun. As you know, the personnel changed a good bit. Jaimoe left, and we had George Weaver on drums for a while. Jaimoe had suggested him to us. He played in Otis Redding's band for a while, then later Joe English. We added Randall Bramblett and Davis Causey to the lineup. And very late in the game we had a guy named Paul Brodeur on bass...great player, but he died of cancer—a tragic thing. Also had Matt Greeley playing percussion and singing for a couple of years, who also died of cancer, but much later, years after the band had broken up. I loved playing with Sea Level. We had wonderful times in the studio and on the road. Stewart Levine [producer on three of the records] is still a very good friend, and I learned a lot from him during those years. I guess the theaters were the most fun for me to play with that band. It just seemed to work better than clubs or big dates. I somehow think that Sea Level never really reached it's potential, and that's a shame. But I don't like looking back over my shoulder, and really all I can say is that I'm grateful for the experience, and think I'm a better musician for it.

Elvin Bishop

I got in on Capricorn because of Duane [Allman] and Dickey [Betts.] I had met those guys, and we just fell right together and made friends. I went to one of their gigs at the old Fillmore in San Francisco or Winterland, and after the show there was a party. And they grabbed Phil Walden, the president of Capricorn and made him come in a room and listen to some of my songs. He just signed me up the next day. But it was all because of Dickey and Duane.

Macon was still like a part of the old South at the time. It hadn't been modernized the least damn bit. There were guys walkin' around with pistols strapped on their sides. You'd go to the barbeque stand and the guy in front of you would have a big ol' pistol strapped on. That cut out any urge you might have to say something smart. Once in a while they would take me out to one of these places way back out in the woods, and they would have picnic tables and sawdust on the floor and get some of that corn liquor. [Laughs] Capricorn Records was the only thing happening in town that was different from anything in a thousand other towns around the South at the time.

Randall Bramblett

The Gregg Allman tour was the first time I ever went on a national, big tour. Before that I was playing with Cowboy and living out at Idlewild with them and doing sessions in Macon at Capricorn Studios. I think it was a blossoming of Southern music going on at that time. It was a real exciting chance for me to go out with a big tour and play some music that was really good too with Gregg. I had been recording and playing some before that in Atlanta and in Athens, but going to Macon I think really helped me get started in the music business. There was just so much going on then. Capricorn was doing real well and Gregg's tours were doing real well. We had an orchestra and everything; it was just a real exciting time.

Jimmy Nalls

Gosh, it was quite a ride. [Sea Level] We had a great band. I think we cut a lot of new ground. I think maybe the band was a little ahead of its time. A lot of it is, unfortunately, a blur. We just sort of jumped on the old horse and rode it 'til it stopped. That again was sort of like going to college for me. It was just a great situation to get involved in. When all that happened with Alex Taylor and the band broke up, I was living back home in Virginia, but I kept an apartment in Macon because I was getting a lot of session work down there. The Allman Brothers were playing in Largo, Maryland. Chuck called and told me they were gonna be in town and did I want to go. I said shoot yeah! He said, "I'll go you one better. Jaimoe and Lamar and myself and possibly Butch will be doing a sound check that afternoon, and Gregg and Dickey won't be there. So you can do the sound check and plug into Dickey's rig." So, I went over and met 'em. So it was Butch, Jaimoe, Lamar, Chuck, and myself playing to an empty stadium for about three hours. When it was over, we kind of looked at each other and said, "Damn, I think we've got something here!" At that time, things were rocky between the three of them and the rest of the band

[Allman Brothers]. So they made a move about six months later, in June of '76. They quit the band. Chuck called and said, "Hey man, we've quit the band and we're going to start another group called Sea Level. Do you want to be involved?" It all went back to the sound check we did that day. I said, sure, I'd love to. So that's how the first Sea Level album got started. That was before Randall and Davis, it was just the four of us. There was a fire on that first album. Not taking anything away from the other albums, because as a body of work I think they all hold up. But I think my favorite one was the first one. We had to overplay to fill up a lot of spaces because it was just a four-piece band. We just played it for everything it was worth.

Tommy Talton (on Kitty Wells's Capricorn album)

I am the one that brought "Forever Young" to Johnny [Sandlin], and to the husband/manager Kitty Wells had, and the way that happened Scott and I had been in Atlanta up from Macon, to do a photographic session for the Boyer/Talton album. The guy who was doing the cover was from New York, and I believe his name was Richard Mantrell. Richard and I were talking in between shoots about album covers. I told him that my favorite cover was by Thelonius Monk and called *Underground*. I asked him if he had ever seen it, and he told me he had done that cover and had won a Grammy for it. [Laughs] So anyway, he had in his possession at the time *Planet Waves*, Bob Dylan's album, before it was released. I am not sure where he got it, or if he was doing some work for Dylan as well, but he gave me that album. I heard "Forever Young" and took it back to the studio. We were doing Kitty Wells in two days, and I showed it to Johnny. We did "Forever Young" with Kitty Wells. It was actually released as a single maybe two days later after we recorded it. What a wonderful, nice, beautiful woman she was and at that time she had done forty-three country albums. She was the queen of country music.

Randall Bramblett

Chuck [Leavell] and Jimmy [Nalls] and Lamar [Williams] and Jaimoe had already formed Sea Level and had done a record as the jazz side of the Allman Brothers. Chuck and my band had been playing some dates together, and for their second album I think Chuck wanted me and Davis [Causey] to come in and help with the writing and the singing. Just expand the group a little bit. That's when I joined, right after my first solo record.

We rehearsed over in Chuck's basement in Macon. It was a really exciting time. We played the Opera House in Macon—I think that was one of our first gigs. It was really fresh and new and exciting, the combination of jazz and funk and rock, or whatever we were doing, it was pretty unique. The first record we made together, *Cats on the Coast*, is a really good record. It had "That's Your Secret" on it, which I think was Sea Level's most successful song—that and "Shake a Leg," I guess. It was a lot of fun at first, but then some of us, like me, were sidetracked with other issues, like partying too much and not writing enough and squabbling inside the organization. It was just a time when there was too much indulgence going on, and we couldn't sustain what we were doing. But we made some more records, and there were some good ones. *On the Edge* was a good one. But it got less and less successful. Capricorn folded and we—I'll speak for myself—I was doing too much of everything. But it was great playing with Chuck. And Jimmy Nalls—all of them.

Elvin Bishop

Guys would get together and jam and not worry so much about being politically correct or what some record company executive thought or worry so much about the show that they didn't want to have anybody on that hadn't rehearsed the tune. They didn't used to think about that. They'd say, oh, there's my buddy, come on up here and play.

Pete Kowalke

One time way back then, I took Gregg Allman home to my Winter Park family home and took him water skiing on my local lake. I barefoot skied for him, and he was way impressed. [Laughs] Then sometime later, don't remember how much later, I went to an Allman's concert. I think it was after a few years, after the original Cowboy had broken up. Anyway, here comes Gregg out of his dressing room with a great looking girl on his arm, looking rather high. [Laughs] I go up to him and say, "Hey Gregg, how you doing man?" He still has a glazed look. "Hey man, it's Pete from Cowboy, remember me?" He turns and looks at me, and in a voice similar to W. C. Fields, says, "Sure do, best damn water skier in the world." [Laughs] And then I must have had a funny look on my face too, as he didn't remember me in Cowboy, just the water skiing! [Laughs] Funny stuff....

Part 6

The Second Wave

34

This Country's Rockin'

With the overwhelming success of the Allmans, the Tuckers, and Skynyrd, a whole series of new bands seemed to spring from the fertile soil of the deep South. While many of these bands had been around for a while, the newfound popularity of Southern rock propelled them into the spotlight. Bands like Doc Holliday and the Winters Brothers Band started shaking things up from Florida to Tennessee.

Dennis Winters

We [the Winters Brothers Band] lived in a smokehouse converted into a bunk room while raising cattle for Marty Robbins on his farm near Franklin, Tennessee. You might say we were sharecroppers. That's where the initial Winters Brothers Band came to be. We also wrote songs for Marty Robbins.

Actually, we have recorded four albums and one with our father, Don Winters. *The Winters Brothers Band* was our first, on ATCO/Atlantic Records; *Coast to Coast*, also on Atlantic; *Keep On Running*, on Star Track Records; and the latest release on SouthStar Records, *Southern Rockers*. The release that featured our father is called *Yodeling King* on Star Track Records.

When we recorded the first two albums at Capricorn Studios in Macon, Georgia, there was always somebody dropping by. There was a rehearsal room in the front, so we were always running into someone from the Allman Brothers, Charlie Daniels, or Marshall Tucker, which was very exciting. One day while in session, we were able to take a day off to go out to visit Dickey Betts at the Allman Brothers Farm near High Falls, Georgia. For Thanksgiving, we took our families to the home of Paul Hornsby for dinner. That was a special treat for all of us.

The worst show we ever had was wonderful because we had the opportunities to open for some of our greatest heroes. When we toured with Skynyrd, Ronnie would come back to the dressing room before the show each night with a bottle of Jack Daniels and a bottle of champagne. He'd always say "A little something for the brothers."

On occasion, he would ask us to come out to jam with them. The Marshall Tucker Band would do the same, but the most memorable was a show at Boston Garden. Toy came out and played steel with us. Jerry played sax, and then they had us come out on their last song. I believe it was "Will the Circle Be Unbroken," and we sang with Doug. Charlie, Taz, and Tommy Crain would jam with us regularly. Once, in New York City, Charlie bought us some amps for our dressing room.

Dickey Betts would also show up at our pre-jam parties [the annual pre-jam jam at the Winters Family Farm the day before Volunteer Jam] to jam with us in Nashville. Memories like these you never forget! There are plenty of stories, maybe one day....

Bruce Brookshire (Doc Holliday)

In the summer of 1971, my brother Bob and I formed a blues band called Roundhouse. My brother plays guitar, piano, and harmonica. Eight years later, Roundhouse, with different members (my brother had gone on to play with Johnny Taylor, Clarence Carter, ZZ Hill, Solomon Burke, and other R&B artists) began to get hot and attracted some attention from Molly Hatchet manager Pat Armstrong. Later on we found the guys that managed a band called Nantucket, Bill Cain and Jet Matthews. We liked them and they managed to get us a record deal with A&M in 1980, and we became Doc Holliday.

We went in the studio for our first LP *Doc Holliday* with Tom Allom, the guy who produced Judas Priest and Pat Travers, which was how we knew him. He did a fabulous job of making us sound like a world-class band. He's a class act all the way.

Our second album, *Rides Again*, was produced by David Anderle, who worked at A&M and was a fan of the band. He later became head of the label. He was a very laid back and supportive producer. Not a Tom Allom, David was more of a "vibes" man. He just sort of sat there and bobbed his head along to the music, and he would stop us every now and then and suggest something. Tom gets in there with both hands and works a band. So, different styles but great results either way. *Rides Again* was pretty successful worldwide and helped to get us a fair amount of European attention.

Our third album was recorded in Munich, Germany, and produced by Mack, a guy who produced ELO, Queen, Billy Squier, lots of superstar bands. Mack scared us and intimidated us a little, but we were pretty strung out on drugs, so he did what he could. We intentionally tried to combine techno music with Southern rock and we failed miserably. That album went cardboard—not gold or platinum. We lost our record deal, our house and tour bus, our equipment, everything. Techno was raging in 1983, and a drugged-out Southern band was not big business. We broke up for about a year and a half and got Doc Holliday back together for another LP in 1986, *Danger Zone*. We were trying to remember how to play rock and roll with that one. In 1988 we recorded *Song for the Outlaw* for a Paris-based label and toured Europe.

In the nineties we found a manager who was our partner and friend, Dave Hulme, a British guy, and we did an album for a German label called *Son of the Morning Star*. We were beginning to remember how to play rock and roll by that time. Next came album number seven, *Legacy*, which was a good representation of the band's live sound. It took us that many years to get back on track since the crash of 1983. That's Doc history in a big 'ol nutshell....

Eddie Stone

We started in Warner Robins, which is right below Macon. I think Bruce was thirteen or fourteen when I met him. I was a couple of years older. He was different, and I liked that. He wasn't playing the same stuff everybody else was. We kind of clicked. We didn't actually form the band until after I was getting out of the army. That was around 1973. I was, in fact, the last person drafted in the state of Georgia. I came home on leave about a year before I was to get out of the service, and Bruce and I started playing. I was dying to play. We opened for Wet Willie down in Albany, Georgia. The band was called Roundhouse at the time.

We signed with A&M Records in 1979. Somebody up in Canada had the name Roundhouse trademarked. At the time, I was heavily into this Time-Life book series on the Old West. I read that the original Doc Holliday was from the state of Georgia. I thought, how cool would that be? I brought it up to the rest of the guys in the band, because we had to change our name. We had three names. I remember two of them, Doc Holliday and Rebel Gray. We had some notoriety in our hometown, with a demo tape that was number two or three on their rotation. So after we signed with A&M, we had a radio interview and let the listeners vote for our name. Doc Holliday won out overwhelmingly.

Bruce Brookshire

The original band made three LPs. When the third album tanked, we imploded. It took a while to recover from that. John, Eddie and I made *Danger Zone* with drummer Jamie Deckard in 1986. Soon after I had a reunion with Daniel Bud Ford—we played together as kids—and we did *Song for the Outlaw* together in early 1988. The lineup was in transition at the time. We joined with Johnny Vaughan, Billy Yates, and the Doc-ettes, June and Karen, for a short time.

The rhythm section became stable later in '88 with the addition of Danny "Cadillac" Lastinger. John and I were the two original members on the next two CDs, *Son of the Morning Star* and *Legacy*, which is one of my all time favorite Doc CDs. Eddie came back for the next two, *A Better Road* and *Good Time Music*. Bud, Cadillac, and I have been together solidly since late 1988. The rhythm section has been together much longer and has done more albums than the original lineup.

I still have a great relationship with Ric Skelton and Herman Nixon from the original band. It has been a real blessing to have these guys in my life. Ric is a monster player, a "Tennessee Natural." I am shocked that no one has picked up any of his bands. I think he cares more about the music than the business, so his head is on straight. I wish we lived closer. I miss him a lot. Herman is an excellent drummer and teaches drums here in middle Georgia. He cares more about having a stable home life than going on the road, I think. Eddie has an ongoing solo career, with one CD out and another in the process. He and John have considerable writing, playing, and vocal talents that don't get enough expression in the Doc format, so it is good for them to stretch out and have fun.

Eddie Stone

We were Roundhouse, from the summer of '71—like I said, I wasn't in the band for two years—we became Doc Holliday in '79, and our first album came out in 1980. Somebody said Southern rock was dead in the early eighties. We went to Germany to do our third album, *Modern Medicine*. A lot of pure Doc fans don't care for that record. It had a lot of new sounds on it. It was produced by Mac, the guy who produced Queen and Billy Squier. We actually had a vision at the time of taking Southern rock to this place. Nobody wanted to buy it until about three years later when ZZ Top did the same thing. They were much cooler than we were. [Laughs] Billy is the epitome of cool. When Rev. Billy said it was cool to do that, it was. Not to say that they were jumping on something we had done. They just had the same idea. The world just wasn't ready for a bunch of redneck Southern rockers to do what we did. I still think the record is a good record. We did that, and then in about '85, I think, Bruce can help us on this, we decided we were going to do something different. Then in about '87, we missed it, and reformed. At one time we had three guitar players and two keyboard players. The guy that plays keyboards in my band, Tony Cooper, was playing in Doc Holliday for a while. We had a different drummer. At one time, Ric Skelton, who was an original member of Doc, rejoined the band. We did the album *Danger Zone*. I left the band again for a while. Then in '88, Europe came knockin.' They said, "Southern rock didn't die over here. We didn't know that." A&M didn't let us know about that. We had a bunch of airplay, a bunch of sales, and a bunch of fans over there. We reformed again and started going to Europe, opening for a Blackfoot and hordes of other bands, Faith No More, different bands. We saw that we had a huge following over there. Then in 1990 I left the band again. The Gulf War was coming, and it was harder get over there and tour. It was dangerous. You know Cinderella was supposed to be on the Pan Am jet that went down. That's scary. I bailed out. They went to Europe a few more times without me; then we started doing the reunions with the original guys and the new guys. I started writing songs. I went to a diaper factory. That'll humble you. So I started writing to cope with the factory job. I'll always be indebted to them for that; they spurred something in me. So I've got kind of the best of both worlds. I've got my own band, which contains some great players, and the Doc reunions.

Bruce Brookshire

It peaked in the eighties the first time at Madison Square Garden with Black Sabbath. Ronnie James Dio is a gentleman and a good friend. He got us there. Lots of gigs were good, dates with April Wine, Loverboy, Charlie Daniels, Pat Travers. I'll tell you, though, some of the best shows we ever did were as a package with Nantucket, our good friends and brothers from North Carolina. That is and was a great band. It peaked again in the nineties with festival shows in England, Scandinavia, and Germany. We played the Marquee in London in the nineties a few times; that was a kick. The way we look at it, it's always peaking. We are just fortunate to have been at it for so long and made good friends and stayed good friends.

Don Barnes (38 Special)

There was an old truck called Big Blue that kept falling apart. It kept eating up all of our profits. I remember coming home with $30 after fixing this truck. Donnie and I would ride around and try to find an obscure place to rehearse. We would find these places for fifty bucks a month to rehearse; of course, we had day jobs then. The guy could not figure out why we wanted to rent this place. There was manure, and we had to shovel it out of there and then get some pallets to stand on for a floor. We had the place fortified and had it vaulted up with 2 x 4s and a big motorcycle chain that went through the hole in the door to lock it with this old rusty lock. Then we had to climb in a window to get in and out. One night we were rehearsing and heard someone banging on the door and when we looked, there were twelve constables banging on the door to get in. We were yelling and telling them we couldn't open the door and one of them yelled that he had a .38 Special to use on the door if we wouldn't let him in. So when we had our first show, we had not thought of a name, so we decided to use that name.

35

Blackfoot

Blackfoot's roots go way back to 1969 in Jacksonville, although they didn't record until 1975. Success would come in 1979 with the release of the Strikes album, yielding both "Train, Train" and "Highway Song," and making them a powerful contender in Southern rock's "second wave."

Jakson Spires

I was in a band in 1969 called Tangerine, and Charlie [Hargrett], Rickey [Medlocke], and Greg [T. Walker], were in a band called Fresh Garbage. We did a lot of stuff together as a combo. When the Allmans first got together, they only had one drum set so they used mine for the double drummer thing. We had a good thing going there, and we had all grown up together since we were five or six years old. Me, Greg and Rickey. I had met Charlie at age fifteen. We had played around together, and we felt that because we got along so well that it could transform into music that same way. It did, and we just kind of took it from there. The two bands merged, and the keyboard player for my band, Tangerine, stayed with us for about one year and then he went on to do other stuff. We called the band Hammer. Then we heard about another band doing an album out on the west coast (this was September 1969), so we changed our name to Free. About one week later we heard about the band [Free] with Paul Rodgers. We knew we had some Indian heritage so we came up with the name Blackfoot. We wanted a strong sounding name. Blackfoot is actually the Blackfeet Indians and Blackfoot is the plural of that, it's reverse English. They were a nomadic tribe that moved seasonally and hunted, and we were very nomadic, moving every night. We played in the South and at the time the Southern thing was real big. Laid back, country blues, or the real jazz-influenced blues of the Allman

Brothers, and then there was Marshall Tucker, Charlie Daniels, and Wet Willie and Skynyrd. Even though we liked all that stuff, we didn't play it. We were more influenced by the heavier stuff, like Deep Purple, Free, the Who, and the Move and stuff like that. So we headed that way. There were not that many places for us to play in the South because we were too heavy for what was going on. So we moved up to New York and did it up there for a while and then moved to New Jersey for a bit. After a few years, Rickey had went with Skynyrd to play drums, and then Greg joined a little later on bass, and the whole thing was maybe a year apart. We re-formed and started the band up again, actually with a different bass player for around a year, in the early seventies—guy out of North Carolina, Lenny Sandler. Greg was working with another band in upstate New York, and I called and asked him if he was doing anything. I went up and got him back, and we stayed together like that for a while. Right up until Charlie left. Then we got Ken Hensley [Uriah Heep], then we got Bobby Barth from Axe right up until 1985. The corporation broke up in 1986. It was a great time and great band, and we did stuff that you would not even believe or comprehend. We still can't talk about a lot of it. [Laughs]

Charlie Hargrett

I first started hanging out with Jakson and his keyboardist, DeWitt Gibbs in 1967. A couple of years later I was jamming at the old downtown Comic Book Club a lot with Jakson's band, Tangerine, the One Percent, and others. Another keyboardist friend of mine, Ron Sciabarasi, told me about two guys who were looking for players. Ron took me over to the bass player's house, and it was Greg Walker, with Rickey playing drums. We set up in Greg's bedroom and played a few songs. They told me later that what got me the job was when we played Cream's "Badge," I nailed the solo perfectly—thank you very much!

We called our new band Fresh Garbage [after a Spirit album title] and started gigging at the Comic Book a lot, playing a bunch of Spirit, Zombies, Doors, stuff like that. After a few months, our keyboard player Ron, who had a day job, started leaving gigs early, leaving the three of us to finish the night. At about the same time,

Jakson's guitar player left Tangerine. We let Ron go and hooked up with Jak and DeWitt. This first lineup was Jakson on drums, Greg on bass, DeWitt on Hammond B-3 and electric piano, Ricky out front singing and playing congas, and myself on guitar.

Rickey Medlocke

Well, my dad Shorty was basically a Mississippi Delta blues country player. He was on a television show called the *Toby Dowdy Show*, and it originated right out of Jacksonville out of a radio station called WJXT and used to be called WMBR. It had a lot of different guests on there. What happened was that, as a kid I learned how to pluck around on a banjo when I was like three, and my dad got me a miniature and strung it up. I was actually a left-hander so, he strung the banjo up for me and taught me some stuff on it, and we would go on the TV show and it was kind of a silly novelty thing. From age three to eight years old I stayed on that show with him. He also did some stints with Roy Acuff's band touring at one time. Then, he played with Toby and his bands throughout the southeast. Me and my mom used to go on the road with him a little bit and I hung around musicians, basically, really all my life. At the age of five I got interested in playing guitar and started learning how to play the guitar, and a couple of guys in his band would play guitar and started teaching me. Actually, my dad taught me three chords, G, C, and D. Watching other players and plunking around on the guitar and stuff, I started playing guitar at that time, and I played and kept playing. That has always been my main instrument of choice although I did learn how to play drums, but only out of necessity. I played with my dad's bands when I was very young, and he had a drummer named Charlie Saddlewhite. He helped teach me and was a really cool guy. I used to think he was like Ringo or somebody. I actually took up playing drums in my dad's bands for quite some time, just as a teenager and going in and out of bands. I got into rock and roll early after seeing Elvis at a baseball park between the ages of six and seven years old. My parents took me to see him, and if Mom was alive today she would be the first to tell you that I kept telling her when we left I wanted to be a musician. It stuck with me for my whole life, and I didn't care too much of anything about any other stuff. Playing probably kept me out of trouble and kept me from doing lots of things that wouldn't have be good for me.

I told some people this before and will always maintain this because a journalist asked me recently what did I consider one of my greatest accomplishments. I told him that the fans had a lot to do with it and the record sales and the traveling and playing shows but, really, to me, probably the greatest accomplishment that I had in my life was being able to share the stage with some of the world's best and legendary rock musicians. Jakson, Greg, Charlie, Ronnie, Allen Collins, Gary Rossington, Leon Wilkeson—and these are some of the guys that I have had the pleasure of standing with and making music. The Blackfoot years were just incredible; we did something that I don't think anybody thought we were going to do. To think about those years of struggling and beating our heads against the wall and traveling like we did and the hopes that we had in our heart that we would do something. Those are some of the best years of our lives and nobody can ever take that away from us.

We impressed somebody from a record company. Then we moved up north to get out of the south because there was limited work around where we were. It's kind of ironic that we were a house band in Gainesville, Florida, and Tom Petty had a group called Mudcrutch, which was there in Gainesville, and Skynyrd used to go play there. It's kind of funny because we went to the northeast, and Tom went to the west coast, and Skynyrd stayed in the south and everyone went to seek their fame and fortune. We hit the big city of New York and stayed in a two-room apartment. It was big with a small bathroom and one small bedroom. It was in the Village and this woman had brought us there; it was her apartment. It is still in the Village because I was there recently and saw it. We were right around the corner from Fillmore East and a block from the Electric Circus. We struggled and starved; we bit the bullet. Then we moved out to New Jersey and that was when I went with Skynyrd. Then I went back with them later. Jakson and Charlie had met a bass player named Lenny Sandler, and they were in North Carolina. Jak asked me if I wanted to do it again, and I told him absolutely, so I went and joined them. Lenny opted to leave the band because of health problems, and he was a born again Christian. So, Greg came back with the band and all of a sudden we were back doing it again. We were up there for years. The Island Records and Epic Records and Atlantic deals all came out of there. Blackfoot, for me, in all sincerity, was a band that was way ahead of its time. We never considered ourselves the typical Southern rock band, but were a very heavy band, heavier than what is on record. We used to give people hell opening for them; there was basically no one that could stand up to us. We were fortunate in our life to cop some hits in that time in our life. We had "Train, Train" and "Highway Song" and others that really made a mark and a dent. We were playing arenas and touring overseas and having the time of our life. Then, for whatever reason, it all unraveled. I do know that there have been things in the press said about whose fault it was, but, to be honest, it was all of our faults. I don't think that it was any one person. When you are a band, you should have control of it. I have the utmost respect for the guys that played in that band. Great musicians like I told you a few minutes ago. They are very talented. For whatever intents and purposes, I do know that the business got in our way. The record business is the most ruthless business that I can even think of; it is funny how some record executives can talk out of both sides of their mouths. The business got in the way. We got caught up in the middle of record company wars, and it was a shame. It took people downhill. There were some hurtful things exchanged between some of us, and to me I don't even want to go back and think of those things. With Blackfoot, we shared some incredible years together and made some incredible music together. Skynyrd had a magic, and Blackfoot had a great magic. We were hell-bent for leather that we were badasses of the South.

Charlie Hargrett

We got along real well for the most part. For a lot of years we spent almost all our time together, living in "band house"-type situations (not always in a house...one year we took over an abandoned Polish summer camp in New Jersey). Like any band we had our share of disagreements. I was going to say that we resolved most of them, but to look back, I guess a lot of them were just simmering beneath the surface, waiting to explode.

Once we started touring, we didn't spend a lot of time off the road. The last several years I was there, we'd go on the road for a few months, go to our individual homes for a couple of weeks (by then we all lived in different cities), and meet in Ann Arbor to get ready for the next tour or album.

Jakson Spires (on highlights of his career with Blackfoot)

Well, I mean touring with Ted Nugent, playing with KISS; the Scorpions are real good friends of ours, AC/DC, toured with Deep Purple, the Who, went to Europe for many tours and had a great time over there. Hopefully, we will be going over there this year too. Touring with the Who was great because we had just come off of eighteen months of touring at the time of the *Strikes* tour. We were doing it worldwide, and I had thought we were going to have some time off. I do remember being offered the thing [the Who tour] by their manager, Bill, at the time and falling and rolling around on the office floor, laughing hysterically that we were getting ready to go to Seattle and start after we had just gotten home. We always seemed to get along with musicians from other countries more than we did with the ones from America. The exception would be Nugent because he took us out when no one else would get near us. That was then and this is now. [Laughs]

Charlie Hargrett

As the years go by and I look at it, there were so many times I can hardly know where to start. I can't start because I would be leaving something out. Monsters of Rock in England, and getting our gold records when we were out on tour with the Who and they did the presentation of the *Strikes* record. We did the spring 1980 tour with them and played with them at the Pontiac, Michigan, show at the Silverdome. It was the first show after their Cincinnati show when those folks got killed [the December 1979 incident where twelve fans were asphyxiated as the crowd surged toward the venue entrance for the Who concert, causing a much-needed examination of general admission tickets]. That was December 1979 when we played at Pontiac, Michigan, and after that show they asked us to do the tour and we went around the country with them and into Canada. It was nice.

Rickey Medlocke

That was one of the cool things about Blackfoot. We were able to open for some of the heaviest rock bands that came out of Europe. We were the darlings of opening acts at one time. We took pride in that and started headlining our own stuff. The guys from AC/DC, I am still friends with today. We struck up a good thing with lots of those guys—Nugent, Foreigner, AC/DC. It is some years that I am very proud of.

Greg T. Walker

One thing comes to mind right off the bat. We did a show in Zurich, Switzerland, and it was an ice hockey arena that was an overblown coliseum that seated 16,000 people. I know when we were doing "Highway Song" there were 16,000 lighters that got turned on at once. I remember looking out there and thinking about being 7,000 miles from home and that all of those people came out to see us. It was a very memorable event.

Then when we did the big festivals in Europe like Castle Donington and Reading where you have got in Reading 80,000 paid attendees, and the other was about 65,000. That was the European part. It was a happy experience for us because we were always glad being out there. To us every night was like the last night we would play. When we were touring with a lot of the bands before we started being able to headline ourselves, we just had a blast. Ted Nugent took us out when no one else would. He said we made him work and he loved a challenge. Foghat, the Nazareth tour, those were a couple that we enjoyed and hung out with everyday. The Who, we did the North American and Canadian tour with them, and Deep Purple was another one that called us and wanted us to tour with them.

Jakson Spires

[On "Highway Song"] I wrote all of it. I've been going through that for years [writing songs and having to credit Rickey as coauthor], but more and more people are finding out. It was put to me by Al Nally that I had to put Rickey's name on songs. What I do is I write on acoustic guitar. Everything's a ballad at first. Then I speed it up or slow it down. I'll bring it to the band, and I'll hum leads and stuff. I have the finished song in my head; I just don't have the ability to play it. I used to be a guitar player, but I got a real bad burn on my left hand, my chording hand, when I was fifteen. That's why I play drums. It took me eight years to get two of my fingers working for half-chords and bass chords and that's how I've written every song I've written—with two fingers. But Al came to me and said, "These songs are great and they're going to be hits. But you know Rickey and his ego. If his name don't start getting on some of these songs, he's going to freak out and the band's going to break up." I said, "Al, like I give a shit." I mean, I put Charlie and Greg's name on songs that they didn't even hear until they were recorded, just to give them extra money.

Charlie Hargrett

No, I didn't play on the *Vertical Smiles* album at all, or tour on it. I do recall suggesting the name, though. I went to Atlanta to work on the album, but my musical input wasn't welcome. I was basically told that the band was trying to come up with a new image and that I "looked and played too old." I kept on working on my parts and was ready and anxious to play, but the album was finished without my participation and was presented to the record company, who rejected it and said to go do it again. I told the band and management that I wasn't going to listen to any more of that "looked and played too old" crap, and that if I heard it again that I was gone. Well, I heard it again.

I quit the band cold, without a lawyer, and just walked away from what was actually a fifteen-year investment. I accepted the pitiful settlement they offered me. I didn't want them to be able to say that I caused the band to fail because I made it harder on them financially when I left.

At the time I was thinking, sink or swim, they couldn't blame me for the demise of the band.... I just gave them what they said they wanted. Of course, looking back on it, I probably should have used a lawyer.

Jakson Spires

Rickey and Al kind of phased Charlie Hargrett out, unbeknownst to everybody else while we were off the road doing the *Vertical Smiles* album. But we had Ken Hensley from Uriah Heep after that, and we burned him out in about two years. Bobby Barth from Axe, another band that Al Nally was managing—his guitar player and him had been in a wreck in Texas and Michael [Osborne] was killed. Bobby was the bass player and he was recuperating. When Ken quit the band, we rehearsed one night and played Chicago at the Vic Theatre the next night and just kept going for the last two years. It was a great band, and we had a great time and stuff. But, to tell you the truth, Rickey was so in debt to Nally and listening to stuff he wanted to do, he [Rickey] kept wanting to change direction and do this and that to sound like everybody else.

People wonder why the band isn't together and why Rickey this and why Rickey that. I just tell them look, the last time they had a song or album that charted, I was in the band. But that was the direction Rickey and Al wanted to go. They tried to change back to it, but it was too late. People could no longer relate to it. It wasn't Blackfoot, that was the thing. When we split the band up, it was put to me that I could hire another singer and guitar player, and me and Charlie and Greg could go out and call the band Blackfoot since I named the band. You know? They said you can do this because we'll never use the name again. So, I go out and I'm doing sessions in L. A. for six weeks, and when I come back Rick Medlocke and Blackfoot was out. It was a mess. He even took an album that me and Greg and Charlie had done, and when we split the corporation up he took the album we had done and put out Rickey Medlocke and Blackfoot.

Blackfoot broke up in 1986, but Rickey continued on with a new group of players until 1997, when he joined Lynyrd Skynryd. The remaining original members played in several different bands, including the Southern Rock Allstars, until 2004 when Spires, Hargrett, and Walker reunited with Bobby Barth for a rebirth of Blackfoot. In March 2005, Spires died suddenly of an aneurysm. The band continued with Christoph Ullman on drums, changing lineups several times until 2011. In 2012, Rickey Medlocke introduced an entirely new group of musicians as Blackfoot, and he acted as their producer.

36

The Outlaws

Like Blackfoot, the Outlaws had actually been around for years before they recorded and before their popularity caught on. Hughie Thomasson had formed the band in Tampa, Florida, back in 1967, but they did not record until 1975. The debut album spawned their hit "There Goes Another Love Song."

Alan Walden

Along the way Ronnie [Van Zant] had recommended I sign a band called the Outlaws, and I did. He said they had themselves a "Bird." That turned out to be "Green Grass and High Tides." Now I had five of the best guitar players in the world!

Henry Paul

By 1969 I had graduated high school, and I had gone to California and hitchhiked to Woodstock from L. A. Then I moved back to Tampa, but I had made the decision that I was going to gather up all my stuff and move to New York. I was going to go to Greenwich Village and make a career for myself in the music business. I started to audition at all of the folk music clubs like the Gaslight, Folk City, the Bitter End—I made the rounds at these places, and I got a job at the Strand book store in the Village. Don Ellis, the head of A&R at Epic at the time, heard that I was around and had an interesting voice, so I went and auditioned for Don, who took me down to the Columbia 55th Street Studios. Myself and a violinist from Tampa named Richard Lepps and Frank McCare all went into the studio and cut like six of my songs. Don Ellis loved it, and he asked me if I'd ever considered going to Nashville. I said no, but I'd do whatever it took to get to the next level. I was really chewed up wanting to make it. I figured if Johnny Cash could make it in the music business, I could too. [Laughs]

I was pretty aggressive. At that time I got a call from my friend in Tampa who was putting a show together of folks from Tampa who had gone on to make progress in the music business, and I was in that group. He was going to put a show on at the Tampa Armory. This was in 1970.

I met Jim Fish through Frank McCare, my friend in Greenwich Village, and Jim lived up in Albany. We just hit it off and played great together and sang harmony. We formed this band called Sienna. The bass player and sax player, both from the Village in New York, and Jim and myself, came to Florida, and Monte Yoho joined the group—that was in like '70 or '71. Then the bass player got a case of homesickness and took off, so Frank O'Keefe joined the band. So there's Monte and Frank and I. So we played the counterculture card for about a year.

Hughie Thomasson was in New York playing with another folk singer at the time, and he got homesick and came back to Florida, and he joined us. He knew Frank and Monte from the Outlaws, the little teenage band they had that played recreation centers and such. Then we changed our name from Sienna to the Outlaws to try and get more bookings. We started playing in the clubs in central Florida and Cocoa Beach, and Billy Jones came back from Colorado and joined the band, and we were writing songs. I had become a fan of folk rock or country rock and was into bands like Poco and the Lost Planet Airmen and New Riders of the Purple Sage. And the Grateful Dead were producing great albums at the time like *American Beauty* and *Working Man's Dead*. So I tried to wrap the Outlaws' musical identity around that type of sound, and it worked. Hughie was really adept at playing that type of music, and Monte, as a drummer was just right for that job.

So we started to catch on in Tampa, and there were five or six bars up around the University of South Florida where we played and became sort of the underground band. I met this guy who wanted to manage the band, and I let him do that, and that got us in touch with a couple of other people. We met Lynyrd Skynyrd out on the road. Ronnie Van Zant was singing our praises to his manager and to anyone who would listen. We wound up getting our record deal in '74 and the first album came out in '75.

Hughie Thomasson

We were on the road and Monte came running in the room yelling "Hughie!! I've got it!!" I told him, "Well, Monte if you've got it, maybe you ought to go see a doctor." He said, "No Hughie, I've got *it*!" He sang the chorus, and I told him I liked it and would see what I could do with it. That became "There Goes Another Love Song."

"Green Grass and High Tides"—I wrote that song in St. Augustine, Florida. We went to a cookout on the beach, and everybody forgot to bring their guitars. I was standing by the ocean, and there was a breeze and the words kept coming to me. It's about all the rock stars I liked that died had come back and were playing a show just for me. Like Jimi Hendrix, Janis Joplin, and Jim Morrison. And eventually more of course.

I wrote "Hurry Sundown" based on an episode of Bonanza. I was in my room, and I had the sound off on Bonanza. There was a wagon of gypsies shaking their tambourines. One had died and they were taking her away. That is how the song came about.

Henry Paul

We were talking the other day about the band Cowboy. They had a record out, and Marshall Tucker was way out there with a very, very popular record. We were still playing clubs; we had not quite arrived. But when we played with Marshall Tucker—we never played with Cowboy. They sort of evaporated before we got going— but the Tucker band was huge and they embraced us, as did the Charlie Daniels Band. David Corlew, Taz, Tommy Crain, Toy and Tommy Caldwell, Paul Riddle especially, George McCorkle—Jerry Eubanks was more of a jazz guy, he was on a different page sort of, but Jerry was a very nice man, but he seemed a little more intellectual. He was a little more sophisticated. But Tommy was the focal point of that group as the gatekeeper and he set the tone. He was enormously huge in our hearts. I would say Tommy Caldwell and Charlie Daniels were the two biggest influences on me as bandleaders and as cultural icons. They were two people who were worthy of imitation. We had this brotherhood. It was us against the world. It was fuck L. A.; fuck the Eagles. I remember feeling it was us and Tucker and Charlie against L. A., the Eagles, and Linda Ronstadt and Loggins and Messina. It was "The South's Gonna Do It Again" and "Dixie." It was tattoos and the flag and a cultural bonding of like-minded spirits.

Hughie Thomasson
The Outlaws did a lot of shows with the Marshall Tucker Band. We were great friends. On the *Southern Spirit* tour, the Outlaws were Toy's backing band. When I was first learning how to play steel guitar we were on tour with them, and I couldn't afford one. On the last night of the tour I go in our dressing room, and there is a steel guitar with a note on it. He [Toy] gave it to me free. I still have that steel guitar. I'll never forget that. I really miss him and the world was a better place for him being here.

Henry Paul
When the Henry Paul Band came along, unfortunately Tommy was gone, Tucker was evaporating. Charlie was still in business, and we shared that relationship with them. Then Hughie and I reconciled our ongoing relationship of difference to put the Outlaws together in 1983. It was weird Hughie wanted me out of the band in '77 because he wanted to go in more of a rock and roll direction, and I was sort of the country rock guy in the band. And there were conflicts between Billy and me and Hughie, and there wasn't a core that held us together like the Tucker band. So Hughie thought it was a good idea for me and him to get back together. Billy Jones was already out of the band and on a downward spiral as far as substance abuse. Frank was not in the music business anymore. Monte was spinning his own web. But Hughie and I continued to move forward from '83–'89 with one album called *Soldier of Fortune*—one odd record. I tried to get us into the modern music scene, but it was like a dog chasing his tail. You're either out in front or you're just jerking off. That record had "Cold Harbor" on it, which I am thankful for. It was an odd song for the record, but it turned out to be the best song on the record. And it

had "What You Don't Do," which I thought was a good song, and the title track which was an interesting, melodic Hughie Thomasson song. But we couldn't get arrested. We were out there playing clubs for very little money, and it was a great job—but it was a labor of love. We started doing things ourselves. Then in '89, I wanted to come to Nashville. I wanted to take the Outlaws with me, but Hughie didn't want to, so I went on my own and ended up forming Blackhawk and had significant success with that band. Then Hughie and I got back together in 2005, and I basically put Chris Anderson in. My job was always to put the band together. I met Chris in a bar in Sarasota and gave him a job. Randy [Threet] and I played together in Blackhawk. And Dave Robbins and I played together in the Outlaws, and he got the keyboard job. And then it was down to [Davis] Dix and me and Monte and Flame [Hughie]. Then when Hughie died, we added Billy Crain, who was perfect for the job. That was huge. I had this idea of consolidating the bands into one, bringing Jon Coleman into the band, and that worked well. I always thought the two-drummer thing for us was not necessary. It was a great entertainment, but musically, Monte was enough. So we decided to move forward as the Outlaws, and we would rehearse the songs, and I would sing the shit out of them and play the damned dog crap out of them and see if we can win over the faithful. And we were able to do that. It was mostly on the strength of the band's heart.

Alan Walden

[After Skynyrd] I went on to work with the Outlaws for twenty-five years until they completely disbanded. We had three gold and one platinum on Arista Records. It was not near as successful as Skynyrd, but I am still very proud of what we did with them! Henry Paul has proven to still be a major recording artist still in the mainstream, and he was asked to leave the Outlaws under very similar circumstances as mine.

Henry Paul

[On Hughie Thomasson] I absolutely loved the guy and miss him a lot. His signature work was the hallmark of that band. His sense of melody and structure was absolute genius. He was such a great and unique singer, both lead and harmony, and he could play the dog shit out of a song on guitar. I miss Flame everyday.

37

Molly Hatchet

Jacksonville, Florida. Dave Hlubek and Steve Holland started a band in 1975 that seemed to help fill the void following Skynyrd's 1977 plane crash. Danny Joe Brown and company had a little heavier rock sound than Lynyrd Skynyrd, but the triple-guitar attack was loud and clear, as was the band's admiration for their Jacksonville neighbors. Hatchet performed and recorded some of the same cover tunes as Skynyrd—songs like "Crossroads," "T for Texas," and they even did their own version of "Free Bird." Their debut album was released in 1978 on Epic Records. Ronnie Van Zant was supposed to produce the album. Sadly, that was not meant to be.

Dave Hlubek

It was after playing in a long line of local bands in the Jacksonville area. After so many years of playing in all the different clubs, I happened to meet Steve Holland at a local music store called Paula's Music in downtown Jax. He had just moved from Virginia Beach to Florida, and I heard this voice behind me saying, "That guitar really sucks." I turned around and asked who he was, and he said, "I'm Steve Holland! Wanna start a band?" We started rehearsing that very afternoon, and that band is what went on to become Molly Hatchet.

Danny Joe Brown

[Ronnie Van Zant] was going to produce the first album. As a matter of fact, Johnny [Van Zant] called me last night. He was at a restaurant where my wife works. We haven't been together in about eight years or something like that. But, she was at the restaurant, and talking to Johnny and she said, "Why don't I call Danny?" And he said, "I'd love to talk to him." And Leon [Wilkeson] wanted my number, so we talked for a few minutes. They sounded good.

Duane Roland

I was working on putting a band together with Banner [Thomas] and Bruce [Crump], but that didn't work out. They joined Dave and Steve, and then Danny. At this point, I was in another band called the Ball Brothers Band. Dave didn't show up for one of Hatchet's gigs, and Banner called me to fill in so they could get paid for the night. They and their management were thinking about going to three guitar players, so one they came down from Macon to hear me play, and after that I was asked to join.

Bobby Ingram

Being that the scene in Jacksonville was a lot of musicians knowing everybody else at the time—Hatchet and [my band] Rum Creek played the same places, and we shared off and on the same rehearsal studios in 1976 'til '78. We were like brother bands, and being great friends with Danny Joe Brown it was hard not to know what both of the groups were doing at the time. When MH would get back into town, they would set up in my rehearsal hall and write songs for the first album. If there was an opening in the lineup at the time, I would have loved to join the band. We all knew each other and our styles in playing were the same. But the band already had three guitar players. MH went on to sign with Epic Records and released two albums.

Then in 1980, Danny had just quit MH and came to my house and talk to me about putting together another band. It was to be the Danny Joe Brown Band. This is where I meet John Galvin who was an up-and-coming keyboard player from Detroit and the best I have ever heard. We rehearsed for six months under the most difficult of situations. There was no money, no heat in the practice hall, and we would rehearse fifteen or sixteen hours a day, seven days a week, and then the break-through happened. Don Dempsey, president of Epic records, came down to Jacksonville and signed the band, and we were off to Nassau, Bahamas, at Compass Point studios to record the first album. Glen Johns was the producer [Rolling Stones, the Who, the Beatles, the Eagles] on the project, and we toured the album in 1981 in support of it. We recorded that album live in the studio. What I mean by that is there were no overdubs except for the vocals. Very old-school style of recording, which is sometimes the best. That band lasted until 1982 and disbanded due to personal reasons. Danny rejoined MH for the *No Guts...No Glory* album. During the live *Double Trouble* album, I was called in by Pat Armstrong to do work on it at LEI Studios in Jacksonville. After that I joined the band full time. As well as touring, I recorded the *Lightning Strikes Twice* album in Orlando with Danny, Duane, and Bruce of the original lineup for Capitol Records.

John Galvin

I am not an original member of Molly Hatchet per se, however I *am* the original keyboard player. I was called in to play some keyboard parts on the *No Guts...No Glory* album in 1983, which was just after Danny Joe rejoined Molly Hatchet. There was some talk at that point of them pulling me into the band, but nothing was concrete. After the album was complete, and the band was on the road, they played here in Detroit with Sammy Hagar at Cobo Hall. I remember going down there and waking Dave up on the bus out in front of the venue, and a few minutes later Sammy came on the bus and was trying to rouse Dave also. After the show that night, Danny Joe and Steve Holland came to my house for a little late-night party, and Steve said, "Wanna be in the band? You can take *my* place, I've had enough." Well, of course he didn't have to ask me twice, and after that tour, I was called to be a full-time member of Molly Hatchet, at which time we went into rehearsals for a new album, *The Deed Is Done*. I also must add that on the first couple MH albums, session man Jai Winding played keys on a few tracks but was not in the band.

Danny Joe Brown

Oh, my God. [Long pause] Well, I had three guitar players who were absolutely and totally different in sound. And I don't think anybody could drive a set of drums harder than Bruce Crump. And it took Steve Holland leaving before John Galvin came in. John was the best keyboard player that I've ever worked with. Ever. And I've worked with all of them as far as Southern keyboard players go. He's the best I've ever heard. And when I left Molly Hatchet because of my diabetes and my pancreas and all that crap, John sent me a tape from Detroit and told me if I ever decided to do something else to please consider him. He sent me a tape that was gospel and country. That's what made me decide to put back together a band. And I knew immediately that Bobby [Ingram] was going to be my lead guitar player. Besides John being the best keyboard player I ever worked with, Bobby was the best guitar player I ever worked with. I felt he was the best and I still do, to this day.

John Galvin

When I first joined the band, it was so overwhelming! The crowds were bigger, the venues were bigger, we were treated like kings. I felt like, "Am I really getting paid for this?" It was really like a nonstop vacation with all expenses paid, and spending money to boot. Kind of like a rolling party with your friends. The only real downside was having to leave my family at home although there were times they could join us on the road. It was hard not to go home and say, "I did this and this, and went here and there," because I didn't want them to feel left out, so I had to suppress some of that. "Yeah, it was pretty rough out there! Pretty much stayed in my room with the door locked." That kind of thing. But the band really made me feel like part of the family right from the get-go. It was an experience I wish everyone could share at least once.

Bobby Ingram

In 1986, I got a call from Pat Armstrong, the band's manager, and Danny, and was asked if I would be interested in coming into the group. At that time, I was really busy with my own project, China Sky, which had a major record deal with CBS/PARC Records. It was my solo project that I had been working on after the Danny Joe Brown Band. Anyway, I went down to Orlando where the management company headquarters were and found out that I was to step in for Duane Roland. I couldn't understand that. The story that was told to me by the band was that he was not getting along with Dave and was going to resign if there were not any changes. At that time, I told the band about my prior obligations, and I wouldn't be able to devote 100 percent of my time to MH due to the China Sky project. A few months later, I get another call from the band. So, I went the second time to Orlando and found out they were replacing Dave Hlubek. There were some strange things going on then, but I agreed to do a tour and I loved it. Dave has mentioned in interviews that he gave me the job, but that is not at all how it happened. I was being called by other members as well as management to come into the band. At that time, the members in the band were Danny Joe Brown, Duane Roland, Bruce Crump, John Galvin, and Riff West. I was to take Dave Hlubek's place in the group. Danny was a great friend, and I had been around the band from the beginning and it made a lot of sense; it felt like home. Danny was the main reason for my decision to join Molly Hatchet, and he was the main reason for the opportunity—I thank him for that—but, it was up to me then. I played the guitar, did my share of the songwriting, carried my own weight, and was paid the same as everyone else in the band. I worked hard and made many sacrifices and gave up my solo career, turned down a major deal with CBS Records to be able to devote all of my time to the band and had no regrets.

John Galvin

It was just a thrill being onstage with all my heroes, and playing behind Danny Joe. He had something that few front men have. We did some videos back then that were a real kick. It was kind of funny to see these video girls come in in the morning, and you wouldn't recognize them, they all looked like they just crawled out of bed, but as soon as the makeup people got through with them, *bam!*—instant supermodels. The transformation was incredible. It was a lot of fun getting to act a little in the videos, but unfortunately, they never got much, if any, airplay, and MTV pretty much refused to play them. They considered us a "classic" act. But all in all it was an enlightening experience. Traveling in a luxury tour bus was also very cool because as a teenager, I was into custom vans and did some custom painting, so the bus was like an extension of that.

At times we could be a hell-raising band, some members more than others. I think that would have to fall into Danny and Dave's lap. They were the hardcore party men—the ones that would take the most risks and hang with the riskiest of people. Bruce was into health and bodybuilding and kind of lived in his own bubble. He would prepare all his own food and rarely ate in a restaurant with the band and only drank bottled water. There was a time in Iowa, at a ballroom, that Bruce and Danny got into a fistfight offstage, right before the encore. I still have no idea what it was about, but soon after they settled their dispute. Incidents like that were not unusual, but the band had pretty much settled down by the time I joined. Of course, we have always had a strong biker following, so it was not unusual to see the Hells Angels, Outlaws, Banditos, or any other bike club at our shows and occasionally onstage with us. They have been with us from the beginning, all over the world, and we welcome them wherever we go.

Everyone in the band, at one time or another, has partied with the best of them and rarely passed on an invitation to join in.

Danny Joe Brown

Well, it was one of those things where they came out with *Beatin' the Odds*, and I came out with my solo thing, and their album sales fell off. I mean just dropped off. We were a platinum act before that. But when my solo album came out, I didn't do but a couple of hundred thousand records. And they dropped off from platinum back down to gold. And it took them a long time to get back up to platinum. And they realized we weren't going anywhere separated. The company didn't push my record, and they didn't back Hatchet. I remember going to the bathroom with the president of the record label. He said, "Danny, you guys have to get back together." I remember looking over at him, and he was in one urinal and I was in the other. [Laughs] Anyway, we decided right there in the bathroom that we would get back together. And that's the truth. Jimmy had to go. He's a great singer, but he's a helluva looking guy. [Laughs] He's a lovely man and I love him to death. And thank God he was on this album, *The Jammin' for DJB* record. He can sing his ass off. I ain't never heard anybody sing "Mississippi Queen" better in my life. I think I about wore out my tape in that spot because I play it so much.

Bobby Ingram

When I joined MH, the band still had three original members—Danny, Duane, and Bruce. Also, John Galvin who took Steve's place and Riff who took Banner's place. The spirit and tradition at that point was carried on from the original band less Dave, Banner, and Steve.

July 8, 1990, in Toledo, Ohio, was this band's last performance with this lineup. Duane was going into locksmithing or computers. Bruce had a new wife and baby (he went home to Virginia), and the other members were getting into other things, and Molly Hatchet had its last show. It was advertised as the last show—management knew it, the agency knew it, and was even announced at the gig in Toledo. Danny and myself continued on and went out on the road, putting together a new band to carry on the spirit and tradition. During that time Duane, Riff, and the other members were asked to come back and get things started again. No one did. They were not interested in it at the time. Duane Roland, who owned the name Molly Hatchet and Pat Armstrong with the management company, offered a licensing deal to Danny and myself, knowing that we were out playing. We accepted and paid Pat and Duane a percentage for the use of the name. We wanted to continue the band, and we did even under that situation. Everyone else left (except Danny and myself) and did other things. The other members of the band left on there own standings. We continued on with a new band and toured for the next five years until Danny was not able due to health reasons. We were best of friends and loved what we did together...making music onstage. Over those five years, from 1990–1995, Danny's health was becoming a major issue with the touring. Steve Green of Artists International Management and myself and the entire band at that time tried to help Danny with his diabetes and with his demons problem. We all loved Danny and didn't want to see anything bad happen to him on or off the road. We had Phil McCormack come out for three months to give Danny time off the road to go into treatment in 1992—to no avail—countless recommendations made to him over the next three years—to no avail—until 1995 when he entered the Memorial Hospital in Jacksonville. He stayed for approximately six weeks, and when [he was] discharged, his mother took him to her Miami home, and he never came back to the band due to his health. At that point in time, Phil McCormack was brought in full time under Danny's recommendations to fulfill all of his studio and touring obligations. And for the record, Jimmy Farrar was the other singer mentioned during this time and was brought out on the road for a week of auditions, and it was best decided to use Phil. So again, the spirit and tradition was carried on, and the torch passed again. At that time, Pat Armstrong and Duane Roland both licensed the name to me exclusively, knowing that Danny was unable to perform.

It was for fifteen years with a five-year option. Let me state this again, the licensing was offered to me. There are some people out there that think I stole the name or obtained it illegally. Let's get this straight—I continued to work and make music and stay dedicated to the band. That is why I received the licensing. It's not brain surgery to figure this out. I stayed true to the band, and Duane and Pat saw this. I'm out here to make music, carry on the legacy, and continue the future of the band. I am not out here to hurt any of the past members. If people want to know all of the dirty laundry that is the business of the band—sorry, it's not public information. I personally believe that the focus should be on the music, not the back-and-forth mud slinging that has been going on far too long. This is not politics; it's a rock band, and what we make is music. If someone doesn't like the music—don't listen to it, and please don't buy it. It's that simple! And for some people that think the band is just slapped together, and there are no ties to the past, I played with Danny and gave him his first singing job; played with Duane, who is a great guitarist and someone I deeply respect as a person and a player; played with Bruce, who is one of the best drummers in the music industry and has a very unique style, and I was hired to take Dave's position in the band.

Yes, there have been many member changes from 1980 and on...recording and non-recording members. The 1978 until 1980s original recording lineup passed the torch and legacy to the eighties recording lineup, during which time I was in the band. The eighties lineup passed the torch and legacy to the nineties recording lineup. I was in the band. The nineties lineup passed the torch and legacy to the now-recording and touring 2000 Molly Hatchet lineup. I'm still in the band, and it will be passed long after I have retired. Molly Hatchet is a generational band. Some bands can succeed and others can't. There might be a time where some of the original members come back in and then leave again. Molly Hatchet is a legacy, spirit, tradition, and future. It started a long time before I joined the band. It started when the first original member left the group, and the band carried on with other members. I have said this before and I'll say it always—if it wasn't for the original six members, there would not be a legacy to continue. The present lineup will continue, and we are very proud to be a part of the mix and look toward the future.

Danny Joe Brown

Steve was absolutely insane, that's why he left. I've seen Steve Holland eat corn flakes, pouring beer on them. I love him to death, don't get me wrong—ain't nobody can play "Gator Country" like Steve. Even though Banner Thomas wrote it. Banner had a dream one night on the bus and came out of his bunk one morning with that written down on paper. I couldn't believe it. How did he do that? I don't know.

Riff West

I joined in 1981 when Banner left. I spent a year with Jimmy [Farrar]. We did the whole *Take No Prisoners* tour. I joined right after that album. Then Danny Joe came back. Molly Hatchet did break up in 1990. I stayed with them through their last show in 1990. There actually was a final tour and a final concert.

We played somewhere in Ohio with Meatloaf, and all of our old friends and old crew came out. That was it. We were taking a break, and were going to get off the road for a year or so. There was really no intention of the band actually breaking up. We just wanted a break.

During that time we figured out we didn't all want to go back out, but Danny did want to go back out. We didn't have any problem with that whatsoever. He went back out as "Danny Joe Brown of

Molly Hatchet." It wasn't Molly Hatchet. He had Bobby Ingram in his band at the time.

Bobby did play with Molly Hatchet there at the end, but he was a hired side man. He had his own band China Sky and was on Polydor Records, so he couldn't be in both bands with two different record companies, so he was a hired side guy. He was unable to sign with Molly Hatchet because of the other contract.

Eventually the management licensed the name to Danny and Bobby. They were partners at the time. None of us wanted to go back out, and as long as Danny was in the band we were fine. We were all for it.

And after a couple of years, around 1993, Danny left, and Bobby became the leader of the band. I admire Bobby for what he has done for ten years. He's kept the name going. I don't have anything at all against Bobby Ingram; he was one of my best friends at one time. I don't begrudge him for trying to keep the name going, for making a living for himself, but I don't agree with it. We always wanted Danny Joe to be the singer of Molly Hatchet when the name was licensed. We always thought it was going to be Bobby and Danny, not just Bobby. But I don't hold grudges; it's just not worth it.

Duane Roland

[On leaving the band] We were only planning to take a year off. But that changed. There was a lot of corporate bullshit going on that's best left unsaid.

John Galvin

Danny Joe and I used to room together frequently. First off, I have to say, if it wasn't for Danny, I wouldn't have been in Molly Hatchet. He is very generous, very kind, and would give anyone the shirt off his back. He was the most non-materialistic person in the band and pretty much lived for the moment. He frequently read the Bible and treated everyone that came his way with respect. He has a good ol' boy persona that's almost Elvis-like. He was a "yes, Ma'am, yes, Sir" kind of guy that appealed to both young and old. He would have made a great actor. He definitely had an aura, and when he entered a room he commanded attention. The women wanted him, and the men wanted to be like him. He is a very likeable guy, but his image created problems for him. People saw him drink onstage, so they wanted to drink with him and bring him liquor as gifts, and buy him drinks, and I think it just got away from him. Now he's having some serious health issues as a result, and I *know*, it wasn't part of the plan, but it's something we all have to face and learn from it.

Back in the eighties, we had this bus driver by the name of Joe "Bear" McEntire. He looked *just like* Willie Nelson, and everywhere we went, people thought he was. He even had the braids, the beard, the whole nine yards, and I think he even played off that a little. Anyway, we were on our way from Georgia up to New Jersey, I think, and everyone was asleep on the bus. Joe Bear stopped at a truck stop for fuel and coffee. Danny usually had a habit of calling his wife whenever we stopped, and for some reason he woke up and got off the bus to find a pay phone. Joe Bear was in the truck stop and unaware that Danny was off the bus calling home from a payphone across the parking lot. After paying for the fuel, Joe hopped in the bus and resumed the trip, unknowing that Danny was gone. In the meantime, Danny finished his call and started back to the bus, realizing it had left. Now you have to picture this: here's a guy with nothing on but a pair of shorts, no ID, no money, except the phone change, with a little Jim Beam buzz going, trying to explain to people that he's Molly Hatchets singer, and needs to get to New Jersey. ("Yeah, right, buddy, and I'm Frank Sinatra!") Meanwhile, the next day we arrive at our destination, when everyone realizes, "Where's Danny?" Suddenly out of nowhere, Danny appears with a big grin. He had borrowed a shirt from a trucker, called our manager at home, who got him a flight, had a state trooper rush him to the airport, and actually *beat us* to New Jersey! So ends the saga of the missing vocalist.

Riff West

From this day until the day I die, I will say Danny is one of my best friends. He's a meathead! I call him that all the time. He knows it. But he would do anything in the world for you. Danny could never beat his demons, you know, the alcohol—he knows that. And being a diabetic, that's a lethal combination. I've known those guys for years, even before they got a record deal or anything. And I'll tell you a story. My mom has been incredibly sick for years. I was already out of the band and in Foghat, and Danny would always ask me how my mom was doing. My mom always thought Danny was like Charles Bronson, the neatest little guy in the world. Danny knew my mom was dying at one time, and luckily she didn't die, and Danny grabbed me and prayed for my mom. Another time he called my mom and prayed with her without me knowing it. For me, my parents are my best buds. I knew right then if Danny ever needed my help, I'd be there for him. So even though Danny can be a meathead, he's had a lot of problems, he's got a temper, he's done things we wish he didn't do, and he's done things that *he* wished he didn't do, he's still a great guy. And I'll do anything in the world for him.

John Galvin

Dave [Hlubek] was the showman. He was the spark that would turn a lead into a flash-fire. Along with Danny, I think he brought a certain "toughness" to the band, and a look that defined Southern rock. Together, they were unstoppable. Dave also had a great gift for doing interviews laced with wit, sarcasm, and pride. Later on, though, I sensed a certain competition within the band for the "top" spot, that I think created a certain edge.

Duane Roland was the unsung hero and really was more of a family guy, but you couldn't tell by looking. He was less flashy, but more precision, and did a lot of his leads in one take, in the studio. I had the pleasure of staying at Duane's house in Jacksonville when I first joined the band. He had a bad hip, which he ended up having replaced, and I think it prevented him from running around onstage too much.

Bruce Crump, also very family oriented, had a style all his own and would blow your mind onstage with some new drum-fills he would throw in. A great drummer and a great guy. Very disciplined in his diet and health issues.

Riff West was the bass player when I came into the band. Riff and I were very close and pretty much hung out together, later to be joined by Bobby Ingram. We dubbed ourselves the "three amigos," because the three of us were the ones that would go exploring in

every city and pretty much were the most compatible. We partied a
little lighter than the rest and would be off to find another adventure
at every turn. The rest of the band would be sleeping off hangovers or
nights on the town, but we didn't realize at the time, that they had
already *done* what we were doing many times over, so they opted to
relax. Riff was a super guy and organizes many charitable events for
animals and the Humane Society, as well as the Jammin for DJB
benefit. We still keep in contact occasionally.

Barry Lee Harwood

Dave and I had the Hlubek-Harwood Band in the eighties. The
lineup included Lonnie Brown and Buzzy Meekins. All my memories
with Dave were fun—he's a funny guy. When we first pulled a band
together, some people were shocked that I chose to work with him. I
was "warned" about Dave's persona, but I honestly never saw Dave's
dark side! [Laughing] Fortunately he caught me during one of my
attempts to "stay on the straight and narrow" so I was in my right
mind at the time, and although it was a flash in the pan, it worked
and we had fun with it. We weren't trying to re-live our past success;
we were just gigging around town—making some money. My
favorite Dave quote: "Three things I like to do and that's eat—play
music—and eat; did I mention eatin'? 'Cause I like to eat!" [Laughs]

Danny Joe Brown

I guess the highlights of Hatchet for me were selling out the
Spectrum in Philadelphia twice in one week. Selling out Madison
Square Garden. Playing with the Who in front of 180,000 people.
Playing straight across from where Hitler stood. And being on tour
with the Outlaws. That was one of the greatest tours I ever had. For
me, anyway. I don't know what everybody else thinks.

Bobby Ingram

Dave came back aboard in 2005. It's been a great thing for the
veteran fans because it adds to the nostalgia of the band. Of course
Dave was one of the founders of the group. I don't like to speak for
Dave, but I believe it's been really great for him to get back out and
play under the Molly Hatchet banner again. It's great for him to be

able to express himself in a different way now, you know. It's like a homecoming. Dave and I knew each other way back before the band got their first record deal in 1978. I think we've known each other since about '73. So it's like looking over and seeing a brother in a lot of ways, a family member.

And Timmy Lindsey is with the group now. He was the original bass player even before Banner Thomas. And John Galvin and I go back over thirty years playing together now. Thirty years, wow. [Laughs] There were a lot of changes prior to *Warriors of the Rainbow Bridge*, but now this is the longest-standing lineup in the history of Molly Hatchet. There have been no changes since 2005. Things have settled in. I mean, things are gonna change as you move along, it's generational. But this combination of musicians seems to work really well to carry on the legacy and tradition of the band. I am really happy with all the band members. Dave, Timmy, John and I are hanging in there, and Phil [McCormack] is hanging in there, and Shawn Beamer is still on the drums. He is something else. A monster. He sparks the guitar lineup because he's on the cutting edge, and that helps me and Dave because we don't ever want to fall back into an easy Holiday Inn-ish kind of feel. [Laughs] Not that there's anything wrong with that, but I still like to turn the amps up and get feedback; I'm still into that. I guess I'm a kid at heart that never grew up, but I don't know if I want to.

John Galvin

Over the last few years there has been a lot of controversy over the "old band" vs. the "new band." I was fortunate enough to be a part of both versions, and I have to say that I had an equally great time in both bands. When I joined the original band, everything was new and exciting, and I was playing with people that were my musical heroes, that I had seen in concert many times before I ever met them. To be a part of that was a gift that can't be compared. That band started it all, wrote the hits that went platinum, and whether or not they are still on stage as a band or not, they will always be in our hearts as Molly Hatchet. The "new" version of the band, which a lot of people think just happened overnight, in fact was an evolvement of sorts, that happened over years. Members would come and go, as early as 1980, when Danny first left the band. It was never the same since.

Bobby Ingram has a heart of gold. He is very driven to make the band a success and is ambitious beyond anyone I know of. He knows what he wants and how to get it. As a guitar player, he ranks with the best. He can play whatever you want him to play and then some. And he gets the tone from hell without even trying!

The new version, in my opinion, has picked up where *Flirtin' with Disaster* left off. It feels fresh again; the songwriting is back on track, and it is self-sufficient. The internal struggles within the band are gone, and music is now the number one priority. Bobby has singlehandedly transformed a band that had one foot in the grave and gave it new life.

Afterword

Today, the Allman Brothers Band continues to play to sold out shows and packed venues, while Dickey Betts & Great Southern play fewer gigs, performing mostly in clubs and festivals. Dickey's son Duane, a spitting image of the *Fillmore*-era Dickey, plays guitar in the band. In early 2014, Warren Haynes and Derek Trucks announced their departure from the ABB. Within weeks, Gregg announced the band would cease touring at the end of 2014.

Lynyrd Skynyrd is also flying high with a single original band member, and even with the plague of deaths over the past few years, the band continues to draw huge crowds that want to hear "Free Bird" live.

The Marshall Tucker Band is down to one original member, but the band tours relentlessly, and they sound great. The MTB has played the Grand Ole Opry twice, and last year took their music overseas to play for the troops in Iraq.

The Charlie Daniels Band continues to entertain huge crowds everywhere they go, with Charlie's obvious country crossover appeal.

Cowboy reunited recently, recorded a live album in Macon, and have played several live shows since. Many of the bands have simply lost so many members that they can never exist again—great bands like Grinderswitch and Eric Quincy Tate.

The Outlaws continue to tour and record, lead by founding members Henry Paul and Monte Yoho. Until a recent doctor's order took him off the road, Billy Crain was in the band, now replaced by one-time Outlaw Steve Grisham.

Molly Hatchet continues to tour and record, lead by Bobby Ingram, with founding member Dave Hlubek and longtime lead vocalist Phil McCormack. Original keyboard man John Galvin performs with the band often.

Southern rock has enjoyed somewhat of a revival over the past few years as many of today's contemporary country stars have expressed their love for the classic sound. There have also been several newer bands who bring a lot of hope of a continued life for the musical genre—bands like Blackberry Smoke, the Zac Brown Band, the Duane Betts Band, the Justin McCorkle Band, Swampdawamp, Silver Travis, and many others are out there keeping it real.

So here we are, some forty-five years since the opening of Capricorn Records, and the music is still alive and well. I have to wonder what Phil Walden and Frank Fenter would say if they were still with us. Most likely, the same thing Ronnie Van Zant once exclaimed on his live album—"Turn it up!"

Special Thanks

My sincere thanks to every one of the hundreds of people who have spent time on the phone or in person over the years allowing me to glimpse into your lives.

Many thanks to the great photographers who contributed to this book: Tom Bell; Peter Cross; John Gellman; John C. Griffin; Roxanne Lark; Bill Thames; Kirk West; and thank you for sharing your archived photos—Robin Duner-Fenter; Tommy Talton; and Alan Walden.

To all who helped me through all of my recent medical trials, I owe you a huge debt of gratitude: MusiCares; Dr. Lori Malvern and T.J.; Hal Stewart; Dr. Paul Ross; Everyone at Weight Loss Services of Spartanburg; Dr. Tommy Bridges; Dr. Nick McLane; Dr. Hollinger and Kendra at Palmetto Pulmonary; Karleen Fenderson and Lincare; Colleen Knights; Tim Shook; Charlie Daniels; Billy Bob Thornton; Henry Paul; Craig Stevens; Joey Parrish; Alex, Abbie and Josie Parrish; Jeff "Burley" Bannister; Jody Weisner; Jay Taylor; Tom Greene; Jaryd Walley; Steve and Laura Flacy; and everyone else who donated time, money or services of offered an ear or a prayer; and all of the musicians and folks who helped with the various benefit concerts.

Love and gratitude: Benjamin and Austin Greene; Hannah Jane Greene, Zoe and Leila Maxey; Scott Greene; Richard "J.R." Smith, Billy Bob Thornton; JD Andrew; Kristen Irving; Michael "Bubba" Bruce; Peter Cross; Bonnie Bramlett; Bekka Bramlett; Alan Walden; Roxanne Lark; Tommy Talton; Billy Eli; Tammy Williams; Tom Coerver; Eric Wenzel; the Rebel Rock crowd; Rebyl and Ms. Rebyl; Southern George and CiCi; John Griffin; David and Peggy Peck; Donnie and Paula Winters; Dennis and Linda Winters; Silver Travis; Dave and Inge Haddox; Greg and Connie Yeary; Lee Ridings;

Michael Proctor; Timmy Fodrey; Denny and Janet Walley; Rick Broyles; all my Facebook friends.

To absent friends: Tony Heatherly; Stuart Swanlund; Brad Lesley; Tommy Crain; Taz DiGregorio; George McCorkle; Jo Jo Billingsley; Delaney Bramlett; Dan Toler; Frankie Toler; Jakson Spires; Toy Caldwell, Sr.; Red Dog Campbell; Tom Dowd; Leonard Skinner; Allen Woody. Your stories were all a major part of this book. I feel blessed to have known you all.

Appendix 1

Southern Rock Lists

Top Ten Guitarists of Southern Rock

1. Duane Allman (Allman Brothers Band)
Duane is pretty much the undisputed King of Southern rock guitarists. No small wonder: Skydog laid down some of the best guitar tracks ever committed to magnetic tape during his brief twenty-five-year life, and anyone who was lucky enough to see Duane play live will certainly never, ever forget it. Vacillating between scorching lead riffs and smoldering slide work, Skydog was the very best. *Definitive guitar work:* the entire *At Fillmore East* album.

2. Toy Caldwell (Marshall Tucker Band)
The lead guitar player from Spartanburg, South Carolina, took the Marshall Tucker Band into the stratosphere in the early seventies as their primary songwriter and the "fastest thumb in the South" on guitar. *Definitive guitar work:* The entire live disc of the *Where We All Belong* double album, especially "Every Day I Have the Blues."

3. Ed King (Lynyrd Skynyrd)
The California kid and former Strawberry Alarm Clocker wrote and played some of Southern rock's most memorable licks as guitarist for Lynyrd Skynyrd. *Definitive guitar work:* Ed's signature lick that opens "Sweet Home Alabama" is one of the most recognizable riffs in rock history.

4. Hughie Thomasson (Outlaws)
The founder of the Outlaws had both a unique vocal sound and a unique guitar style that set him apart from everyone else in the pack.

There were times when his guitar artistry seemed to stem from another realm of time and space. *Definitive guitar work:* "Green Grass and High Tides."

5. Allen Collins (Lynyrd Skynyrd)
The high energy, tall and lanky, dancing and leaping Lynyrd Skynyrd guitarist blazed across the strings and consistently raised the bar for Southern rockers everywhere. *Definitive guitar work:* "Free Bird," especially the end jam, live version. Wowzer.

6. Dickey Betts (Allman Brothers Band)
The Allman Brothers Band guitarist blended his vast array of influences, from Django Rhinehardt to Robert Johnson and brought a country rock and blues style into a band that blended blues, Southern soul, and jazz to create a one-of-a-kind sound that set the bar for all the bands in their wake. *Definitive guitar work:* "Jessica" and "In Memory of Elizabeth Reed."

7. Dave Hlubek (Molly Hatchet)
Co-founder of Molly Hatchet and one of three guitarists in the band, Dave played his instrument like a renegade outlaw biker on steroids. *Definitive guitar work:* "Dreams."

8. Gary Rossington (Lynryrd Skynyrd)
One of the three original guitar slingers of Lynyrd Skynyrd, and the man who today still carries their flag into the future. *Definitive guitar work:* The opening slide to "Free Bird."

9. Tommy Crain (Charlie Daniels Band)
Tommy joined the Charlie Daniels Band in 1975 and brought in a new energy. Whether playing dual leads with Charlie or smoking on a solo, Crain ruled the roost for more than fifteen years of hits. He would spend ten years prior to his death fronting the Crosstown Allstars, a red-hot blues band based in Atlanta. *Definitive guitar work:* "Still in Saigon," "The Devil Went Down to Georgia."

10. Tommy Talton (Cowboy)
A true master of acoustic and electric lead and slide, Talton played some of the most brilliant music of the Capricorn Records era with his band Cowboy. *Definitive guitar work:* The entire *5'll Getcha Ten* and *Reach for the Sky* LPs.

Top Ten Singers of Southern Rock

1. Jimmy Hall (Wet Willie)
I am sure to get some flack for choosing Jimmy above Gregg as the number one contender here, but I truly believe that his huge body of work with Wet Willie, with Jeff Beck, and all of his ongoing projects over the years, Jimmy has proven to be one of the overall finest singers in not only Southern rock, but in all of music. *At his best:* "Grits Ain't Groceries" (live), "Shout Bamalama," "Street Corner Serenade."

2. Gregg Allman (Allman Brothers Band)
What an amazing, smoky blues voice. Gregg won me over with the *Fillmore* album, and his *Laid Back* solo record is always in my CD player. *At his best:* "Whipping Post" (live versions from *At Fillmore East*), "Queen of Hearts," "Come and Go Blues."

3. Doug Gray (Marshall Tucker Band)
When he locked his legs together and planted his feet on stage like tree roots, you could tell he was about to let fly with vocal pyrotechnics like you ain't never heard in all your born days. An amazing singer, steeped in blues, country, and good ol' rock and roll. *At his best:* "Ramblin'" (live version from *Where We All Belong*), "The Thrill Is Gone" (live, *Volunteer Jam*), "Singing Rhymes," "My Jesus Told Me So."

4. Bonnie Bramlett

Before she came to Capricorn Records, Bonnie had already recorded some of the finest music ever with husband Delaney Bramlett (e.g., *Motel Shot*, which also featured Duane Allman, Gram Parsons, and a cast of thousands), but when she hit Macon, Georgia, her Southern rock roots came to the surface. Whether singing with the Allman Brothers Band, Dickey Betts solo, Gregg solo, or on her own solo records, Ms. Bonnie always rocked. *At her best:* "It's Time" (*It's Time*), "Two Steps from the Blues" (duet with Gregg), "Superstar" (*Delaney & Bonnie*).

5. Ronnie Van Zant (Lynyrd Skynyrd)

One of the most unique singers in all of Southern rock, Ronnie was the conduit that held all of Lynyrd Skynyrd together. His songwriting was as honest as his vocals. *At his best:* "Free Bird" (live version from *One More from the Road*); "Ballad of Curtis Loew," "On the Hunt."

6. Hughie Thomasson (Outlaws)

Another original voice that you can spot immediately upon hearing just a few notes, Hughie blended a cowboy sound, country rock, and a huge dose of originality into a vocal style that was just plain good. As amazing a singer as he was a guitarist. *At his best:* "Green Grass and High Tides," "There Goes Another Love Song," "Hurry Sundown."

7. Dale Krantz-Rossington (Rossington-Collins, Lynryd Skynyrd)

The first time I heard Dale sing with the Rossington Collins Band, it blew my mind. She reminded me of Janis Joplin and Grace Slick wrapped up in an Ann Wilson vibe. I'd love to see her front and center once again. *At her best:* "Prime Time" and "Don't Misunderstand Me"

8. Rickey Medlocke (Blackfoot)

The wild and crazy front man of Blackfoot, who these days acts as a guitarist for Lynyrd Skynyrd, Medlocke was a true powerhouse vocalist and show stopper with Blackfoot. *At his best:* "Gimme, Gimme, Gimme," "Highway Song," "Train, Train."

9. Danny Joe Brown (Molly Hatchet)
Another powerhouse singer and one of the true legends of Southern rock, Danny Joe belted out the tunes like nobody else and worked the stage like a true rock star. *At his best:* "Flirtin' With Disaster," "Dreams," "The Creeper" (live version from *The Agora Ballroom*).

10. Dickey Betts (Allman Brothers Band)
Dickey brought a country element into the Allman Brothers Band that really gave them their unique sound. His voice is clear and smooth and perfect for his style of music. *At his best:* "Blue Sky," "Ramblin' Man," "Long Time Gone."

Top Ten Drummers of Southern Rock

1. Jakson Spires (Blackfoot)
In my opinion, Jakson was the greatest drummer who ever swung a pair of Vic Firth 2-B drumsticks. One of the most intense moments of my life was playing "Train, Train" with Jak, standing three feet away from his bass drum. I was truly afraid a stick was going to break, a shard of 2-B would fly out and pierce my jugular, and I'd bleed out before the song finished. Thunderfoot Spires played with the power of ten men. *At his best:* "Train, Train," "Highway Song."

2. Artimus Pyle (Lynyrd Skynyrd)
If ever there was a legendary name in Southern rock, it has to be Artimus Pyle. While he was not the original drummer for Lynyrd Skynyrd as many folks believe, he came in on the third album and became a legend. An iconic, super-talented percussion machine. *At his best:* The entire *One More from the Road* double LP.

3. Paul Riddle (Marshall Tucker Band)
Truly a jazz drummer with licks that recall Buddy Rich and Gene Krupa, Paul brought his own style into the Marshall Tucker Band,

blending with the bands country, R&B and gospel elements to create a whole new sound in Southern rock. *At his best:* "Ramblin'" (live), "Last of the Singing Cowboys."

4. Jaimoe (Allman Brothers Band)
One of the two legendary Brothers drummers, Jaimoe has always brought solid R&B influenced drums to the table. *At his best: At Fillmore East.*

5. Butch Trucks (Allman Brothers Band)
Numbers four and five are truly a tie, considering the fact that together, Butch and Jaimoe make up a machine that hits the note every single time, playing the original—and still the best—double drum kits in music. *At his best: At Fillmore East.*

6. Robert Nix (Atlanta Rhythm Section)
The multi-talented Robert Nix, who also wrote many of the band's biggest hits, was also a rock-solid drummer, with a flair for excellent cymbal work and subtle percussive elements. *At his best:* "Champagne Jam," "So into You," and as guest drummer for Lynyrd Skynyrd on "Tuesday's Gone."

7. Bob Burns (Lynyrd Skynyrd)
The drummer for Skynyrd's red-hot first and second albums, Floridian Bob Burns is another solid beat-oriented wailer of the skins. *At his best:* "Sweet Home Alabama," "Free Bird."

8. Frank Beard (ZZ Top)
It takes three mighty heavy players to pull off a power trio, and ZZ Top has been doing it for nearly forty (count 'em!) years. Beard is rock solid and a true powerhouse on the kit. *At his best:* "Manic Mechanic," "Just Got Paid," the entire *Fandango* record.

9. Tommy Aldridge (Black Oak Arkansas)
Tommy wasn't the original BOA drummer, but he is a true "Jim Dandy" (pun intended). My memories of him live in the seventies are

all great, both as a drummer and as a showman. *At his best:* The entire *Raunch 'n Roll* live LP, especially the epic "Up."

10. Freddie Edwards (Charlie Daniels Band)

One of two drummers with the CDB early on, Freddie was always steady and played with near-perfect timing. He was a staple at many a Volunteer Jam and appears on the Volunteer Jam DVD. *At his best: Fire On the Mountain* and the first *Volunteer Jam* album.

The Top Ten Bass Players of Southern Rock

1. Tommy Caldwell (Marshall Tucker Band)

According to all of the members of the Marshall Tucker Band, Tommy Caldwell was their rock, the bandleader, and one of the finest musicians in all of Southern rock. When Tommy died in 1980, the band changed and would never be exactly the same again. He drove the band with that Fender bass. *At his best:* "24 Hours at a Time," (Live), "Cattle Drive."

2. Berry Oakley (Allman Brothers Band)

Like his brother Duane Allman, Berry died far too young, but while he was with us, he recorded some amazing music that will live forever. *At his best:* the entire *At Fillmore East* record.

3. Leon Wilkeson (Lynyrd Skynyrd)

Ed King was originally hired as a bass player for Lynyrd Skynyrd, and he says that after he heard Leon play, he decided to hand the bass over to Leon. Wilkeson had a unique style and personality that added tons to the Skynyrd band's legacy. *At his best:* "Free Bird," "On the Hunt."

4. Jack Hall (Wet Willie)

Mobile, Alabama, son Jack Hall, who played bass with brother Jimmy Hall and sister Donna Hall in Wet Willie, remains a major force on the instrument even today. *At his best:* the entire *Drippin' Wet Live* LP.

5. Charlie Hayward (Charlie Daniels Band)

Prior to joining the Charlie Daniels Band in 1975, Hayward played on Gregg Allman's *Laid Back* and Cowboy's *Boyer and Talton* albums, as well as with Dr. John, Alex Taylor, and more. He has been rocking the country with the CDB for more than thirty years. *At his best:* "The Devil Went Down to Georgia," "Still in Saigon," "In America."

6. Johnny Sandlin

Producer, engineer, drummer, guitarist and bass player, Johnny Sandlin is a master of music. He simply does it all and does it all well. *At his best: Live at 2nd Street Music Hall* (Capricorn Rhythm Section).

7. Dusty Hill (ZZ Top)

Solid, artistic, Southern, bluesy, rockin'—ZZ Top's Hill is a true legend. *At his best:* "Beer Drinkers and Hell Raiders," "LaGrange."

8. Banner Thomas (Molly Hatchet)

As bassist for the original Molly Hatchet, Banner was always in the pocket with drummer Bruce Crump, driving the gator train to new heights of rock and roll mayhem. *At his best:* "Flirtin' with Disaster," "Gator Country."

9. Greg T. Walker (Blackfoot)

Founding Blackfoot member Greg Walker was one of the heaviest rock bassists in classic rock history, and along with Jakson Spires created an ultra-tight rhythm section behind Charlie Hargrett and Rick Medlocke. *At his best:* "Highway Song," "Train, Train."

10. Riff West (Molly Hatchet)

With the departure of Banner Thomas from Molly Hatchet in 1985, Riff West came in on bass. The former Foghat bassist was a solid addition and created a firm foundation with new drummer B. B. Borden. *At his best:* "Fall of the Peacemakers," "Bounty Hunter" (live).

The Top Ten Keyboard Players of Southern Rock

1. Chuck Leavell (Allman Brothers Band)
Take one look at the Georgia boy's resume: Besides being a former member of the Allman Brothers Band, Chuck remains a touring member and musical director for the Rolling Stones; plus he has recorded and performed with everyone from Gov't Mule to Marshall Tucker to the Black Crowes. *At his best:* "Jessica," the Allman Brothers Band.

2. Gregg Allman (Allman Brothers Band)
The master of the B-3, Gregg has a way of channeling his very soul into the keys. *At his best: At Fillmore East, Laid Back, Searching for Simplicity.*

3. Billy Powell (Lynryd Skynyrd)
The classically trained Powell could play Beethoven and Fats Domino riffs with equal fervor. The story of his move from Lynyrd Skynyrd roadie to key player is the stuff of legend. *At his best:* "Free Bird" (live).

4. John Galvin (Molly Hatchet)
Another versatile keyboard man, Molly Hatchet kicked their sound up several notches when they added John. *At his best: Double Trouble Live.*

5. Edgar Winter
Texan Edgar Winter is certainly a man of many talents who covers many genres. While he is not normally considered a Southern rocker, he is a Southerner who rocks as well as he plays jazz, blues, or gospel. *At his best:* The *Roadwork* LP by Edgar Winter's White Trash, *They Only Come Out at Night* LP, the Edgar Winter Group.

6. Bobby Whitlock
From his work with Delaney and Bonnie and Friends, to the seminal
Derek & the Dominos LP *Layla and Other Love Songs* and his four
Capricorn solo albums, Whitlock never ceases to amaze as a multi-
instrumentalist and singer-songwriter. *At his best: Layla and Other
Assorted Love Songs, Rock Your Socks Off.*

7. Taz DiGregorio (Charlie Daniels Band)
After nearly forty years as sideman to Charlie Daniels, Taz was a true
legend of Southern rock. *At his best: Fire on the Mountain*, any
Volunteer Jam LP.

8. Al Kooper
Kooper is a legendary producer, if for no other reason than his work
with Lynyrd Skynyrd (which is just the tip of his iceberg), but he is
also a top-notch keyboard man. *At his best: Pronounced* by Lynyrd
Skynyrd, *Super Session* with Mike Bloomfield and Stephen Stills.

9. Paul Hornsby
Another fine record producer and engineer, Paul was a member of
the pre-Allmans band Hour Glass and played keys on many sessions,
including the Marshall Tucker Band. *At his best: The Marshall Tucker
Band* (debut), "Heard It in a Love Song," *Live at Second Street Music
Hall* by Capricorn Rhythm Section.

10. Eddie Stone (Doc Holliday)
Doc Holliday's own keyboard whiz kid, Eddie is another great
guitarist, singer, and songwriter who can wail on a B-3. *At his best:
Doc Holliday Rides Again, Doc Holliday* (first LP), *Right Tonight*, solo.

Top Ten Instrumentalists (Other than Guitar/Keys/Drum Kit) of Southern Rock

1. Charlie Daniels (Charlie Daniels Band) (fiddle)
Nobody does it better. Besides being a super hot guitar picker, Charlie is an amazing fiddler. Heck, he beat the devil in a contest! Still the Godfather of Southern rock. *At his best:* "The Devil Went Down to Georgia," "Orange Blossom Special."

2. Jimmy Hall (Wet Willie) (sax, harp)
An amazing vocalist and an equally impressive sax man and harp player. Whether fronting Wet Willie, working with Jeff Beck or as band director for Hank, Jr., Jimmy does it all so well. *At his best:* "Street Corner Serenade," the whole *Drippin' Wet Live* LP.

3. Toy Caldwell (Marshall Tucker Band) (pedal steel)
One of Southern rock's very best guitar players was also a very tasty steel player. *At his best:* "Fire on the Mountain," "Desert Skies."

4. Thom Doucette (harp)
You've got to be a helluva harp player to sit in with the Allman Brothers Band. *At his best: At Fillmore East* and *Live at the Atlanta International Pop Festival.*

5. Jerry Eubanks (Marshall Tucker Band) (sax, flute, keys)
The super-talented multi-instrumentalist of the (original) Marshall Tucker Band. *At his best:* "Heard it in a Love Song," "Can't You See," "This Time I Believe."

6. Jim Dandy Mangrum (Black Oak Arkansas) (washboard)
Black Oak Arkansas front man Jim Dandy can play a washboard like nobody's business. A truly unique skill. *At his best:* The whole *Raunch 'n' Roll Live* LP, especially "When Electricity Came to Arkansas."

7. Jo Jo Billingsley (Lynryd Skynyrd) (percussion)
One of the original Lynryd Skynyrd Honkettes, Deborah Jo is a
phenomenal singer, but she also shakes a mean set of maracas. *At her
best: One More from the Road.*

8. Donnie McCormick (Eric Quincy Tate) (Chicken Coup)
Founding father of Eric Quincy Tate and a super talent. *At his best:*
EQT *Drinking Man's Friend*, solo *Howl.*

9. Norton Buffalo (harp)
Buffalo was the bomb, playing on so many great albums and
jamming live during the heyday of Southern rock. *At his best:
Dedicated* (Marshall Tucker Band), *We've Got a Live One Here*
(Commander Cody).

10. Edgar Winter (sax, keys, percussion)
The jury is still out as to whether Edgar can be called a "Southern
rocker." Hell, he is from Texas, and he plays rock, jazz, blues, and
gospel equally well. I love him, so here he is. A monster sax player
and excellent percussionist. *At his best:* "Frankenstein" (keys, synth,
drums, sax), Edgar Winter's White Trash *Roadwork.*

Top Ten Songwriters of Southern Rock

1. Dickey Betts
Dickey brought something to the Allman Brothers Band table that
nobody else had. That something was a true country music passion,
fueled by other influences from blues and jazz, like Robert Johnson
and Django Reinhardt. Dickey has written some of the most
memorable tunes ever. *At his best:* "Blue Sky," "Ramblin' Man,"
"Seven Turns," "In Memory of Elizabeth Reed."

2. Toy Caldwell
Marshall Tucker's Toy wrote about life. He could take a subject like
fishing, driving on the highway, or walking his property line and

make it sing. *At his best:* "Heard it in a Love Song," "Can't You See," "Bob Away My Blues," "Hillbilly Band."

3. George McCorkle
George wrote one of Marshall Tucker's biggest ever hits, as well as a bunch or excellent LP tracks. Prior to his death in 2007, he was becoming one of Nashville's finest writers as well, aging like a fine wine. *At his best:* "Fire On the Mountain," "Last of the Singing Cowboys," "American Street," "Peace Stories."

4. Charlie Daniels
Charlie can write a story, a blog, or a song with equal skill. He's a natural writer like Toy was. *At his best:* "The Devil Went Down to Georgia," "Caballo Diablo," "The Legend of Wooley Swamp," "Simple Man."

5. Ronnie Van Zant
Another writer who wrote from his heart and wrote about what was going on around him. If you listen to Ronnie's songs, they reflect where he and the band were at the time of the writing, almost telling their story like a musical journal. *At his best:* "Free Bird," (with Allen) "Sweet Home Alabama," (with Gary and Ed), "On the Hunt" (with Allen).

6. Gregg Allman
Not as prolific a writer as Dickey, Gregg has nonetheless turned in some of the most timeless Southern rock tunes of all time. *At his best:* "Melissa," "Queen of Hearts," "Whipping Post."

7. Ed King
The Lynyrd Skynyrd guitar hero wrote some of Southern rock's most loved tunes and guitar riffs, including one of the most instantly recognizable in "Sweet Home Alabama." *At his best:* "Sweet Home Alabama" (with Gary and Ed), "Saturday Night Special" (with Ronnie).

8. Dru Lombar

The Grinderswitch front man was not only a great guitarist and singer, but also a great songwriter. *At his best:* "Kiss the Blues Goodbye," "Peach County Jamboree."

9. Don Barnes

Don Barnes of 38 Special has written some of the greatest songs— from Southern rock to pop rock. *At his best:* "Caught Up in You" (with Jeff Carlisi/Jim Peterik), "Stone Cold Believer" (with Carlisi/Johnny Van Zant).

10. Bruce Brookshire

The leader of Doc Holliday plays and sings Southern rock and gospel equally well, and his writing is always top drawer. *At his best:* "Lonesome Guitar," "Hoodoo Man," "Workin' Man."

Top Ten Great Southern Rock Towns

1. Macon, Georgia

During the seventies, Capricorn Records in Macon was the hub of the Southern rock world. Phil Walden was the crown prince of the movement, which featured the Allman Brothers, Marshall Tucker, Wet Willie, and many other greats. The old studio is being turned into a museum, and the Big House on Vineville Avenue is the official Allman museum. Duane Allman and Berry Oakley are buried in town at Rose Hill Cemetery.

2. Jacksonville, Florida

The birthplace of Ronnie Van Zant, Lynyrd Skynyrd, 38 Special, and Molly Hatchet, among others. In 1960, a band called the Escorts was formed here that would eventually become the Allman Brothers Band.

3. Muscle Shoals, Alabama

A mecca of great recording during the sixties and seventies, from FAME Studios to Jackson Highway to Muscle Shoals Sound. It was at Rick Hall's FAME Studios that Duane Allman first began his rise to the top. Of course, Lynyrd Skynyrd recorded their first tracks here. *"In Muscle Shoals they've got the Swampers..."*

4. Nashville, Tennessee

The home of country music and the home of Charlie Daniels (well, the Nashville area, anyway), Nashville was also the birthplace of brothers Gregg and Duane Allman.

5. Austin, Texas

The great music scene of Austin is by no means a secret, from the PBS TV series *Austin City Limits*, to the legend of Stevie Ray Vaughan. Austin was also the home of the Armadillo World Headquarters, which became the Texas home of Southern rock during the seventies. Among the bands to take the stage on multiple occasions were the Charlie Daniels Band, the Marshall Tucker Band, Wet Willie, Dickey Betts, Elvin Bishop, Grinderswitch, ZZ Top, Goose Creek Symphony, Atlanta Rhythm Section, Black Oak Arkansas, Hydra, and Eric Quincy Tate, just to name a few.

6. Tampa, Florida

In 1972 Hughie Thomasson and company formed the legendary Outlaws in Tampa. These days, Tampa plays host to Charlie Daniels's annual gathering of Southern rock and country superstars at the Angelus benefit golf tournament and concert.

7. Spartanburg, South Carolina

The birthplace of the Marshall Tucker Band and all six of its original members, as well as the long time home of Lynyrd Skynyrd drummer Artimus Pyle. Charlie Daniels attended school here, and Wet Willie discovered Marshall Tucker while gigging downtown at the Ruins. Oh, it's also the birthplace of yours truly.

8. Athens, Georgia
Besides being the home of rockers like R.E.M. and The B-52s, Athens gave birth to Southern rockers the Drive By Truckers and former Capricorn records recording group Widespread Panic. The college town has always drawn great music to her venues, including the best Southern rock. Clubs like the Georgia Theatre and the 40 Watt have become legendary venues.

9. Wilmington, North Carolina
The birthplace of Charlie Daniels. Need I say more?

10. Tupelo, Mississippi
The birthplace of Elvis Presley, "the original Southern rocker." Also the birthplace of singer/songwriter/Southern entertainer Paul Thorn.

Top Twenty-five Songs in Southern Rock

1. "Free Bird" (Lynyrd Skynyrd)
As if there was any doubt whatsoever. Not only Southern rock's number one, but one of the top two in classic rock. Ronnie Van Zant's crowning glory.

2. "Can't You See" (Marshall Tucker)
The Marshall Tucker Band's biggest hit ever wasn't sung by their lead singer; it was sung by its writer, the great Toy Caldwell. Toy said many times that he was not really a singer, but the honest truth is, nobody else, not even the great Doug Gray, could have sung this song. It is Toy all the way.

3. "Whipping Post" (Allman Brothers)
Especially the live version from *At Fillmore East*. Never has there been a more passionate vocal—Gregg Allman sings his own composition with heart and soul to spare, and the band, led by brother Duane, simply smokes.

4. "The Devil Went Down to Georgia" (Charlie Daniels Band)
Charlie hit his stride with this one, his biggest hit ever, a song that received as much airplay on country radio as on rock radio. The tale of the fiddler battling the devil has become one of the most recognizable songs in history, and Charlie's fiddle couples with Tommy Crain's guitar and a brilliant story lyric to create a timeless masterpiece.

5. "Queen of Hearts" (Gregg Allman)
When I asked Gregg his favorite song of his own, he didn't hesitate in telling me it was "Queen of Hearts." No small wonder, as Gregg sings his song straight from the heart, and plays some amazing B-3. The *Laid Back* album's centerpiece.

6. "Sweet Home Alabama" (Lynyrd Skynyrd)
No, Ronnie didn't hate Neil Young. That was record company hype. Things have really changed since the single originally dropped. The record is now a staple of country radio, which is a perfect example of how much Southern rock has influenced today's country.

7. "Green Grass and High Tides" (Outlaws)
An epic Southern rock song, like "Free Bird," a real classic, with Hughie Thomasson singing and playing to beat the band.

8. "Highway Song" (Blackfoot)
The third "epic" in our trilogy, featuring the patented "start slow and then speed up" formula. Powerhouse drums from Jakson Spires, bass from Greg T. Walker, and guitars from Rick Medlocke and Charlie Hargrett. Classic, man.

9. "Melissa" (Allman Brothers)
Although Gregg had recorded it before, the definitive version recorded for *Eat a Peach* took on a whole new meaning following the death of brother Duane Allman. You'd be hard pressed to find a Southern rock fan who doesn't immediately think of Duane when they hear "Melissa."

10. "Sang Her Love Songs" (Winters Bros. Band)
Another "long" song, and perhaps the best loved of the Winters Brothers catalog. Moody and rockin' the country, like Marty Robbins meets Marshall Tucker Band.

11. "Blue Sky" (Allman Brothers Band)
Dickey Betts's love song to his former wife Sandy Blue Sky, a beautiful, country rock track with amazing guitar twin leads. A song I never, ever get tired of.

12. "Please Be With Me" (Cowboy)
Scott Boyer's classic, with Tommy Talton and all the rest, and with Duane Allman on Dobro. One of the downright prettiest songs ever recorded.

13. "Mean to Your Queenie" (Point Blank)
Rusty Burns and the Texas rockers rip it up. What the hell did you expect?

14. "South's Gonna Do it Again" (Charlie Daniels Band)
The ultimate roll call for Southern rock bands, and a rebel yell if ever there was one. Be proud you're a rebel!

15. "Jessica" (Allman Brothers Band)
The greatest instrumental in Southern rock history, with amazing piano from Chuck Leavell and some of Dickey's best lead work ever.

16. "Don't Misunderstand Me" (Rossington Collins Band)
One kick-ass Southern rock song, with Dale Krantz wailing like Janis Joplin and Ann Wilson combined. Damn, that woman can sing! My favorite part is the cowbell solo. (More cowbell!)

17. "Dreams (I'll Never See)" (Molly Hatchet/Allman Brothers Band)
A true Allmans classic, and the Hatchet version just rocks the house. Danny Joe rules.

18. "Fire on the Mountain" (Marshall Tucker Band)
George McCorkle wrote one hell of a western themed song, and Toy's pedal steel is as smooth as Tennessee sipping whiskey. Doug Gray outdoes himself on the vocal.

19. "Ramblin' Man" (Allman Brothers Band)
Another Dickey Betts tune I could listen to over and over. I just love Dickey's voice as well as his guitar style.

20. "Flirtin' with Disaster" (Molly Hatchet)
Can I get a big "Hell, yeah!?" Every time I have heard this on radio or on record I have automatically turned the volume up to eleven. The song begs to be played loud.

21. "Heard It in a Love Song" (Marshall Tucker Band)
True confessions. The first time I heard it, I would have sworn Doug was singing "Purty little love song." That being said, the song is another all time favorite. Jerry's flute makes the song.

22. "Homesick" (Atlanta Rhythm Section)
I love the signature riff; I love the lyrics. An amazing song that is great live and also fun to *perform* live.

23. "In Memory of Elizabeth Reed" (Allman Brothers)
Dickey Betts' absolutely breathtakingly beautiful instrumental. 'Nuff said.

24. "La Grange" (ZZ Top)
Ah, that little ol' band from Texas singing about a Texas whorehouse. It don't get no better than that, does it? My favorite song when I was in ninth grade.

25. "Hold On Loosely" (38 Special)
Okay, "Caught Up in You" is my personal 38 favorite, but "Hold On" was my first ever exposure to Donnie Van Zant and Don Barnes, so it holds a special place in my heart, as well as in the hearts and minds of Southern rockers the world over.

Appendix 2

Band Member Histories

The Allman Brothers Band

Present members

Gregg Allman—organ, piano, guitar, vocals (1969–1976, 1978–1982, 1986, 1989–present)

Butch Trucks—drums, tympani (1969–1976, 1978–1982, 1986, 1989–present)

Jai Johanny "Jaimoe" Johanson—drums, percussion (1969–1976, 1978–1980, 1986, 1989–present)

Warren Haynes—guitar, slide guitar, vocals (1989–1997, 2000–present)

Marc Quiñones—drums, percussion, background vocals (1991–present)

Oteil Burbridge—bass, vocals (1997–present)

Derek Trucks—guitar, slide guitar (1999–present)

Past Members, in order of appearance

Duane Allman—guitar, slide guitar (1969–1971; died October 29, 1971)

Dickey Betts—guitar, slide guitar, vocals (1969–1976, 1978–1982, 1986, 1989–2000)

Berry Oakley—bass, vocals (1969–1972; died November 11, 1972)

Chuck Leavell—piano, synthesizer, background vocals (1972–1976, 1986)

Lamar Williams—bass, vocals (1972–1976; died January 21, 1983)

Dan Toler—guitar (1978–1982, 1986; died February 25, 2013)

David Goldflies—bass (1978–1982)

David "Frankie" Toler—drums (1980–1982; died June 4, 2011)

Mike Lawler—keyboards (1980–1982)
Allen Woody—bass, background vocals (1989–1997; died 2000)
Johnny Neel—keyboards, harmonica (1989–1990)
Jack Pearson—guitar, vocals (1997–1999)
Jimmy Herring—guitar (2000)

Live Personnel
Thom Doucette—harmonica, percussion (for the *At Fillmore East* concert)
Rudolph "Juici" Carter—saxophone (for the *At Fillmore East* concert) (died May 6, 2013)
Bobby Caldwell—percussion (for the *At Fillmore East* concert)
Elvin Bishop—vocals (for the *At Fillmore East* concert)
Steve Miller—piano (for the At Fillmore East concert)
Bruce Waibel—bass (1986 reunion concert; died September 2, 2003)

Lynryd Skynyrd

Present Lineup
Johnny Van Zant—lead vocals (1987–present)
Gary Rossington—guitars (1969–1977; 1987–present)
Rickey Medlocke—guitars, backing vocals (1970–1971, drums) (1996–present)
Mark Matejka—guitars, backing vocals (2006–present)
Johnny Colt—bass, backing vocals (2012–present)
Michael Cartellone—drums, percussion (1999–present)
Peter Keys—keyboards (2012–present)

Present Honkettes
Dale Krantz-Rossington—backing vocals (1987–present)
Carol Chase—backing vocals (1991–present)

Past Members
Ronnie Van Zant—lead vocals (1969–1977)
Allen Collins—guitars (1969–1977)
Larry Junstrom—bass (1969–1970)
Greg T. Walker—bass (1970–1971)

Bo Burns—drums (1968-1974)
Artimus Pyle—drums (1974-1977, 1991)
Ed King—guitars (1972–1975; 1987–1996)
Leon Wilkeson—bass, backing vocals (1972–1977; 1987–2001)
Billy Powell—keyboards (1972–1977; 1987–2009)
Steve Gaines—guitars, backing vocals (1976–1977)
Randall Hall—guitars, backing vocals (1987–1993)
Kurt Custer—drums (1990–1994)
Mike Estes—guitars (1993–1996)
Owen Hale—drums (1994–1998)
Hughie Thomasson—guitars, backing vocals (1996–2007)
Rickey Medlocke—guitars, backing vocals
Hughie Thomasson—guitars, backing vocals
Jeff McAllister—drums (1998–1999)
Kenny Aronoff—drums (1999)
Hughie Thomasson—guitars, backing vocals (2001–2007)
Ean Evans—bass, backing vocals (2001–2009)
Michael Cartellone—drums, percussion
Ean Evans—bass, backing vocals
Michael Cartellone—drums, percussion
Robert Kearns—bass, backing vocals (2009–2012)

Honkettes
Leslie Hawkins—backing vocals (1975–1977)
Jo Jo Billingsley—backing vocals (1975–1977)
Cassie Gaines—backing vocals (1975–1977)
Carol Bristow—backing vocals (1987–1991)

The Marshall Tucker Band

Present Lineup
Doug Gray—vocals
Pat Ellwood—bass
Rick Willis—guitar
Chris Hicks—guitar
B. B. Borden—drums
Marcus James Henderson—sax/flute/keys

The Original Lineup, 1972–1980
Toy Caldwell—guitar/pedal steel (died February 25, 1993)
Doug Gray—vocals
Jerry Eubanks—saxophone/flute
Paul Riddle—drums
George McCorkle—guitar (died June 29, 2007)
Tommy Caldwell—bass (died April 28, 1980)

Past members
Franklin Wilkie
Ronnie Godfrey
Rusty Milner
Bobby Ogdin
Bob Wray
James Stroud
Tom Robb
Ace Allen
Tim Lawter
Stuart Swanlund (died August 4, 2012)
Don Cameron
Frankie Toler (died June 4, 2011)
Mark Pettey
Ronald Radford
Paul Thompson (died 1999)
Garry Guzzardo
David Muse
Chris Hicks
Clay Cook
Tony Heatherly (died May 15, 2013)

Molly Hatchet

Present members
Dave Hlubek—guitars vocals (1978–1987, 2005–present)
John Galvin—keyboards (1984–1991, 1995–present)
Bobby Ingram—guitars (1987–present)
Phil McCormack—vocals (1996–present)

Tim Lindsey—bass (2003–present)
Shawn Beamer—drums (2001–present)

Former members
Duane Roland—guitars (1978–1990; died 2006)
Steve Holland—guitars (1978–1984)
Bruce Crump—drums (1978–1982, 1984–1990)
Banner Thomas—bass (1978–1981)
Danny Joe Brown—vocals (1978–1980, 1982–1996; left band, died
    2005)
Melvin Powell—keyboards (1978)
Jimmy Farrar—vocals (1980–1982)
Riff West—bass (1981–1990)
B.B. Borden—drums (1982–1984)
Andy McKinney—bass (1990–2003)
Mac Crawford—drums (1990–1999)
Bryan Bassett—guitars (1993–1999)
Sean Shannon—drums (1999–2001)
Mike Owings—guitars (1999–2000)

Former touring musicians
Steve Wheeler—bass (1980)
David Feagle—drums (1980, 1989–1991)
Jimmy Glenn—drums (1980)
Kenny McVay—guitars (1980)
Eddie Rio—bass (1990)
Rob Sweat—bass (1990–1993)
Rob Scavetto—keyboards (1990–1993)
Rik Blanz—guitars (1990–1993)
Kevin Ryan—bass (1991–1993)
Kenny Holton—drums (1991)
Eric Lundgren—guitars (1991)
Mike Kach—keyboards (1993)
Andy Orth—guitars (1994–1995)
Buzzy Meekins—bass (1994–1995)
Chuck Modrey—vocals (1996)
Tim Donovan—keyboards (1997–2002)

Doc Forrester—guitars (1995–1997)
Dale Rock—drums (2001)
Scott Woods—keyboards (2002)
Doc Warnock—bass (2002–2003)
Jerry Scott—bass (2002–2003, 2004)
J. J. Strickland—bass (2003–2004, 2004)
Richie Del Favero—guitars (2004–2005)

Index